T0327457

After Heritage

Critical Perspectives on Heritage from Below

Edited by

Hamzah Muzaini

Department of Southeast Asian Studies, National University of Singapore, Singapore

Claudio Minca

Department of History and Culture, University of Bologna, Italy and Department of Geography and Planning, Macquarie University, Australia

 Edward Elgar
PUBLISHING

Cheltenham, UK • Northampton, MA, USA

© Hamzah Muzaini and Claudio Minca 2018

Cover image: Tirta Empul, Bali, Indonesia. *Source:* Hamzah Muzaini

All rights reserved. No part of this publication may be reproduced, stored in a retrieval system or transmitted in any form or by any means, electronic, mechanical or photocopying, recording, or otherwise without the prior permission of the publisher.

Published by
Edward Elgar Publishing Limited
The Lypiatts
15 Lansdown Road
Cheltenham
Glos GL50 2JA
UK

Edward Elgar Publishing, Inc.
William Pratt House
9 Dewey Court
Northampton
Massachusetts 01060
USA

Paperback edition 2020

A catalogue record for this book
is available from the British Library

Library of Congress Control Number: 2018932703

This book is available electronically in the **Elgar**online
Social and Political Science subject collection
DOI 10.4337/9781788110747

MIX
Paper from
responsible sources
FSC   FSC® C013604
www.fsc.org

ISBN 978 1 78811 073 0 (cased)
ISBN 978 1 78811 074 7 (eBook)
ISBN 978 1 83910 445 9 (paperback)

Typeset by Servis Filmsetting Ltd, Stockport, Cheshire
Printed and bound by CPI Group (UK) Ltd, Croydon, CR0 4YY

After Heritage

Contents

Figures

Contributors

Ana Aceska is Lecturer at the Cultural Geography Group at Wageningen University. She received her PhD degree at Humboldt University Berlin in 2013. Her core research is focused on the processes of place-making and identity-formation in post-war Bosnia-Herzegovina and on questions of migration, heritage and well-being in cities.

Richard Carter-White completed his PhD in Geography at the University of Exeter, and is now Project Assistant Professor in the College of Arts and Sciences at the University of Tokyo. His research focuses on themes of disaster and witnessing, particularly in the context of geographies of the Holocaust, and he has previously published on the spatial historiographies generated by literary, cinematic and testimonial representations of the Holocaust. His current research is concerned with the spatialities of violence in the Holocaust, drawing on ideas of community and witnessing to analyse the organization and unfolding of genocidal violence.

Matthew R. Cook is Assistant Professor of Historic Preservation and Cultural Geography at Eastern Michigan University. Broadly trained in cultural and historical geography, he earned his PhD from the University of Tennessee at Knoxville. His scholarly interests lie at the intersections of geography, historical interpretation, race, public/critical pedagogy and popular culture. Past research has included the historical-geographical counter narratives of slavery in the American South; the Stolpersteine Project in Europe and public memory of the Holocaust; and urban landscape change in Berlin. He is currently studying how museums interpret African American history, looking particularly at their responses to expanding geographies of racism and racial violence in the US.

Danielle Drozdzewski is a human geographer and Senior Lecturer at UNSW Australia. Her research focuses on cultural memories and the interlinkages of these with identity and place. She is interested in how memory is encountered in public spheres through monuments and public discourse, as well as in private spaces, between and within generations of families, in homes and with migrants in diaspora. Her research has looked at the outcomes of these encounters for national identities, especially within the context of multicultural societies and in post-war landscapes.

Jamie Gillen is Assistant Professor of Geography at the National University of Singapore. His research interests centre on the human geographies of Vietnam and Southeast Asia. At NUS his teaching covers tourism, cultural, urban and social geographies. Recently completed research projects include tourism and Vietnamese state power, drinking alcohol, the role of the motorbike in Vietnam, and entrepreneurialism in the tourism industry (the latter resulted in a book entitled *Entrepreneurialism and Tourism in Contemporary Vietnam*, 2016).

Claudio Minca is Head and Professor of Human Geography at Macquarie University, Sydney. His research centres on three major themes: tourism and travel theories of modernity; the spatialization of (bio)politics; and the relationship between modern knowledge, space and landscape in postcolonial geography. His most recent books are *On Schmitt and Space* (with R. Rowan, 2015), *Hitler's Geographies* (with P. Giaccaria, University Press, 2016) and *Moroccan Dreams* (with L. Wagner, 2016).

Hamzah Muzaini is a cultural geographer with the Department of Southeast Asian Studies, National University of Singapore. His research interest relates to war heritage and memoryscapes, conceptualized around postcolonial theory, materiality and the spatial politics of remembering by state and non-state actors in Malaysia and Singapore. He is author of *Contested Memoryscapes: The Politics of Second World War Commemoration in Singapore* (with Brenda Yeoh, 2016) and has also published on backpacking, dark tourism in Southeast Asia, international peace museums, and Singapore's transborder geographies and histories. His present research looks at 'heritage from below' within the contexts of cultural theme parks; and migrant and transnational heritage.

Meghann Ormond is Associate Professor in Cultural Geography at Wageningen University. A human geographer, her research is mainly focused on the intersections of transnational mobility, health and care at a range of scales. She is the author of *Neoliberal Governance and International Medical Travel in Malaysia* (2013) and numerous journal articles and book chapters on citizenship, consumption, tourism, migration and healthcare.

Amy E. Potter is Assistant Professor in the Department of Geology and Geography at Georgia Southern University in Savannah, Georgia. Her PhD is in Geography from Louisiana State University. Most of her research is connected to the larger themes of cultural justice and Black Geographies. She has conducted extensive ethnographic fieldwork in the Caribbean and the US South. On the island of Barbuda, she explored the complex relationship between transnational migrants to their common property, while also examining how tourism is transforming Barbudan's sense of place. Her most recent research, building on her experience as a tour guide at a Louisiana plantation and funded by the National Science Foundation, focuses on historic Southern plantation culture, particularly in terms of the theorization of the transformation of racialized Southern heritage landscapes.

Iain J.M. Robertson is Reader in History in the Centre for History at the University of the Highlands and Islands, Scotland, but is a historical geographer by inclination and training! He has two principal research interests: the intersection of land, landscape and identity found in struggles of dispossession and resistance in the Scottish highlands in the early twentieth century; and critical heritage studies. He published *Heritage From Below* in 2012 and, since then, has concentrated on developing and deepening the concept via case studies. Working with colleagues from England, Denmark and Australia, he will publish *Creating Heritage: Unrecognised Pasts and Rejected Futures* with Routledge in 2019.

James A. Tyner is Professor of Geography at Kent State University. His research operates at the intersection of political and population geography with a focus on war, violence and genocide. He is the author of 15 books, including *War, Violence, and Population: Making the Body Count*, which received the AAG Meridian Book Award for Outstanding Scholarly Contribution to Geography, and *Iraq, Terror, and the Philippines' Will to War*, which received the Julian Minghi Award for Outstanding Contribution to Political Geography. His most recent books include *Landscape, Memory, and Post-Violence in Cambodia* (2016) and *From Rice Fields to Killing Fields: Nature, Life, and Labor under the Khmer Rouge* (2017).

Preface

Tirta Empul (translated as 'holy mountain spring') located in the Gianyar province of Bali, Indonesia, is a temple complex of shrines and purification/bathing pools sourced from the Pakerisan River. Built during the Warmadewa dynasty (1000–1100 AD), locals have for centuries frequented it to pay respect to and, in turn, receive blessings from, the spirits believed to reside in situ. This is done by making offerings, bathing in its pools, or bringing home 'healing' water from one of its elaborately designed spouts (see cover picture). Since its UNESCO designation as part of the 'Cultural Landscapes of Bali' in 2012, the complex is also, these days, a popular tourist attraction, its heritage touted for its spiritual values where people (mainly locals) still perform age-old traditions and customs. Yet, actual experiences on the ground tell different stories, ranging from awe to annoyance, owing to criticisms of overcrowding, commercialization, and the pollution of its waters from its use as a bathing pool and the concomitant use of the river as sewage channels by surrounding residents. While there are locals who go to the site for its sacred values, there are also those motivated to visit purely for its aesthetics as a tourist site. This underscores how heritage sites can be formally *represented* in one way – here as a religious site (with an enforced dress code and suggested visiting practices) – although how it is actually *experienced* differs from person to person.

The above speaks to how 'heritage from below' (HFB) is conceptualized in this book, as a call to consider beyond how heritage is manufactured from the 'top down' and put into the service of collective identity-making towards the ways in which heritage is encountered in myriad fashions on the level of the individuals themselves, even as these experiences, positive or negative, are fleeting, not aired publicly or detract from one's enjoyment of the site (given how, despite the issues associated with the site, visitor numbers remain unabated). It is, however, still salient to seek out these less visible or vocalized experiences of heritage for what they tell us about the ways in which non-state agents encounter heritage and how plural interpretations (or even alternative sites) of heritage may emerge out of these. It is this desire to critically analyse ephemeral/intimate stories of heritage-making – particularly as they supplement/subvert dominant ideas of heritage – that is the driver for *After Heritage*.

Drawing on international case studies, and building upon the work of Laurajanne Smith and Iain Robertson in particular, *After Heritage* sheds critical light on heritage/heritagescapes that are, more frequently than not, located in virtual, less conspicuous and/or more everyday spaces. The book also considers, as highlighted above, the personal, often ephemeral, individual – vis-à-vis collective – experiences of (in)formal ways the past is folded into contemporary societies. In doing so, it unravels merits of examining 'closest to the body' materializations of heritage – often hidden 'in the shadows' and, therefore, less scrutinized by scholars – not only as a check against, but also complementary to, more formal heritage representations. Even so, the book argues against the tendency to romanticize how these alternative forms of heritage-making are produced, performed and patronized. Thus, ultimately, this book offers a much needed clarion call to reinsert the more individual/transient into heritage processes.

The realization of this edited book would not have been possible without the support of very patient and highly cooperative contributors, the encouragement of family, friends and other loved ones and, subsequently, the highly responsive and efficient production team behind Edward Elgar Publishing. We would especially like to thank Katy Crossan for broaching with us the idea of producing this book, as well as other scholars, whose comments and suggestions indirectly contributed much to the ideas within the book.

Hamzah Muzaini and Claudio Minca
Singapore and Sydney, December 2017

1. Rethinking heritage, but 'from below'

Hamzah Muzaini and Claudio Minca

INTRODUCTION

There is, really, no such thing as heritage. (Smith 2006, p. 11)

As counterintuitive as this statement may sound, the basic idea introduced by Laurajanne Smith (2006) in her much vaunted *Uses of Heritage* is the starting point for this collection. Indeed, for all its grand pronouncements, within national(ized) canons, global heritage lists, tourism brochures or the agenda of organizations such as the European Union (EU), or when mouthed from the lips of laypeople asked to define their respective identities, 'heritage', even as it owes its lineage from historical events, is nothing more than a manipulation of the past. Thus, it should not surprise that critical heritage scholars have largely engaged with the idea of 'heritage' not as a priori, or fixed in its essence, but as a process folded into the service of the present through what Harvey (2001, p. 332) refers to as 'heritage-isation'. In line with this idea, Smith (2006) also coined the term Authorized Heritage Discourse (hereafter AHD) to describe how the past is mobilized to attain socio-economic and political objectives, and how audiences are persuaded to accept particular versions of the past as true, even as these may be nothing but strategically selected narratives of people and events belonging to another time.

There is now a burgeoning amount of work centred, implicitly if not explicitly, on the political and cultural issues associated with AHD, especially as these are undertaken as part of nation-building or nationalistic projects. Yet, there is comparatively lesser attention on heritage as a process understood, practised *and experienced* on the ground by the people themselves. This includes heritagescapes (or heritage landscapes) spearheaded by non-elites, and the ways in which these same actors may engage heritagescapes in more affective ways, thus exercising their own agency as both producers *and* consumers of 'the past'. What we would like to emphasize in the critical reading of heritage proposed by this book is the fact that heritage(scapes) are fashioned not only in spectacular manners, or even in highly public spaces; they may also be materialized 'in the shadows' by individuals and communities within erstwhile everyday spaces, or manifested in more embodied (vis-à-vis emplaced) ways (see Connerton 1989). We also believe that not enough focus has been given in the relevant literature to how individuals themselves engage 'heritage' on a more personal register, cognitively and emotionally, regardless of mandates of official 'top-down' heritage(scapes). These two aspects constitute how we will conceptualize Heritage from Below (hereafter, HFB) in this collection, deliberately building upon how Iain Robertson introduced the concept in his path-breaking book with the same title (2012, see also 2008).

Moreover, while cases of HFB do occasionally rear their heads in scholarship, they are often framed as checks to AHD, such as in the shape of counter-narratives of what constitutes one's heritage (see Hoelscher and Alderman 2004 for a review). These counter-narratives, so the argument goes, are particularly useful in revealing the biases, partiality and selectivity of official versions of the past, hence turning them on their heads, or in representing counter-sites of memory and heritage as necessarily reviving what AHD has forgotten (see, among others, Legg 2005a). Yet, even as it has become almost a truism to say that, regardless of what is formally presented, people engage heritage in their own ways, there is a tendency in the literature to romanticize alternative heritage formulations, even as many of these formulations may also be subservient to dominant official discourses, be driven by only a select grassroots, or even have their own hidden agendas. For sure, if *all* 'heritage' is nothing more than the past as imagined from the perspectives of the 'here and now', it is perhaps too simplistic to frame AHD as a process of strategic forgetting and HFB as a positive process of collective memory recovery; things, we suggest, are far more complex even when the past is actualized 'from below'. Accordingly, one of the aims of this book is that of questioning all forms of heritage produced 'from below', while maintaining a critical stance towards AHD. As much as we like to read in a critical perspective all formal renderings of heritage(scapes), we also believe that such a critical perspective should be applied to cases where individuals and groups manifest alternative forms of 'heritage', thus problematizing the myriad ways the past may be subsequently engaged, both personally as well as collectively.

The purpose of the edited collection is thus two-fold. First, to unravel some of the blind-sights of scholarship centred on a critique of AHD, but also to reflect on how a critical positioning of HFB may look like. Specifically, this involves seeking out heritages(scapes) beyond that which is formalized, visual, tangible, spectacular and spatially bounded, to also include those that are made, unmade and remade within the present but within the vernacular and the everyday, frequently motivated by more than just the desire to revive the reified past. In other words, every form of heritage valorisation, from the 'top down' to the 'bottom up', is inherently selective and responds, in various degrees, to the position of the respective promoters and advocates. There is therefore no neutral ground out there to stage an apolitical and objective actualization of history. Secondly, the book departs from interpretations based on the overtly simplistic binary of 'AHD-evil'-'HFB-good'. Drawing on critical heritage studies (Winter 2013), this book thus argues for pathways in and through which HFB and AHD should not necessarily be seen as antithetical but possibly complementary to one another.

In what follows, the chapter does some conceptual ground-clearing. It first examines the idea of AHD (Smith 2006) and its limitations. The chapter then presents what we understand by HFB and why there should be more emphasis on studying it. Drawing on recent debates (see Winter and Waterton 2013), we also explain how we envision taking HFB in more critical directions, not only to enhance our understanding of what heritage is *or does*, but also to take better account of *individual practices of heritage-making and engagement*, particularly those situated in less conspicuous forms and spaces. Indeed, as Halbwachs (1925 [1992], p. 51) once said of memory, equally valid for considerations of heritage:

> [Even as a] man must often appeal to others' remembrances to evoke his own past . . ., one remembers only what he himself has seen, done, felt and thought . . . our own memory is never confused with anyone else's.

Through this book therefore we seek to also incorporate the individual – with its imperfections and imperiousness – back into the heritage process (see Crane 1997), and to show how HFB may be seen as a missed opportunity for AHD. Finally, we provide a summary of the chapters composing the book and propose how to read them together.

'FROM AUTHORIZED HERITAGE DISCOURSE . . .'

> [H]eritage, far from being fatally predetermined or God-given, is in large measure our own marvellously malleable creation. (Lowenthal 1997, p. 226)

'Heritage' is defined in this book as elements drawn from the past seen as valuable to be preserved within the present for the benefit of current and future generations, where 'the present selects an inheritance from an imagined past for current use and decides what should be passed on to an imagined future' (Tunbridge and Ashworth 1996, p. 6). While this may also refer to 'natural' elements, the focus in this edited book is extracted from the cultural realm – such as in the form of material artefacts, rituals, practices, customs, traditions, as well as memories of what transpired before – that have survived the winds of time and are part of the lived or represented realities of contemporary societies. Thus, although many of these expressions of heritage may have been hitherto co-opted in the form of material artefacts within museums, choreographed heritage festivals, cultural theme parks and hardy monuments (Hardy 1988; Young 1989; Harvey 2001), others may also refer to aspects of everyday life not yet marked as 'heritage', despite having deep roots in the past. Furthermore, heritage may be 'tangible' or 'intangible', the latter standing for *meanings* behind the tangible and for heritage as 'practised' (i.e., as embodied, for instance, in story-telling and dance).

Taken in this way, 'heritage' can be anything and everything. This is why critical scholars of heritage have tended to home in less on what constitutes 'heritage' – as heritage practitioners, such as policy makers and curators are more inclined to do, sometimes unquestioningly – and more on *what* heritage is meant to achieve and *how* the past is crafted to achieve objectives set for it (Hanna et al. 2004). Usually done by elites (including the heritage practitioners mentioned earlier, but also national governments and supranational organizations such as UNESCO), it is to these crafted forms of dominant heritage-making that Smith (2006) applies the idea of the AHD. Highly presentist in nature, AHD is often perceived negatively in terms of how it privileges certain interpretations of the past, but marginalizes others when these do not conform to its overarching purpose (Tunbridge and Ashworth 1996; Crampton 2003; Muzaini and Yeoh 2005; Graham and Whelan 2007). The need for heritage as pushed by AHD is also often couched in the need to salvage the past as bulwark against the harm of conflicts and threats such as modernization, exploitative urbanization, unmonitored tourism trends and the socio-cultural impact of prevailing economic crises (see also Winter 2013).

Since hegemonic discourses about heritage seek to influence the way 'we think, talk and write about heritage', Smith (2006, p. 11) focuses primarily on the tendency for AHD to *naturalize* the practices (and products) of preserving a certain interpretation of the past by obscuring the 'work' that goes into its making, expressing it as 'common sense', reliant:

> on the power/knowledge claims of technical and aesthetic experts, and insti-
> tutionalized in state cultural agencies . . . This discourse takes its cue from the
> grand narratives of nation and class . . . privileges monumentality and scale,
> innate artefact/site significance tied to time depth . . . social consensus and
> nation building . . . to establish claims about itself that make it real.

Such is the anointing of narratives and understandings of the past as the 'right' heritage, even as this suppresses other aspects, other narratives, other understandings rendered 'invisible' by 'hegemonic conceptualizations of history and identity' (Dwyer 2000, p. 661; see also Leib 2002; Dwyer 2004; Hoelscher and Alderman 2004). Furthermore, AHD is conceived as 'a discrete "site", "object", building or other structure with identifiable boundaries that can be mapped, surveyed, recorded' (Smith 2006, p. 31), often freeze-framed as it was in the past to render it 'more authentic', even as this may alienate it from the masses. One may recall how the appropriation of *Sukhotai*, an ancient temple complex in Thailand, as AHD had not only meant the removal of newer temples and settlements established since the period of the ancient kingdom, but also the displacement of rituals seen as incongruent with the status of the site of 'national' heritage and of tourist attraction (Byrne 2014). Taken this way, hence, 'heritage is not simply practised but also authorised and ascribed with value, legitimacy and social and cultural capital', such that what is seen to not align nicely with AHD is erased (Roberts and Cohen 2014, p. 243).

Some scholars, geographers in particular, have also intimated how this sleight of hand – where the value of heritage is determined by a small elite group appointed as its stewards, even as it is expressed as being for the betterment of many – is done spatially, since memory, as even historian Nora (1989, p. 9) has famously averred, 'takes root in the concrete, in spaces, gestures, images, and objects' (in geography, see Edensor 1998; Johnson 1999, 2011; Crampton 2003; Gough 2004; Hoelscher and Alderman 2004; Tolia-Kelly 2010). These sites of heritage are then packaged in ways that hide their partiality. Far from being representative of the views of the people for whom one specific heritage is meant, AHD is forged out of the mills of politicians, archaeologists and historians who are 'speaking for' rather than 'speaking from' the platform of the masses. The privileging by AHD of the materiality of heritage also implies that their intangible elements – even as these have increasingly been recognized, by nations and supranational organizations (e.g., UNESCO) alike, as important to consider as part of heritage to be preserved (Harrison 2013) – often fall by the wayside either in the interest of secularizing discourses (so as not to interest some groups more than others, thus appealing to more visitors) or ensuring that visitor behaviour and action does not threaten the integrity of preserved heritages (Byrne 2014).

AHD strives to naturalize its formally appointed version of the past so that this is accepted by the people unquestioningly. Thus, ironically, while this is meant to be the heritage of many, it is often an inherently distancing reconstruction of the past, according to which visitors are often told what to remember and what they can or cannot do while at heritagescapes. As a result, they tend to be fundamentally estranged from the 'work' that goes into the making of heritage, its selection, interpretation, value. As Smith (2006, p. 31) proceeds to say:

> AHD constructs heritage as something . . . engaged with passively – while it may be the subject of popular 'gaze', that gaze is a passive one in which the audience will uncritically consume the message of heritage constructed by heritage experts. Heritage is not defined . . . as an active process or experience, but rather it is something visitors are led to, are instructed about but are then not invited to engage with more actively.

Although this has changed with the shift towards more participatory, consensus-building and 'community-based' approaches to heritage-making (see Dicks 2000; Atkinson 2007; Smith and Waterton 2013), this has at times been found to merely pay lip service (what Smith 2006, p. 38 refers to as 'gestural politics') or done in a way in which 'the expert' still reigns supreme (on this, see Waterton and Watson 2011). While laudable in how excluded groups may, in this way, be recruited into existing practices of valuing the past, unfortunately it is merely a case of co-opting vernacular heritage without effectively challenging the status quo of the day.

Having said that, AHD is not always embraced by those for whom it is intended. Realizing how '[o]fficial memorials . . . [may] not simply testify a "real" history but rather represent what some want to believe, or what some want others to believe, in the monument' (Tyner et al. 2012, p. 856), scholars have highlighted how individuals may show up, and speak against, the partiality that surrounds the formal constitution or re-enactment of the past. Curthoys (2000, p. 129), for instance, has shown how indigenous populations of Australia have critiqued national historiography as having excised their own stories within the white settler society (see also Johnson 1999; Leib 2002; Dwyer and Alderman 2008), while Enloe's work (1998, pp. 51–2) has put the emphasis on how official war remembrances have tended to be biased against representations of women's war experiences given 'it had been men whose ideas and actions had been crucial shapers of [memory] processes', thus showing AHD as not only racist but gendered (see also Dwyer 2002). Gough (2004, p. 238) also illustrates how the hegemony of formal heritagescapes may be offset by the lack of patronage on the part of the people themselves, such that: 'without frequent reinscription, the date and place of commemoration fades away as memory atrophies [and] the commemorative space loses its potency to reinvigorate memory'.

The key thing to note here is that there is never only one 'heritage' but many. If indeed there is no such thing as an a priori heritage, and heritage is what is inherited and then valued about the past within the present, then there may be as many ways of 'valuing' heritage as there are individuals in any given society. While interpretations about the past – both AHD and those produced by the masses at large – may coalesce such that they serve to consolidate a particular understanding of history, in other contexts they may collide, for instance when AHD is resisted by alternative ways of interpreting history, hence giving rise to its contested nature (Hewison 1987; Tunbridge and Ashworth 1996; Leib 2002; Hoelscher and Alderman 2004; Legg 2005a; Graham et al. 2016; Muzaini 2016a). It is in this sense, then, that AHD can work to undermine ideas about 'heritage' that may be seen to go against presentist objectives such as nation-building and tourism. Consequently, AHD may also result in saturating public expressions of place attachment, lending to a sense of dispossession and alienation (Smith and Waterton 2013).

'. . . TO A HERITAGE FROM BELOW'

> To look only at large scale and/or commercial and tangible sites is to place limits on the counter hegemonic possibilities written into the expression of the past at these sites. (Robertson 2012, p. 13)

While the scholarship pertaining to the politics of heritage-making that emphasizes the contentious interplay of heritage-making has provided us with much fodder with regards to revealing the appropriative politics of 'top-down' heritage-making (Harrison 2013), there exists a lacuna in terms of considering heritage made 'in the shadows' and away from the public eye, as well as how individuals themselves experience heritage at the more local level. In this regard, Robertson's (2008, 2012) work on HFB has clearly paved the way. As Robertson (2012, p. 6) puts it himself:

> [D]iscussion of the manifestations of heritage at the local scale has been somewhat superficial despite the fact that it is in the local context that the relationship between heritage and identity establishment and maintenance is often most meaningful.

In his reckoning, heritage is not just something political, commodified and spectacular, but also something personal, sometimes invisible – 'a sense of inheritance that does not seek to attract an audience' (Robertson 2012, p. 2) – although still pertinent for a more complete understanding of the past. Here, he points to the need to recognize the value of popular heritage crafted by the ordinary people themselves, as active agents in their own right such that they become not only consumers of heritage but also makers/keepers of their own pasts.

In doing so, it becomes possible to overcome the elitism of history and refocus towards what may be called unofficial histories, especially those which may not be overtly presented as 'counter-memory' (Legg 2005a) or even remotely interested in engaging with AHD. Indeed, as much as heritage may be used to serve the realm of politics (i.e., nation-building) or to serve more economic imperatives (i.e., tourism) 'from above', they can also be 'cultural resources for counter hegemonic expressions' (Robertson 2012, p. 1). Having said that, HFB can also function beyond these explicitly incited purposes to include more implicit intentions to, as Muzaini (2012, p. 216) puts it, 'mak[e] memories our own way'. In his work, Muzaini directs attention to how non-elite individuals in Perak, Malaysia, have sought to recuperate memories sidelined by formal heritage-makers by materializing their own memorials and through their own practices of 'story-telling' to overturn the biases of AHD. Furthermore, there are also times when it is inappropriate or even unsafe to make personal or community heritages public especially when these pertain to sensitive histories (Muzaini 2012).

This is not to say, however, that there has been complete paucity in the critical scholarship interested in how heritage has survived in these less palpable spaces, shapes and forms. In fact, there have been many studies that have taken into consideration often overlooked ways of remembering that had served as 'anti-hegemonic possibilities ... [and] resources for expressions of identity and ways of life that run counter to the dominant' (Robertson 2012, p. 2). Examples of these would be Legg's (2005a) investigation of sites of counter-memories in India, where the formally marginalized past has been found to still play important roles in the everyday practices of locals, Tolia-Kelly's (2004, 2010) work on how South Asian migrants preserve their heritage in Britain, Atkinson's (2007) reflections on the retention of everyday, 'kitchified', social memories in the docklands of Hull, as well as Byrne's (2014) ruminations on the 'numinous' in Asian forms of heritage-making (see also Alderman 2003; Hebbert 2005; Crooke 2007; Alderman and Campbell 2008; Lin 2011; Waterton and Watson 2011; Robertson 2012; Byrne 2013; Muzaini 2014, 2016a, 2016b; Drozdszewski 2016). Of note here is how HFB may emerge not only as reaction to AHD but also for many other reasons, albeit in less visible fashion and spaces. Even as such heritage may be, as Tyner et al. (2012, p. 854) put it, '"hidden in plain sight": those places that are not commemorated through official channels ... [but] experienced on a day-to-day basis', they may still have an impact especially on those who know of the stories (see also Till 2005). In these regards, the concept of HFB thus rests on the idea that, as much as it is important to consider forms of heritage-making (and resultant heritagescapes) that are 'top-down', high profile, bounded and representational, we should also seek out those that are 'from below'.

In line with what Robertson and Webster (2017, p. 313) refer to as 'the turn towards the exploration of heritages that are local, particular, mundane', Robertson (2012, p. 2, see also Robertson 2015) has conceptualized HFB as 'an expression of, and draws on, the ordinary and quotidian that [. . .] is underscored by *embodied* practice', highly personal in its 'assertion of a right to dwell: an engagement with and expression of landscape as an enduring record of the lives and works of past and present generations who have dwelled within it' (emphasis added). This calls for more attention to be paid to how the people themselves engage with heritagescapes on a more intimate register. With reference to Angkor Wat in Cambodia, for instance, Winter (2004, p. 337) speaks of how popular understandings of the site's heritage are never fixed or dormant; rather, heritage sites are constantly reinterpreted (and therefore rejuvenated) by the people themselves who use and claim it as their own 'living heritage' – in an 'interweaving of leisure, tourism and religion as visitors continually move between swimming, picnicking, temple visits and prayer' – thus making their own experiences even as these may collide with the mandated status of the temples as a revered heritage site (see also Muzaini 2012).

For Byrne (2013, p. 603), despite the suppression of public commemoration of the killings in Indonesia by the government of General Soeharto in 1965–66 to purge the country of (alleged) communists which led the deaths of at least half a million people, the island of Bali is 'replete with reminders, for those left behind, of the cataclysm and those who perished with it', in the form of memories embodied not in stones and plinths but in the individuals themselves. Here, Byrne (2013, p. 597) insists on how memories may at times survive not in the physical landscape but 'are constituted in the sensory, the emotional and the imaginary. . . steeped in affect'. This emphasis on 'affect' draws from the cognate field of cultural geography (see Lorimer 2005; Thrift 2008) that considers heritage(scapes) as more than just what it (they) represent but also how they make us feel, the emotions they incite, and how they are reproduced, sometimes unwittingly, within our own persona. This literature tends to shift emphasis on heritage-making from just the ways in which heritagescapes are to be 'read' to, as Lorimer (2005, p. 84) puts it, 'how life takes shape and gains expression in shared experiences, everyday routines, fleeting encounters, embodied movements, precognitive triggers, practical skills, affective intensities, enduring urges, unexceptional interactions and sensuous dispositions' (see also Crang and Tolia-Kelly 2010; Park 2010; Jones 2011; Muzaini 2016b).

In previous work, again Muzaini (2016a, 2016b) reported on how visitors sometimes engage in their own chosen routes, movements and behaviours within carefully scripted cultural theme parks, thus 'making their own heritage', or have memories triggered at war memorial sites that can escape the messages intended by the sites' initiators and managers, some not even related to the past itself. In fact, much production of heritage and its related practices may be missed, especially if one is not deliberately seeking them or if the respondents simply do not care to bring these up in interviews. Central to the approach guiding this book, therefore, is the extent to which our experiences of formal as well as informal heritage sites are frequently influenced not only by the carefully choreographed routes and narratives of heritagescapes, but also by the material surroundings and by our own positionalities, which then form an ever transient and evolving assemblage determining how we feel and what we think at any given time (Muzaini 2015). Our aim here is thus to capture the more fluid ways in which individuals and groups not only participate in the production of, but also engage with, heritagescapes that may be overlooked in more conventional ethnographies of (sites and practices of) heritage.

For sure, there is much more to heritage than the AHD, and the practice of making and consuming heritage extends beyond the efforts of elites – be it of the state, representatives of the UNESCO World Heritage committee, or similar – to include non-state individuals and groups seeking to create public heritage in their own private capacities (Dwyer and Alderman 2008). In fact, practices of heritage-making, and the wide range of ways in which people can engage with them, vary tremendously. While the literature on the politics of heritage may give some clues as to the existence of discourses counter to AHD, the 'occularcentrism' (Harvey 2001) of much heritage studies tends to obscure heritagescapes that may not be visible (or kept obscured by the community themselves), as well as perpetuate that tendency for AHD to be centred only on the spectacular. Further, there is also the inclination for many studies to be focused primarily on bounded sites. This might be attributed to the work of early thinkers such as Halbwachs (1925 [1992]) and Nora (1989), whose emphasis upon *sites* of memory provided a convenient *entrée* for geographical studies. However, as Atkinson (2007, p. 523) reckons, 'an excessive focus upon bounded sites of memory risks fetishizing place and space too much [while] obscur[ing] the wider production of social memory throughout society'.

Another theme pertinent to the discussion developed in this book, and in our view lacking in Robertson's early conceptualization of HFB, is the role of technology and the extent to which this has allowed for HFB to get a more public presence, and how this has impacted upon AHD. Living in an age of advanced computer-mediated communication (CMC) and Web 2.0 technologies as well as its tools (first and foremost, the Internet), it is inevitable that this would play a role in how heritage is made/unmade within societies today. Affordances that such technologies have given rise to – in terms of increasing the extent of memory to be virtually preserved, allowing for contact without geographical propinquity, and democratising heritage-making such that it is no longer just the purview of elites but for anyone with a computer and something to say! – have definitely served to provide a platform in which alternative interpretations of the past can emerge and AHD be subverted (Muzaini and Yeoh 2015). Having said that, such technologies have also been co-opted by elite heritage-makers in terms of ensuring not only the increase of (right and accurate) information to be disseminated, but also the added possibility to reach an even wider audience, for instance, via the online presence of, or the use of audio-guided trails within, formal heritagescapes (Reading 2003).

Yet, the Internet has also translated into a portal through which ordinary men and women may voice their views, thus allowing for a certain 'democratization' of memory and heritage-making, even if these may go against official heritage discourses and practices, such as in the form of e-memorials or social media (see, for sampling, Drinot 2011; Blackburn 2013; Muzaini and Yeoh 2015). For others, the Internet has also been a means through which heritage formally excised may find sanctuary, and also where otherwise alienated individuals may be brought together and united in the reproduction of HFB. For sure, regardless of how watertight an AHD may be, once it has entered the realm of cyberspace it becomes hard to put it down, hence indicating how the new technologies may actually serve to impede AHD (Muzaini and Yeoh 2015). More than that, it has also given rise to questions related to how heritage may be consumed differently – at times antagonistically – by the public at large, particularly as the past is now represented not in the physical forms of memorials, museums and monuments, but fashioned as Instagram photographs, web dialogues or virtual memory communities (de Vries and Rutherford 2004; Hess 2007; Maddrell 2012). Thus, in *After Heritage*, we consider not only how virtual platforms may allow for HFB to perpetuate itself, but also the ways in which they play out the challenges and contestations as embodied by their physical counterparts.

TOWARDS A MORE CRITICAL HFB

It is evident heritage studies has embarked upon a critical turn, and the question thus arises, what should 'critical' mean precisely? (Winter 2013, p. 532)

In the light of the discussion so far, it would be tempting to consider HFB as a champion of different forms of heritage – more 'authentic' and ideal-ized versions of the past – that have been marginalized or even excluded within AHD, thus offering vast possibilities for subversion. However, it is salient to note that, even as informal interpretations of the past may emerge as necessary checks to AHD, or provide a space where individuals and groups may engage with history in their own unique ways, they should not be romanticized. In fact, HFB may also serve to (sometimes inadvertently) reproduce dominant official discourses or even be motivated by hidden agendas (Aigner 2016). Some work has indeed shown how, in cases of 'difficult heritage', individuals too may seek to play down or forget altogether the past (see Till 2005; Dwyer and Alderman 2008; MacDonald 2010; Muzaini 2014, 2015). Witcomb and Buckley (2013, p. 563), for instance, suggest for us to 'move away from the idea that critique should only come from the bottom up', lamenting the lack of concern for the fact that HFB as 'critique does not need to be accountable to issues concerning its implementation'.

Thus, far from privileging the extent to which HFB may resuscitate suppressed histories and memories, such as within ordinary rituals and spaces (Muzaini 2012), the book seeks to interrogate how these too may be influenced by their own ulterior motives as much as they may also be constrained by AHD. Often manifested as criticism to how formalized heritage has led to the marginalization or, worse, erasure of the past, leading to disenfranchisement of certain individuals or collectives, HFB, as crafted by non-elite actors, may easily be seen as the last bastion before the eventual demise of societal memories perceived as superfluous or antithetical to dominant discourses and, thus, discarded. Framed this way, it is therefore hard to see these actors as anything but acting against the evils – of selective remembering – as committed by states (and corporations). Yet, one should not forget how states and heritage practitioners are also increasingly seeking to incorporate people's everyday and community heritages into their formal heritage-making, even if their efforts may not be as inclusive as they seem (see Atkinson 2007; Crooke 2007; Smith and Waterton 2013). Furthermore, HFB, like AHD, may also serve their own economic and political functions (e.g., in strategies of ethnic revivalism) such that it too can be selective, biased and partial to the actual past itself.

Additionally, it is also important to note that, while HFB's versions of the past may be framed as being 'more inclusive' or 'less biased' than what formal AHD offers, support for HFB from the masses is far from unequivocal. Given that there can be as many alternative interpretations of the past as there are interpreters, HFB can also be responsible for having its own preferred heritages (as defined by a few, driven by their own motives) such that it too may be culpable, as AHD, of playing down or eliding altogether elements of the past. It is not uncommon to find, for instance, examples of visitors to a heritage site who do not want to hear stories that diverge from rehearsed, 'well-known', narratives about a particular past, or situations in which the public may be divided in terms of how they feel the past should be represented (Dwyer 2000; Smith 2006; Muzaini 2015). There are also those who feel that, while everyone may have a personal story or understanding of the past, these stories are not always to be emphasized since they may risk bringing up unwanted and traumatic memories (see Muzaini 2012, 2014). As such, HFB is not only something frowned upon by AHD, where, as Robertson (2012, pp. 19–20) writes, '[o]fficial recognition of, and support for heritage from below therefore remains fleeting at best and oppositional at worst . . . [given how it] is often itself oppositional and is often best expressed in the illusive, ephemeral and everyday', but also something that can invite dissent among non-elites with respect to physical heritagescapes and in the virtual world (Drinot 2011).

In this regard, the contributions to this book offer a novel way of interrogating informal 'heritagescapes' that intends not merely to react to (or critique) 'top-down' AHD, but also to cast a critical eye on these so-called alternative forms of heritage-making. More fundamentally, however, our conceptualization of HFB also raises the question of what 'heritage' actually is. Inspired by early thinkers such as Halbwachs (1925 [1992]) and Nora (1989), heritage and heritage-making in the modern age is frequently seen as something that is distanced from, and external to, the body – as 'sites of memory' – such that 'we have to some degree divested ourselves of the obligation to remember' (Young 1993, p. 5; see also Hewison 1987). Yet, the past may also survive in more embodied, even ephemeral, ways. For example, Küchler (1999) demonstrates how, during the Malangan ceremony in Papua New Guinea, the act of remembering the ancestral dead entails the iconoclasm (vis-à-vis the retention) of 'traces' of the dead, while Legg's (2005b) work shows how the past can reside in the embodied actions, rituals and practices of the people rather than in the form of 'sites of memory' (see also Bender 1993; Muzaini 2012, 2014; Byrne 2014). Thus, central to this book is also the aim of decentring what we mean when we say 'heritage'. For sure, it is too simplistic, not to say Western-centric, to focus on heritage as what is (in)tangibly *presenced*, or instrumentalized towards the achievement of certain objectives; heritage may also be marked by *absence* (or the absence of physical reminders), perceived in this case in ways that have less to do with valuing something as heritage, but reproduced as part of daily life, where it is more salient what we seek not to forget than what we remember (Tyner et al. 2012).

Finally, the chapters collected here also seek to position critical perspectives of HFB in relation to heritage-making on other scales, including that of the dominant 'national' (when heritage is nationalized) or 'global' AHD (such as promulgated by the work of UNESCO). For sure, the 'local' here does not exist independently from these other scales of heritage-making, where HFB may often be limited in what it can or cannot actually do by actors and narratives operating at different scales. Formed on the bedrock of discussions related to 'alternative' or 'peripheral' critical geographies generally (see Minca 2003; Berg 2010) and critical heritage studies specifically (Winter and Waterton 2013), the 'critical' in the subtitle also relates to the undoing of the binary that often pitches AHD as 'bad' and HFB as 'good'. What clearly emerges in the chapters that follow is that the two are at times almost impossible to disentangle, especially when AHD seeks to (or at least appears to) co-opt HFB for its purposes (Blackburn 2013), or where HFB may rely heavily on what AHD affords it in order to do its tasks, such as to achieve more visibility (see Johnson 2011; Muzaini 2015).

Stemming out of this, the primary idea that we seek to unpack in *After Heritage*, therefore, is that there is no clear line in these days to separate what is AHD from HFB, be it in terms of what of the past is made valuable or who is doing the valuing. In fact, they often overlap and constantly interact with one other, such that clear-cut distinctions are frequently blurred. Having said that, while recognizing that HFB may be seen as a threat to AHD – especially when it disrupts or destabilizes the version of history that has been authorized as heritage, or when it reveals how it is categorically impossible for AHD to ever be fashioned in a way that will please everyone – HFB is nevertheless pertinent to understanding how the people themselves value, appreciate *and practice* heritage. This is why we think it is more instructive to do away with a hierarchical view of heritage from the 'top down' (AHD) or the 'bottom up' (HFB): after all, and here we go back to the quote from which we started: '[t]here is, really, no such thing as heritage' (Smith 2006, p. 11). Rather, all heritages are constructed and crafted; and what is important is to what purpose they are activated and reproduced.

STRUCTURE OF THE BOOK

Following this introduction, **James A. Tyner**'s chapter juxtaposes official heritagescapes with the recollections of ordinary individuals to compare how the actions of the brutal regime of the Khmer Rouge in Cambodia are memorialized by the state as well as the population at large. He argues how the formal memorialization related to events that led to millions massacred – primarily signified by the S21 Museum and the killing fields of Choeung Ek –may be criticized as partial, although the people themselves have sought to ensure that formal memory erasure is incomplete, not by building their own physical memorials but merely by ensuring that they do not forget. Through an account of what he refers to as HFB 'hidden in plain sight', Tyner demonstrates how people in Cambodia subscribe to an alternative idea of how to remember, where it is less important to materially *presence* the past (as formal heritage-making, that is AHD, tends to do) than to honour memories in more intangible ways (such as through oral histories) even as the sites of atrocity themselves have been destroyed, remain unmarked or have erstwhile been rehabilitated to more modern uses.

This is then followed by **Jamie Gillen,** whose chapter highlights the ways in which the motorbike, despite its ubiquity and relatively recent emergence on the country's roads, has been adopted by many ordinary Vietnamese as part of their identity, even as the automobile has become the vehicle of choice for many today. Using the concept of 'aspirational heritage', and comparing the motorbike with other modes of transport, he discusses HFB as something that is defined less by the past, or even by formal policy makers in the country, than by how it fulfils needs within the present and the future in Vietnam. More importantly, this chapter shows clearly how heritage should not only be seen as something 'local' to be protected 'from above' but also something that is 'lived' and claimed by the people themselves although this is often overlooked and not acknowledged by AHD. More than that, Gillen also highlights the provisional status of HFB, as something evolving along with societal trends and aspirations. In other words, far from 'fixed', heritage should be seen as always in a process of becoming.

While the first two chapters focus on some of the mundane ways in which HFB has been interpreted and materialized (or not) by local people, which do not outwardly challenge or resist AHD, the next chapter by **Ana Aceska and Claudio Minca** shifts the attention to the erection of the Bruce Lee monument in the city of Mostar, in Bosnia-Herzegovina. Here, the authors reflect on how the statue dedicated to the *kung fu* star is not only one initiated 'from below', but also a statement to the failure of AHD to bridge the physical and symbolic barriers that separate Muslims and Catholics in the post-war city. Yet, while there are locals who embraced the value of using a popular icon as a means to bind the divided city, there are also others who reneged against it, revealing how the statue does not necessarily receive the support 'of the people' despite it being proclaimed as being 'for the people'. In doing so, Aceska and Minca reflect on the partiality and biased agenda underlining this HFB initiative. While it may be seen to represent the 'voice' of the people on the ground, it is still, at the end of the day, the efforts of a select group of elites purporting *to speak for* the masses, hence a reminder of how HFB should never be overly romanticized even as it may emerge out of the failure of AHD.

The following chapter by **Richard Carter-White** reprises the idea of heritage-making as a contested process, with the case of visitors who have turned to Instagram as a way to memorialize their time in the former concentration camps of Auschwitz and Birkenau in Poland. Here, the emphasis is on the ways in which images taken at what are perhaps the most sacrosanct sites of the Holocaust were uploaded on the social media platform and how this has resulted in ambivalent responses, thus showing how support for HFB can be varied; while some responses serve to destabilize institutional scripting of AHD, others show how heritage as crafted within social media 'from below' may also be a platform for reproducing, and even extending the reach of, dominant elite narratives. Ultimately, Carter-White demonstrates not only the extremely blurred lines that exist between AHD and HFB but, more broadly, the ways in which technology has reshaped how societies relate to 'the past' and how, due to the algorithmic logic of Instagram and arguably all forms of social media, one should never overstate the role of technology in reckoning an era of more democratic heritage-making.

Also building on the theme of technology, **Matthew Cooke and Amy Potter**'s chapter focuses on how social media, films as well as the practice of tour guiding in former plantations where slavery was practised, have provided spaces where individuals can 'speak against' AHD in the United States, that is, in a context in which narratives of slavery have often times been underplayed or silenced at such formalized heritagescapes writ large. More significantly, their work reveals how such alternative interpretations are not always well accepted on the ground, especially by the visitors who seek to avoid difficult conversations related to the country's history of slavery, thus showing how popular attitudes to HFB are far from unequivocal. More than that, through rich interview materials with memorial entrepreneurs working at the plantations, Cooke and Potter also reflect upon the labour and difficulties that are faced in initiatives to revise dominant narratives of slavery in sites of national history.

The next two chapters then narrow down the emphasis to heritage-making on the more personal and intimate level of the individual. **Danielle Drozdzewski**, for instance, focuses on the ways in which the Holocaust is memorialized in Berlin albeit not through its well-known, AHD-driven Topography of Terror, and Memorial to the Murdered Jews in Europe, but by the ubiquitous Stolpersteine, small plaques emplaced in everyday spaces within the city, to commemorate named individuals who lost their lives during the tragic event. Unlike the conspicuous Bruce Lee statue in Mostar, the Stolpersteine may be easily missed; in fact, they are often overlooked, stepped on rather than engaged with. Yet, they undoubtedly hold very personal meaning for the families who commissioned them, and are capable of 'stickily' and deeply affecting others who do encounter them. Despite how the Stolpersteine may be seen to counter the deindividualizing tendency of AHD in Berlin, Drozdzewski reflects on how these 'stumbling stones' remain symbolic; while they ensure memorialization of some individuals who died during the German Third Reich, they do not memorialize all, hence pointing to its selectivity. More than that, she also shows how this effort to manifest heritage 'from below' is not always appreciated such as by those who seek not to associate the city with the past.

In the penultimate chapter, **Meghann Ormond** considers the phenomenon of personal heritage of her own mother who sought to investigate her genealogy as a child adoptee. Here is a case of heritage that does not seek an audience but simply aims at recovering one's history, where Meghann's mother used both AHD (e.g., public records) and HFB (e.g., in the form of 'search angels', genealogical associations and commercial organizations) to put together the jigsaw puzzle that was her life prior to adoption; even as she managed to achieve a measure of success, however, this was not accomplished without hurdles and difficulty. This again demonstrates how we should not see AHD and HFB as pitted against one another; they should instead be seen as different elements of a whole that can be drawn upon in constructing a personalized heritage. More than that, Ormond's chapter also reflects upon how challenges faced by both her and her mother may emerge not only 'from above' but also 'from below'.

Rounding up *After Heritage* is the Afterword by **Iain Robertson** who provides concluding notes to what he understands about HFB as conceptualized in this book, particularly since this relates to his own work that has highly inspired the collection. Additionally, Robertson charts some of the ways in which further research on HFB should proceed moving forward.

What ties all the chapters is our interest in investigating how HFB may be seen to be giving voice to the people even if it too may just be responsible for being partial to history. Indeed, while HFB is often framed as a check to AHD, it is also a process that can sow discord, especially when it privileges some readings of the past and not others. In fact, what the chapters show is that, regardless of heritage as spearheaded by elites or non-elites, it is more important to consider how selected histories are actualized in terms of today's practices, since each actualization, either of the AHD or HFB variety, is nothing more than an attempt to force a specific coding on the past to achieve contemporary objectives. The chapters here also make evident how AHD and HFB are, more often than not, overlapping and intertwined, such that it is problematic to pit one against the other; rather, we should seek to refine their relationships and promote their collaborations towards mutually beneficial purposes. However, what is most salient to recognize is that *people do remember different pasts*, and experience or are affected by heritage in highly subjective ways. This, we argue, is possibly the true value of HFB, in terms of unravelling how individuals read, understand and practice heritage *at the more personal level*, so we can ensure that whatever heritage is produced it can resonate with, and serve the needs of, those for whom 'heritage' is intended.

REFERENCES

Aigner, A. (2016), 'Heritage-making "from-below": the politics of exhibiting architectural heritage on the Internet – a case study', *International Journal of Heritage Studies*, **22** (3), 181–99.

Alderman, D.H. (2003), 'Street names and the scaling of memory: the politics of commemorating Martin Luther King, Jr. within African American community', *Area*, **35**, 163–73.

Alderman, D.H. and R.M. Campbell (2008), 'Symbolic excavation and the artefact politics of remembering slavery in the American South: observations from Walterboro, South Carolina', *Southeastern Geographer*, **48**, 338–55.

Atkinson, D. (2007), 'Kitsch geographies and the everyday spaces of social memory', *Environment and Planning A*, **39**, 521–40.

Bender, Barbara (1993), *Landscape: Politics and Perspectives*, Oxford: Berg.

Berg, L.D. (2010), 'Critical human geography', in Barney Wharf (ed.), *Encyclopedia of Geography*, London: Sage, pp. 617–29.

Blackburn, K. (2013), 'The "democratization" of memories of Singapore's past', Journal of the Humanities and Social Sciences of Southeast Asia, **169** (4), 431–56.

Byrne, D. (2013), 'Love and loss in the 1960s', *International Journal of Heritage Studies*, **19** (6), 596–609.

Byrne, Denis (2014), *Counterheritage: Critical Perspectives on Heritage Conservation in Asia*, London: Routledge.

Connerton, Paul (1989), *How Societies Remember*, Cambridge and New York: Cambridge University Press.

Crampton, A. (2003), 'The art of nation-building: (re)presenting political transition at the South African National Gallery', *cultural geographies*, **10**, 218–42.

Crane, S.A. (1997), 'Writing the individual back in collective memory', *The American Historical Review*, **102** (5), 1372–85.

Crang, M. and D. Tolia-Kelly (2010), 'Nation, race, and affect: senses and sensibilities at national heritage sites', *Environment and Planning A*, **42** (10), 2315–31.

Crooke, Elizabeth (2007), *Museums and Community: Ideas, Issues and Challenges*, London: Routledge.

Curthoys, Ann (2000), 'National narratives, war commemoration and racial exclusion in a settler society: the Australian case', in T.G. Ashplant, Graham Dawson and Michael Roper (eds), *The Politics of War Memory and Commemoration*, London and New York: Routledge, pp. 128–44.

De Vries, B. and J. Rutherford (2004), 'Memorializing loved ones on the World Wide Web', *Omega*, **49**, 5–26.

Dicks, Bella (2000), *Heritage, Place and Community*, Cardiff: University of Wales Press.

Drinot, P. (2011), 'Website of memory: the war of the Pacific (1879–84) in the global age of Youtube', *Memory Studies*, **4**, 370–85.

Drozdzewski, Danielle (2016), 'Encountering memory in the everyday city', in Danielle Drozdzewski, Sarah de Nardi and Emma Waterton (eds), *Memory, Place and Identity: Commemoration and Remembrance of War and Conflict*, London and New York: Routledge, pp. 19–37.

Dwyer, O. (2000), 'Interpreting the Civil Rights movement: place, memory and conflict', *Professional Geographer*, **52** (4), 660–71.

Dwyer, O. (2002), 'Location, politics and the production of Civil Rights memorial landscapes', *Urban Geography*, **23** (1), 31–56.

Dwyer, O. (2004), 'Symbolic accretion and commemoration', *Social and Cultural Geography*, **5** (3), 419–35.

Dwyer, Owen and Derek H. Alderman (2008), *Civil Rights Memorials and the Geography of Memory*, Chicago, IL: The Centre for American Places at Columbia College.

Edensor, Tim (1998), *Tourists at the Taj: Performance and Meaning at a Symbolic Site*, London and New York: Routledge.

Enloe, Cynthia (1998), 'All the men are in the militias, all the women are victims: the politics of masculinity and femininity in nationalist wars', in Lois Ann Lorentzen and Jennifer Turpin (eds), *The Women and War Reader*, New York: New York University Press, pp. 50–62.

Gough, P. (2004), 'Sites in the imagination: the Beaumont Hamel Newfoundland Memorial on the Somme', *cultural geographies*, **11** (4), 235–58.

Graham, B. and Y. Whelan (2007), 'The legacies of the dead: commemorating the Troubles in Northern Ireland', *Environment and Planning D: Society and Space*, **25** (3), 476–95.

Graham, Brian, Gregory J. Ashworth and John E. Tunbridge (eds) (2016), *A Geography of Heritage: Power, Culture and Economy*, London and New York: Routledge.

Halbwachs, Maurice (1925), *On Collective Memory*, reprinted in 1992, trans. Lewis A. Coser, Chicago, IL: University of Chicago Press.

Hanna, S.P., V.J. Del Casino, C. Selden and B. Hite (2004), 'Representation as work in "America's most historic city"', *Social and Cultural Geography*, **5**, 459–81.

Hardy D. (1988), 'Historical geography and heritage studies', *Area*, **20** (4), 333–8.

Harrison, Rodney (2013), *Heritage: Critical Approaches*, London and New York: Routledge.

Harvey, D.C. (2001), 'Heritage pasts and heritage presents: temporality, meaning and the scope of heritage studies', *International Journal of Heritage Studies*, **7** (4), 319–38.

Hebbert, M. (2005), 'The street as locus of collective memory', *Environment and Planning D: Society and Space*, **23**, 581–96.

Hess, A. (2007), 'In digital remembrance: vernacular memory and the rhetorical construction of web memorials', *Media, Culture and Society*, **21**, 812–30.

Hewison, Robert (1987), *The Heritage Industry: Britain in a Climate of Decline*, London: Methuen.

Hoelscher, S. and D.H. Alderman (2004), 'Memory and place: geographies of a critical relationship', *Social and Cultural Geography*, **5**, 347–55.

Johnson, N. (1999), 'The spectacle of memory: Ireland's remembrance of the Great War, 1919', *Journal of Historical Geography*, **25** (1), 36–56.

Johnson, N. (2011), 'The contours of memory in post-conflict societies: enacting public remembrance of the bomb in Omagh, Northern Ireland', *cultural geographies*, **19**, 237–58.

Jones, O. (2011), 'Geography, memory and non-representational geographies', *Geography Compass*, **5**, 875–85.

Küchler, Susanne (1999), 'The place of memory', in Adrian Forty and Susanne Küchler (eds), *The Art of Forgetting*, Oxford: Berg, pp. 53–73.

Legg, S. (2005a), 'Sites of counter-memory: the refusal to forget and the nationalist struggle in Colonial Delhi', *Historical Geography*, **33**, 180–201.

Legg, S. (2005b), 'Contesting and surviving memory: space, nation and nostalgia in les lieux de mémoire', *Environment and Planning D: Society and Space*, **23**, 481–504.

Leib, J.I. (2002), 'Separate times, shared spaces: Arthur Ashe, Monument Avenue and the politics of Richmond, Virginia's symbolic landscape', *cultural geographies*, **9** (3), 286–312.

Lin, Jan (2011), *The Power of Urban Ethnic Places: Cultural Heritage and Community Life*, London: Routledge.

Lorimer, H. (2005), 'Cultural geography: the busyness of being "more-than-representational"', *Progress in Human Geography*, **29**, 83–94.

Lowenthal, David (1997), *The Heritage Crusade and the Spoils of History*, Cambridge: Cambridge University Press.

MacDonald, Sharon (2009), *Difficult Heritage: Negotiating the Nazi Past in Nuremberg and Beyond*, London: Routledge.

Maddrell, A. (2012), 'Online memorials: the virtual as the new vernacular', *Bereavement Care*, **312**, 46–54.

Minca, C. (2003), 'Critical peripheries', *Environment and Planning D: Society and Space*, **21** (2), 160–8.

Muzaini, Hamzah (2012), 'Making memories our own (ways): non-state war remembrances of the Second World War in Perak, Malaysia', in Owain Jones and Joanne Garde-Hansen (eds), *Geography and Memory: Explorations in Identity, Place and Becoming*, London: Palgrave Macmillan, pp. 216–33.

Muzaini, H. (2014), 'The afterlives and memory politics of the Ipoh Cenotaph in Perak, Malaysia', *Geoforum*, **54**, 142–50.

Muzaini, H. (2015), 'On the matter of forgetting and "memory returns"', *Transactions of the Institute of British Geographer*, **40** (1), 102–12.

Muzaini, H. (2016a), 'Informal heritage-making at the Sarawak Cultural Village, East Malaysia', *Tourism Geographies*, **19** (2), 244–64.

Muzaini, Hamzah (2016b), 'Personal reflections on formal Second World War memories/memorials in everyday spaces in Singapore', in Danielle Drozdzewski, Sarah de Nardi and Emma Waterton (eds), *Memory, Place and Identity: Commemoration and Remembrance of War and Conflict*, London and New York: Routledge, pp. 38–55.

Muzaini, H. and B.S.A. Yeoh (2005), 'Reading representations of women's war experiences in the Changi Chapel and Museum, Singapore', *Geoforum*, **36**, 465–76.

Muzaini, H. and B.S.A. Yeoh (2015), 'An exploration of memory-making in the digital era: remembering the FEPOW story online', *Tijdschrift voor economische en sociale geografie*, **106** (1), 53–64.

Nora, P. (1989), 'Between memory and history: les lieux de mémoire', *Representations*, **26**, 7–24.

Park, H.Y. (2010), 'Heritage tourism: emotional journeys into nationhood', *Annals of Tourism Research*, **27** (1), 116–35.

Reading, A. (2003), 'Digital interactivity in public memory institutions: the uses of new technologies in Holocaust museums', *Media, Culture and Society*, **25**, 67–85.

Roberts, L. and S. Cohen (2014), 'Unauthorising popular music heritage: outline of a critical framework', *International Journal of Heritage Studies*, **20** (3), 241–61.

Robertson, Iain J.M. (2008), 'Heritage from below: class, social protest and resistance', in Brian Graham and Peter Howard (eds), *The Ashgate Research Companion to Heritage and Identity*, Aldershot, UK and Burlington, VT: Ashgate, pp. 143–58.

Robertson, Iain J.M. (ed.) (2012), *Heritage from Below*, Farnham, UK and Burlington, VT: Ashgate.

Robertson, I.J.M (2015), 'Hardscrabble heritage: the ruined blackhouse and crofting landscape as heritage from below', *Landscape Research*, **40** (8), 993–1009.

Robertson, I.J.M. and D. Webster (2017), 'People of the croft: visualising land, heritage and identity', *cultural geographies*, **24** (2), 311–18.

Smith, Laurajane (2006), *Uses of Heritage*, London and New York: Routledge.

Smith, Laurajane and Emma Waterton (2013), *Heritage, Communities and Archaeology*, London and New York: Bloomsbury Academic.

Thrift, Nigel (2008), *Non-Representational Theory: Space, Politics, Affect*, London and New York: Routledge.

Till, Karen E. (2005), *The New Berlin*, Minneapolis, MN: Minnesota University Press.

Tolia-Kelly, D. (2004), 'Locating processes of identification: studying the precipitates of re-memory through artefacts in the British Asian home', *Transactions of the Institute of British Geographers*, **29** (3), 314–29.

Tolia-Kelly, Divya P. (2010), *Landscape, Race and Memory: Material Ecologies of Citizenship*, London and New York: Routledge.

Tunbridge, John E. and Gregory Ashworth (1996), *Dissonant Heritage: The Management of the Past as a Resource in Conflict*, London: Wiley.

Tyner, J.A., G.B. Alvarez and A.R. Colucci (2012), 'Memory and the everyday landscape of violence in post-genocide Cambodia', *Social and Cultural Geography*, **13**, 853–71.

Waterton, Emma and Steve Watson (2011), *Heritage and Community Engagement: Collaboration or Contestation?* London and New York: Routledge.

Winter, T. (2004), 'Landscape, memory and heritage: New Year celebrations at Angkor, Cambodia', *Current Issues in Tourism*, 7 (4–5), 330–45.

Winter, T. (2013), 'Clarifying the critical in critical heritage studies', *International Journal of Heritage Studies*, **19** (6), 532–45.

Winter, T. and E. Waterton (2013), 'Critical heritage studies', *International Journal of Heritage Studies*, **19** (6), 529–31.

Witcomb, A. and K.A.M. Buckley (2013), 'Engaging with the future of "critical heritage studies": looking back in order to look forward', *International Journal of Heritage Studies*, **19** (6), 562–78.

Young, J.E. (1989), 'The biography of a memorial icon: Nathan Rapaport's Warsaw Ghetto Monument', *Representations*, **26**, 69–106.

Young, James E. (1993), *The Texture of Memory: Holocaust Memorials and Meaning*, New Haven, CT: Yale University Press.

2. Official memorials, deathscapes, and hidden landscapes of ruin: material legacies of the Cambodian genocide

James A. Tyner

INTRODUCTION

In Cambodia, we see clearly that how we document the past – and how that past is spatially inscribed – matters. It matters, as Lunstrum (2010, pp. 131–2) writes, 'for who has access to and who can legitimately claim ownership of certain spaces; it matters for whether and how certain spaces can be transformed and reinvented; and it matters for who can reap the benefits of these transformations and equally who must make sacrifices to enable them'. As part of a larger project that addresses the political economy of Cambodia's past violence (Tyner 2008, 2014, 2017a, 2017b), in this chapter I juxtapose the various 'writings' of violence on Cambodia's present-day landscape. More precisely, I call attention to the remembrance of Cambodia's past violence 'from below', that is, the mundane spaces of quotidian life that remain unmarked and all-too-often unremarked.

Between 1975 and 1979, the Communist Party of Kampuchea (CPK), also known as the 'Khmer Rouge', carried out a program of mass violence that led to the deaths of approximately 1.7 million people. In just under four years, upwards of one-quarter of the country's pre-genocide population died as a result of famine, exhaustion, disease and murder. Their deaths were the direct result of a series of policies and plans designed and calculated by the CPK to affect a wholesale transformation of Cambodia's pre-1975 society. In theory, Democratic Kampuchea – as Cambodia was renamed – was to be reconfigured as a communal utopia, a society free of oppressive foreign interference, exploitative economic practices and class-based rule (Kiernan 1996; Tyner and Rice 2016; Tyner 2017b). To achieve these ends, the CPK embarked on a policy of eradication, executing thousands of perceived enemies of the revolution, evacuating towns and cities and forcing inhabitants into work-camps to supply forced labor for rice cultivation and the development of infrastructure (Tyner and Will 2015).

Decades after the cessation of direct violence, the question of reconciliation in Cambodia remains fraught, in part because of competing claims over the meaning of reconciliation (Manning 2015, p. 388), but also because of the 'authorship' of Cambodia's past (see Long and Reeves 2009; Norén-Nilsson 2011). To address this latter component, I contrast the material legacies of genocide as exemplified by state-sanctioned memorials that, on the one-hand, cater to a largely Western clientele of 'dark tourists' and, on the other hand, hidden landscapes of past violence that are lived in the everyday by survivors and descendants of the genocide. These latter sites for the most part remained unremarked and unvisited.

We readily understand concrete monuments or bronze plaques as sites of memory. Less often do we consider a lone fence post, drainage ditch or abandoned well as part of the memorial landscape. And yet, it is precisely the banality of ordinary landscapes that conceals the extraordinary landscapes of past violence. Space precludes an in-depth discussion of the methodological parameters of studying hidden landscapes of 'heritage from below'. Briefly, my concern has been to document sites associated with Khmer Rouge practice through (1) archival research and (2) field-based observations. The archives at the Documentation Center of Cambodia offer thousands of pages of Khmer Rouge-era documents; these provide information on specific projects initiated by the Khmer Rouge, including dams, canals, reservoirs and security centers. Over the past decade, I have visited many of these sites, documenting what, if anything, remains on the landscape. It is through the juxtaposition of archived accounts of past landscapes with the present-day material landscape that I attempt to recover that which remains hidden. In so doing I highlight how the current efforts to *remember* the genocide are bounded; and that this bounding serves to construct a particular 'heritage from above' while simultaneously silencing the ongoing living of a 'heritage from below'.

THE PAST MATERIALIZED

Given that monuments and memorials are important symbolic sites in the articulation of political space, the decision to commemorate or even to obliterate a site is frequently made by individuals and institutions of some importance. Indeed, many prominent memorials and monuments constitute official or state-sanctioned actions designed to promote a particular vision of the past in an attempt to provide legitimacy for present and future rule. This is often associated with efforts to formally designate certain places as 'heritage' sites, that is, those deemed worthy of preservation (Harrison 2013). Crucially, many decisions to memorialize or not are predicated on particular (and selective) deployments of authenticity. Itself a much contested term (DeLyser 1999; Lane and Waitt 2001; Schnell 2003; Rickly-Boyd 2009; Alberts and Hazen 2010), claims of authenticity are often wielded as blunt instruments for political or economic purchase. Indeed, the official memorialization of Cambodia's past violence illustrates well how 'the concept of authenticity provides an avenue for understanding how certain views of place, time and culture gain more authority than others and inform decision making processes' about what to preserve, restore, reconstruct or adapt (Lane and Waitt 2001, p. 382; see also Alberts and Hazen 2010).

Not all memorials or places of historic importance are promoted or even supported by governments. Geographers and other scholars are increasingly turning their attention to less formal memorials. Indeed, as Robertson and Webster (2017) write, one of the most exciting recent trends in heritage studies has been the turn toward the exploration of heritages that are local, particular and mundane. Variously termed grassroots memorials, public memorials or vernacular memorials, these are sites remembered through the everyday actions of ordinary men and women (Doss 2008; Stangl 2008).

Frequently of a temporary nature, grassroots memorials are intended for an immediate audience; these also – but not always – have a firmly political component, as silent witnesses to violence and pain (Sánchez-Carretero and Ortiz 2011, p. 107). Such sites provide counter-memories to official narratives and thus call attention to the legitimacy or efficacy of governments. The growing number of privately established roadside memorials that mark vehicular accident sites, for example, may be viewed as more than simply marking the spot where a loved one perished. Kate Hartig and Kevin Dunn (1998, p. 5) suggest that roadside memorials 'are symbolic of societal flaws' and that these landscapes are 'imbued with meanings'.

Memorials and other places of remembrance – whether state-sanctioned (e.g., official heritage sites) or grassroots-initiated (e.g., 'heritage from below' sites) – are not always so prominent on the landscape. Indeed, with few exceptions, scholars have not explicitly considered unmarked landscapes as memorial landscapes. Too often we are myopic in our studies; and for many who toil in the memory and landscape fields, attention is unavoidably directed first-and-foremost toward the visible and tangible memorials and monuments. Recently, however, a handful of scholars are beginning to engage with those sites that remain hidden in plain sight, those sites where the traces of past violence remain unmarked and unremarked on the landscape (Steinberg and Taylor 2003; Tyner et al. 2012; Tyner et al. 2014; Colls 2015). Often, these scholars have focused attention on the material remnants: the traces, ruins or relics of the past that remain spectral-like on the landscape (Edensor 2005, 2008; DeSilvey 2007; Jonker and Till 2009; DeSilvey and Edensor 2012; Till 2012). Tim Edensor (2008, p. 314), for example, notes that 'traces of the past linger in mundane spaces', while DeSilvey (2007, p. 403) reminds us that 'every object left to rot in a dank shed or an airless attic once occupied a place in an active web of social and material relations'. So conceived, the landscape is composed of innumerable remnants and tangible reminders that connect the present with the past. In this way, following Till (2005, p. 9), landscapes 'are not only continuously interpreted; they are haunted by past structures of meaning and material presences from other times and lives'.

Both visible and non-visible markers of Cambodia's violent past remain on the landscape. Former *wats* (temples) and school buildings, for example, had been converted by the Khmer Rouge into prisons or warehouses. *Wat Baray Chaon Dek*, located in the province of Kampong Thom, for example, was used as a prison; an estimated 15,000 men, women and children were buried in scores of mass graves surrounding the site. Other sites remain on the landscape, but are largely unrecognized to outsiders. Here, we understand that 'the landscape is the world as it is known to those who dwell therein, who inhabit its places and journey along the paths connecting them' (Ingold 1993, p. 156). Throughout the Khmer Rouge regime thousands of infrastructure projects were initiated, most notably reservoirs and irrigation schemes. These sites are hidden in plain sight and yet retain an enduring day-to-day presence both for those old enough to have lived through the violence and also for those who continue to earn their living on and around these former sites of brutality. Many of the reservoirs, dams and canals constructed through the use of forced labor continue to function; farmers still obtain water from these structures; and fish continue to be caught in the artificial lakes. The presence of these material sites contributes to the ongoing writing and rewriting of Cambodia's historical geography, in that their material afterlife remain as constant reminders of the violent past (Tyner 2017a, pp. 6–7).

To see again these sites of past violence, my present work is informed by recent developments in critical heritage studies (Smith 2006; Harrison 2009, 2013; Watson and Waterton 2010; Lazzari and Korstanje 2013; Winter 2014). First, we should acknowledge, as Hardy (1988, p. 333) explains, that 'the task of clarification is one that is critical to the sound advance of the study of heritage as a whole'. Indeed, as Winter (2014, p. 557) writes, tracing the historical roots, or origins, of what we understand today as heritage is fraught with problems. Central to this task, Hardy (1988, p. 333) continues, 'is an understanding of the meaning of *heritage* itself'. On the one hand, the term refers to those things – artifacts, ruins, cultural traditions – that are inherited from the past; on the other hand, heritage is also understood as 'a value-loaded concept, embracing (and often obscuring) differences of interpretation' (Hardy 1988, p. 333). Critical heritage studies call attention to the present-ness of heritage processes and practices; it seeks to destabilize the privileged position of technical experts and authorities – members of the so-called heritage industry – who presume the existence of an untarnished past (Harvey 2001). As Tunbridge and Ashworth (1996, p. 6) suggest, 'the present selects an inheritance from an imagined past for current use and decides what should be passed on to an imagined future'. A 'heritage from below' provides a counter-landscape; thus, it 'draws heavily on the cultural realm where a sense of inheritance needs no memorial and instead finds its mnemonic in everyday performances' whereupon 'emphasis is often placed on domestic spaces, routine material culture and the quotidian as prime sites of memory work' (Robertson and Webster 2017, p. 314).

Working from a historical realist presumption, for those in the heritage industry, truth is revealed by experts, aesthetes and professionals to produce an authenticated past; and when further selected and assembled in the social and cultural world view of a particular society, an *authorized discourse* which reproduces its concerns, priorities and content also emerges (Watson and Waterton 2010, pp. 85–6). Here, the concept of an authorized heritage discourse therefore calls attention to the power and performativity of narratives.

In Cambodia, we are presently witness to an ongoing struggle over the representation, interpretation and remembrance of mass violence. More often than not, however, this struggle caters more to the promises of financial reward than truth and reconciliation. The selective preservation of some sites over the recognition of others highlights a political process of memorialization that literally values atrocity over understanding, of death over life. Conversely, a consideration of a 'heritage from below' provides flesh to the skeleton of official memory for, as Robertson and Webster (2017, p. 316) write, such an approach provides 'an engagement with and an expression of the landscape as an enduring record of the lives and works of past and present generations who have dwelt within it'.

STATE AUTHORSHIP OF THE CAMBODIAN GENOCIDE

For the vast majority of international tourists, the legacy of the Khmer Rouge-era is demarcated by two officially recognized and 'authentic' locations: the former security center, S-21, and its attendant mass graves at Choeung Ek (see Ledgerwood 1997; Williams 2004; Hughes 2008;

Tegelberg 2010; Sion 2011; Benzaquen 2014). Located in Phnom Penh, Tuol Sleng had once been a high school. Under the Khmer Rouge, the site was converted into a 'security center', designated as S-21. Throughout its brief existence, approximately 12,000 prisoners were arrested, detained and tortured at the facility. Most were subsequently executed approximately 15 kilometers outside the city at a former Chinese cemetery known as Choeung Ek. Exhumations at this latter site in the 1980s unearthed approximately 9,000 victims.

The memorialization of Tuol Sleng and Cheoung Ek illustrates well the political production of a politicized cultural heritage. On 25 December 1978, Vietnamese forces totaling over 100,000 surged into Democratic Kampuchea. They were joined by approximately 20,000 Cambodians, most of whom were former Khmer Rouge cadre who had established a government-in-exile known as the National Salvation Front (NSF). In the face of this onslaught, the Khmer Rouge retreated into the northern and western highlands of Cambodia. The military defeat of the Khmer Rouge ushered in a decade of Vietnamese occupation and sporadic guerrilla fighting with the still-active Khmer Rouge. According to Chandler (1999), the fledgling People's Republic of Kampuchea (PRK) – as the country was renamed – and its Vietnamese advisors faced enormous economic, organizational and social problems. Of equal importance, however, was how Democratic Kampuchea was to be remembered. Politically, the PRK consisted largely of former Khmer Rouge cadre. Furthermore, the ostensibly socialist PRK faced the problem of how the socialist Democratic Kampuchean period should be remembered. Superficially, one communist government overthrew another communist government. For the PRK, it was imperative to distance them politically from that of the Khmer Rouge.

In the days following the defeat of the Khmer Rouge, two Vietnamese photojournalists were walking through Phnom Penh when they were drawn toward Tuol Sleng by the smell of decomposing bodies (Chandler 1999). There, the photojournalists discovered the bodies of several recently murdered men; some were still chained to iron beds in rooms that once had been classrooms. Over the next several days, as the Vietnamese and their Cambodian assistants searched the former school, thousands of documents were recovered: mug-shot photographs and undeveloped negatives; thousands of written confessions, hundreds of cadre notebooks; numerous Khmer Rouge publications, and myriad instruments of torture and detainment (Chandler 1999).

The language and narrative of national reconciliation emerged in 1979, when Vietnamese troops and Cambodian rebel factions captured Phnom Penh and removed the Khmer Rouge from power (Manning 2015, p. 389). The conversion of S-21 into a site of memorialization began immediately after the defeat of the CPK by occupying Vietnamese forces (Ledgerwood 1997; Chandler 1999). However, the Tuol Sleng Museum of Genocide was *never* intended to promote healing among the survivors of the Khmer Rouge regime; nor was it intended to facilitate reconciliation between the so-called perpetrators and their victims. Indeed, from its opening to the present-day, the intended audience of Tuol Sleng has been an international audience, initially for political purposes and more recently as an economic resource. Accordingly, the museum was, from its inception, designed to promote a particular narrative of the past, a past based not on the historiography of Democratic Kampuchea but instead of a homogenized appropriation of Holocaust-related discourses. In other words, Vietnamese officials explicitly and consciously sought to model Tuol Sleng after existing Holocaust memorials in an effort to substantiate their claims that their own military action was justified to remove a genocidal regime from power. As Judy Ledgerwood (1997, p. 87) explains, providing evidence to the outside world that the invasion by the Vietnamese army was an act of 'liberation' was the primary concern of those who designed Tuol Sleng as a museum. Indeed, a report from the Ministry of Culture, Information and Propaganda dated October 1980 stated that the aim of the museum was 'to show the international guests the cruel torture committed by the traitors to the Khmer people' (Benzaquen 2014, p. 791).

Simply put, the leadership of the PRK saw a political as opposed to a humanitarian opportunity at S-21. Rather than provide a means to engage seriously with either reconciliation or remembrance, officials deliberately used the brutality of S-21 in an effort to provide legitimacy to a fragile regime. According to Hughes (2003, p. 26), the long-term 'national and international legitimacy of the People's Republic of Kampuchea hinged on the exposure of the violent excesses of Pol Pot . . . and the continued production of a coherent memory of the past, that is, of liberation and reconstruction at the hands of a benevolent fraternal state'. Consequently, Mai Lam, a Vietnamese colonel who was fluent in Khmer and had extensive experience in legal studies and museology, was appointed to oversee the rehabilitation of the security center into a museum of genocide (Chandler 1999, p. 4). Previously, Lam had curated Ho Chi Minh City's American Atrocities Museum, a site designed to bolster anti-American support for a newly reunited Vietnam (Schlund-Vials 2012, p. 33). Now, Lam set about designing S-21 to align with the established narrative that the Vietnamese successfully overthrew a genocidal regime. Mai Lam traveled throughout Eastern Europe, visiting former Nazi concentration camps and extermination camps, in an attempt to recreate S-21 as an 'Asian Auschwitz' (Ledgerwood 1997; Williams 2004). On 25 January 1979 – a mere two weeks following the 'discovery' of Tuol Sleng – a group of journalists from socialist countries was invited; these were the first official visitors to Tuol Sleng (Chandler 1999, p. 4). The museum was officially opened to the public in July 1980. For Sion (2011, p. 5), the rush to turn a death site into a gallery for visitors is a telling sign that the new leadership had less concern about the memory of the victims than about using the site for immediate political purposes.

Much has been written on the Tuol Sleng Genocide Museum and so I will be necessarily brief. The power of Tuol Sleng, as a memorial site, is in its purported authenticity. As a museum, S-21 was kept largely intact with only minor modifications to the compound made. Surrounded by a corrugated tin fence topped with coils of barbed wire, Tuol Sleng consists of four three-story concrete buildings arranged in a U-shaped pattern around a grassy courtyard dotted with palm trees. In the middle is the former administrative building and current site of the museum's archives. To the left of the courtyard are 14 tombstones and hanging poles. Visitors, upon their entrance, are directed first to Building A, located at the southern end of the compound.[1] This building includes the torture rooms. All are empty save for the rusty metal beds and shackles and various torture instruments. Grainy photographs of corpses discovered in January 1979 hang forlornly on the walls. Adjoining Building A are two buildings that were used to detain prisoners. Building B consists of large classrooms that were converted into communal holding cells. Now, these vacuous rooms are filled with thousands of black-and-white photographs taken of the unnamed prisoners upon their entry to Tuol Sleng. Building C was likewise used to detain prisoners. However, in this building the former classrooms were sub-divided with brick walls to create individual 'private' cells for important prisoners (Figure 2.1). Inside the smaller cells are shackles and chains. Directly opposite Building A, on the northern end of the compound, is Building D. Under the Khmer Rouge, this building was also used to detain prisoners. It now houses various instruments of torture, thousands of shackles and disinterred skulls.

There is little textual material provided at the museum; most photographs and exhibits are unmarked (Ledgerwood 1997; Williams 2004; Tyner 2014). Such a minimalist approach was (and is) deliberate. At one level, the museum seemingly provides an authentic experience, one where visitors can enter into cells or interrogation rooms *just as the rooms were* when prisoners were actually detained and tortured. The intent is clear: to signify that these crimes took place.

Guttormsen and Fageraas (2011, pp. 449–50) suggest that 'heritage as cultural capital becomes symbolic capital when master narratives, images and monuments are used in the construction of . . . a national . . . identity and for branding products, places and peoples'. S-21 as an official museum

After heritage

Source: Author's own.

Figure 2.1   Detention cells, Tuol Sleng Genocide Museum, Phnom Penh, Cambodia

capitalizes on the site's authenticity – it is, after all, the actual building in which prisoners were detained, tortured and often forced to confess prior to their execution. However, as an authentic site, S-21 is very much a *dead* space. As Chhabra (2005, p. 65) explains, 'authenticity is often staged and commodified to meet the needs of the tourist'. And in fact, S-21 has been highly commodified to serve purposes other than remembrance. For example, the attendant question of *why* these crimes took place remains unasked and unanswered. We unconsciously experience the museum as a political lesson, ironically, not unlike the detainees who suffered and died at S-21, for they too were kept ignorant of the reasons for their arrest.

The graphic display of physical horrors – the shackles, instruments of torture and skulls – serves political goals: the legitimacy of political rule in the country (Sion 2011). For it was the intent of Mai Lam, and the PRK more generally, to provide not a conceptual or contextual understanding of S-21, or of the Khmer Rouge, or even of the genocide, but rather to affect a separation between the crimes of the Khmer Rouge and the newly installed government of the People's Republic of Kampuchea – itself dominated by former Khmer Rouge members. As Chandler (1999, p. 5) explains, 'Mai Lam wanted to arrange Cambodia's recent past to fit the requirements of the PRK and its Vietnamese mentors as well as the long-term needs, as he saw them, of the Cambodian people'. The former would take precedence over the latter.

Memorial exhibits at S-21 are graphic and poignant reminders of the past and yet ironically are devoid of history. While visitors viscerally experience the photographic stares of people long since dead, there is little to indicate who they were or why they died. Only a select few are named as the genocide was to be re-presented as the product of a small clique of Khmer Rouge cadre, notably Pol Pot, Ieng Sary, Nuon Chea and Khieu Samphan. Moreover, their actions are portrayed as isolated events, devoid of any assistance from the Vietnamese Communist Party. These re-presentations are important, given that the PRK was both dominated by former Khmer Rouge cadre who either participated in, or witnessed, crimes (Sion 2011). Thus, rather than directly addressing the violent past, the new regime promoted (and continues to promote) national 'reconciliation' through a selective remembrance of the past.

The problem is not simply the politics of authenticity at S-21 as it is the 'representativeness' of the site. Barring any textual explanation, visitors are confronted with mute images of death. Exhibits are graphic and poignant: grainy black-and-white photographs of people staring death in the face; postmortem photographs of beaten prisoners; photographs of mass graves partially exhumed. Most photographs, however, are untitled. Visitors have no way of knowing who is in the image, or why the photograph was shot. The Cambodian genocide and its victims becomes a generic event of mass atrocity; nothing exists that allows visitors to make connections between S-21 as a security center and the larger context of Democratic Kampuchea. No mention is made, for example, of the fact that the face in the photograph may – or may not be – a Khmer Rouge soldier; there is no indication that the person immortalized in the image could possibly have been an interrogator or executioner at S-21.[2] As Ledgerwood (1997, p. 83) concludes, 'the state narrative presented at the museum and the standardized remembrances of the DK times . . . present a prepackaged, summarized, public version of events for view both by Khmer and by foreigners'. Consequently, Tuol Sleng provides an interpretive framework that does ring true to the horrendous experiences of the Khmer Rouge-era; however, it also condenses those experiences into a series of generic and senseless images devoid of context. On that point, the commodified authenticity of S-21 belies its uniqueness and obfuscates conditions experienced elsewhere.

A similar ossification is underway at Choeung Ek (Figure 2.2). In 1989

Source: Author's own.

Figure 2.2   Main stupa *at Choeung Ek Genocidal Center, Cambodia*

the site was opened to the public and, in the intervening years, has become
a monstrous commodified landscape of abstract violence. Throughout the
1990s – prior to the phenomenal rise of tourism to Cambodia – the mass
grave site remained relatively undisturbed, exceptions being the erection
of a central *stupa* filled with skeletal remains and the placement of simple
wooden structures marking the location of mass graves. Visitors arrived
via a dirt road; there was no formal entrance to the site and a lonely
wooden gift shop sat to the side. In 2005, however, a Japanese corporation,
JC Royal, obtained from the Cambodian government a 30-year license to
operate the site. Now, visitors to the site – the overwhelming majority of
whom are foreigners – are confronted with an elaborate gated entrance,
a ticket counter, public toilets, a renovated gift shop periodically selling
replica Khmer Rouge clothing, and an air-conditioned screening room
showing a brief documentary of the genocide. The once-dirt road has
been replaced by tarmac, lined with bars, cafes, hotels and football pitches.
Billboards advertising a shooting-range stand faded near the entrance to
the site.

Tuol Sleng and Choeung Ek have become as iconic – and ossified – as the World Heritage Site of Angkor. The complexities and contradictions of the Khmer Rouge period have become spatially fixed, thereby rendering silent other landscapes of violence. As of 2015, for example, over 300 mass grave sites have been mapped; to these are added approximately 200 security centers and other places of mass detention. By far, the vast majority of these sites remain unmarked and, consequently, unvisited. Neither are the thousands of infrastructure projects initiated by the Khmer Rouge: irrigation canals, dams, reservoirs, airfields, warehouses and outdoor schools. Accordingly, the ossification of only a select few Khmer Rouge sites has contributed to the emergence of a pattern of dark tourism which largely erases Cambodia's living heritage of mass violence. For it is not simply that tourists do not visit these unrecognized sites; it is more a matter that these sites have been excluded from the collective memory of Cambodia's past.

THE LIVED SPACES OF TRAPEANG THMA DAM

Architectural landscapes are typically valued and preserved as a cultural heritage of a time past (Winter 2014). The historical preservation of Tuol Sleng and Choeung Ek, for example, serves to materially situate Cambodia's genocidal past as a fixed present and cautionary futurity. In so doing, however, the bounding of Cambodia's recent violent past to Tuol Sleng and Choeung Ek obscures other landscapes of violence that remain hidden in plain sight – deathscapes that remain very much lived (Tyner et al. 2012; Tyner 2014, 2017a). One such place is the Trapeang Thma Dam, located in the Phnom Srok District, Banteay Meanchey Province (see Tyner 2017a).

During the Khmer Rouge regime, the irrigation scheme at Trapeang Thma was proposed and developed by the Chief of the Region 5 Mobile Work Unit, a man named Val (alias Aok Haun).[3] According to Pann Chhuong, a former Khmer Rouge cadre who served as Deputy Chief of Region 5, Val initially wanted to build a road to Thailand, a project that aligned with objects specified by key members of the Standing Committee of the CPK.[4] It is possible that these transportation systems were preferred as a means to more effectively transport rice and other resources. Perhaps also these efforts indicate a desire to increase international trade with Thailand. Pann Chhuong recalls that during the early months of 1977 work-teams began clearing forests in anticipation of road construction. At the same time, surveys were also taken for the formulation of plans to develop a rail line. In the end, however, both of these projects were placed

Source: Author's own.

*Figure 2.3   Floodgate at Trapeang Thma Dam, Banteay Meanchey
            Province, Cambodia*

on hold as it was determined that a network of irrigation projects was
more important.[5]

The construction of Trapeang Thma Dam was a monumental task
(Figure 2.3). The size of the work-force is estimated to have been anywhere
from 15,000 men, women and children to over 20,000. Most workers were
'recruited' from the four districts that composed Region 5; witnesses also
report that 'new' people were brought in from other zones (OCIJ 2010,
p. 88). Initially, after dense forest was cleared, mobile units began to survey
the area, cordoning off areas for excavation.[6] Then the actual digging,
transporting and building began. At the work-site men, women and children were grouped into working units. Each work-unit was composed of
approximately ten people; these work-units in turn formed platoons, companies and battalions, consisting of 30, 100 and 300 people, respectively.
Work-groups were divided into three levels, depending on the strength of
the worker.[7] According to My Mao, the first group was assigned to excavate three cubic meters of earth per day per person; the second and third
groups were assigned quotas of two and one cubic meters, respectively.[8] In

practice, the amount assigned varied based on the unit chief. Muong Ry, for example, remembers that members of the first group were required to dig 3.5 to 4 cubic meters while Nhoun Soeum says that he was responsible for carrying five cubic meters.[9]

Exposed to the elements, men, women and children were subject to horrific working and living conditions. People succumbed to a host of diseases, including malaria, dysentery and hermeralopia.[10] Some were bitten by poisonous snakes.[11] Most witnesses remember that hunger and thirst were ever-present (OCIJ 2010, p. 89). To supplement these meager rations, many former workers describe having to scavenge for food, for example, catching frogs or gathering wild mushrooms.[12] Workers were subject to swift punishment and possible execution for any number of infractions – including food scavenging. Soeu Saut recalls how a 'new' person was discovered to have caught a rat to eat and was subsequently executed.[13] Persons found guilty of moral offences were often killed outright. Witnesses also recall 'pregnant women being beaten, killed and thrown into the reservoir basin, as the CPK cadre would say that "the dam would hold firmly only if pregnant women were killed and placed at the sluice gate"' (OCIJ 2010, p. 90).

The Trapeang Thma project was widely seen as a key milestone in the development of CPK water management practice. Once completed, the main dam – located some 50 kilometers northwest of the town of Sisophon – was approximately 10 meters wide at the top, 18 meters wide at the base, and between 3 to 5 meters in height; it formed a reservoir approximately 70 square kilometers in size (OCIJ 2010, p. 86). An inauguration ceremony held in December 1977 was attended by Pol Pot, other senior CPK cadre and a delegation from China. As described in an official CPK publication, the dam composed part of a nation-wide labor offensive whereby workers 'sacrificed everything for maximum rice production' (quoted in OCIJ 2010, p. 86). Survivors recall that Khmer Rouge musical troupes performed at the ceremony; that cows and pigs were cooked, and that everyone had much to eat.[14]

The Trapeang Thma Dam – and hundreds of other structures – remains on the landscape and, in many respects, assumes a prominent place in the lives of many Cambodians. Banteay Meanchey Province currently is home to over 55,000 households with upwards of 250,000 people living in the immediate vicinity of the dam. Currently, many of the secondary canals built during the Khmer Rouge-era have fallen into disrepair; however, the overall scheme remains in use. Farmers in the neighboring villages cultivate rice on fields located south, east and north of the reservoir. During the rainy season, roughly between June and December, the reservoir fills with water and rice is cultivated in the flooded areas. During the dry season, irrigation allows a smaller area to the east to be used for rice cultivation. For many local residents, the reservoir provides the main source of water, protein and income (Loeung et al. 2015). Many poor farmers, for example, supplement their diet and income through fishing, the gathering of aquatic plants and the collection of water snakes.[15] Administratively, water issues in the region are managed by the Ministry of Water Resources and Meteorology (MOWRM). In partnership with other entities, the dam has been partially rehabilitated. In 2004, for example, a joint Cambodian-Japanese project rebuilt the principle floodgate and plans have been developed to repair the entirety of the canal network connected to the dam. The massive earthen dike forms part of the region's transportation network (Farmer et al. 2009; Loeung et al. 2015). Moreover, in 1998, scientists discovered the presence of the Sarus crane (*Grusantigone sharpie*) and Eld's deer (*Rucervus eldii*), both globally endangered, along with other threatened wildlife (Loeung et al. 2015).

Consequently, the area was designated in February 2000, with 12,650 hectares set aside, to form the Ang Trapeang Thma conservation area. Overall, the wetlands system includes Trapeang Thma reservoir, flooded forests, grasslands, irrigated canals, creeks, ponds and rice paddy fields. Today, signs indicate this conservation effort; however, there are no markers indicating that the dam was originally constructed by forced labor under the Khmer Rouge regime. Nor is there any indication that skeletal remains of those who perished or were executed during the construction of the irrigation project may still lie buried beneath the soil.

For the most part, landscapes such as that at Trapeang Thma do not immediately convey a sense of horror and, as such, have little to offer to so-called dark tourists. And yet, perhaps more than Tuol Sleng and Choeung Ek, these sites hold great importance in the everyday lives of those who experienced first-hand the trauma of war and mass violence, as well as those of the later generations who carry this legacy forward in the form of post-memories. Of those sites that retain a physical presence on the landscape – the canals and reservoirs, for example – there is little public information that speaks of their dark past.

The myriad infrastructure projects initiated by the Khmer Rouge problematize the presumption that a site only becomes fully authentic when marked (Rickly-Boyd 2009, p. 3; see also MacCannell 1976; Voase 1999). Indeed, while many of these structures have been rehabilitated, they largely retain the same functions as they did during the Khmer Rouge regime. Consequently, the daily act of farming, fishing or gathering water provides a tangible link between past and present. As Robertson and Webster (2017, p. 316) explain, the daily working of land and water reconnects the individual to past practices and places work-tasks and the intersection of the human and non-human at the center of localized and spatialized identity-making. Those who lived through the Khmer Rouge years speak of a disconnect between the official narrative of genocide and their lived reality of violence – a reality that they relive daily as they utilize the dams, the reservoirs and the roads constructed during the genocide. For these individuals, the need to document these landscapes grows out of a perceived duty to not forget as opposed to an obligation to remember. In other words, for many survivors – and it is not my intent to generalize – it is far more important to not forget what happened, rather than to actively memorialize the landscape. This act of forgetting transfers to the remembrance of the forced labor utilized in the construction of Khmer Rouge infrastructural projects (Tyner 2017a).

To date, scholars have paid minimal attention to these structures in their accounts of memory and memorialization. Here, and elsewhere, I provide a corrective to this omission (Tyner et al. 2012; Tyner 2017a). My purpose is to view the myriad dams and dikes, canals and reservoirs, not simply as material objects of a despotic regime but rather as material objects of ruination. In so doing, I recast these sites of past atrocity as present landscapes of living heritage. Ruins, Stoler (2008, p. 194) explains, are often thought of as enchanted, desolate spaces, large-scale monumental structures abandoned and grown over, which 'provide a quintessential image of what has vanished from the past and has long decayed'. Counter to this image, she calls (p. 194) not for a 'turn to ruins as memorialized and large-scale monumental "leftovers" or relics . . . but rather to what people are "left with": to what remains . . . to the material and social afterlife of structures, sensibilities, and things'.

The remnants of Khmer Rouge infrastructure developments remain palpable on the landscape. Neither marked nor memorialized, these structures are hidden in plain sight, their past visible only to those who experienced first-hand the horrific conditions occasioned by the Khmer Rouge. Efforts are underway to document these experiences, of past-and-present workings on the landscape. The Documentation Center of Cambodia, for example, has conducted thousands of interviews, both with Khmer Rouge cadre and non-Khmer Rouge survivors. Other non-profit organizations, such as Youth for Peace, have facilitated survivors to reflect upon their past experiences as a means of conveying their memories to the next generation. Notably, survivors are often encouraged to use art as a means of sharing their experiences; in the process, survivors actively represent past landscapes of violence while, in the process, problematize landscapes of the present (see Tyner 2017a).

As ruins, the dikes and dams, canals and reservoirs remain ever-present features in everyday life. Some have fallen into disrepair; others have been rehabilitated. Still more continue to function as designed. As spaces of everyday life, these material landscapes are anything but static, bearing instead 'traces of other, earlier experiences there and elsewhere, merging the ways in which landscape happens, relationally' (Crouch 2010, p. 13).

CONCLUSION

The ruins of Democratic Kampuchea remain ever-present, both in the memories and post-memories of the survivors and their descendants. Many of these ruins also remain viable and continue to serve the original functions for which they were built. They are 'constituent parts of "past-present systems", formations of lived social experience characterized by the mutual constitution of past and present realities' (Lazzari and Korstanje 2013, p. 395). They are, in effect, living landscapes. And herein lays the problem. In part, the variegated cartographies of landscape memorialization in Cambodia results from a historical miasma that clouds the visible representation of violence. In other words, the continued privileging of S-21 as *the* paradigmatic authentic site of mass murder overshadows myriad other places of violence throughout the country. Moreover, the continued demonization of all-things-Khmer-Rouge sits uneasily with these other structures, for it is still difficult to see (or say) anything remotely positive or beneficial as resulting from the so-called Pol Pot times. But how are we to remember sites such as the Trapeang Thma Dam, a site of atrocity literally built on the bodies of the dead? A site that provides to thousands of men, women and children ample supplies of water, a resource that was denied to those who were forced to build the dam? A site that now offers protection to endangered species when protection was denied to those who lived and died in its construction?

Some survivors, perhaps strangely, look upon the site with a sense of accomplishment. Vann Teav, for example, explains that '[o]f course, we suffered during the regime and were put to work tirelessly'. However, she adds that 'when the project was complete and now we have this dam . . . I am pleased that we have water from Trapeang Thma Dam and we can even fish there'.[16] Perhaps the comments of Vann Teav may be interpreted as trying to make sense of the past; of trying to find some meaning in the sacrifices made. In *The Sunflower*, Simon Wiesenthal (1997, p. 98) recounts an incident where a dying Nazi soldier made a deathbed confession and asked for forgiveness. And while feeling pity for the man, Wiesenthal said nothing. He concludes that 'forgiveness is an act of volition, and only the sufferer is qualified to make the decision'. I cannot speak for the survivors or for the dead; nor can I offer forgiveness or reconciliation to those responsible. In this chapter and with my work in general, I have tried to provide a context for the past; to trouble the reductionist portrayal of the Cambodian genocide that is all too apparent in the marketing of atrocity to dark tourists.

The landscape of Cambodia reveals a legacy of living ruins, populated by thousands of people, each with their own stories to share. These sites, such as Trapeang Thma Dam, remain visible on the landscape. These are not the ruins of castles long-since abandoned or ghost towns left to the elements. Indeed, ruins need not be seen as discarded sites. A focus on ruins does, however, provide a critical vantage point from which to view landscapes of violence. As Stoler (2008, p. 196) writes, '[a]sking how people live with and in ruins redirects the engagement elsewhere, to the politics animated, to the common sense they disturb, to the critiques condensed or disallowed, and to the social relations avidly coalesced or shattered around them'. Authorized heritage discourses, such as those narrated at S-21 and Choeung Ek, are not so much wrong as they are incomplete. Accordingly, an engagement with the everyday heritage of violent landscapes hidden in plain sight, framed as a form of heritage-making but from below, provides an enlargement of our remembrance and interpretation of the past.

NOTES

1. To facilitate the 'standard' tour of the site, in 2010 the main entrance gate to S-21 was relocated from the center wall to the southeastern corner.
2. At least 155 staff members of S-21 were themselves arrested, detained and executed; of these, at least 34 interrogators were executed. See Document Number D288/6.68.39, archived at the Documentation Center of Cambodia, Phnom Penh.
3. Interview with former Khmer Rouge cadre, 18 July 2014. See also 'Trapeang Thma Dam Worksite', at http://www.eccc.gov.kh/en/crime-sites/trapeang-thma-dam-worksite" (accessed 23 May 2016). Other individuals responsible for the management of the project included Hat (member of the Phnom Srok District Committee), Man Chun (alias Hoeung; Secretary of Region 5) and Muol Sambat (alias Ta Nhim; Secretary of the Northwest Zone). Most of these men, however, would not survive to see the completion of the dam. Val and Hat were arrested and sent to S-21 in June and September 1977, respectively; both were accused of traitorous activities. Man Chun likewise was arrested in September 1977, to be replaced by Heng Rin, until his arrest and execution in 1978.
4. Pann Chhuong, interviewed by Long Dany, 18 June 2011, transcript archived at the Documentation Center of Cambodia, Phnom Penh.
5. Pann Chhuong, interviewed by Long Dany, 18 June 2011, transcript archived at the Documentation Center of Cambodia, Phnom Penh. Both documentary evidence and individual testimony provide contradictory dates as to when construction on the dam site began. Some witnesses recall that building work began in early 1976; others maintain that work was started in 1977. The completion date is also unclear. While most witnesses claim that work finished in 1977, some recall that construction continued in 1978. According to one account, Trapeang Thma Dam was built on the site of a previous dam. See Tuy Sophal, interviewed by Hin Sothearny, 18 June 2011, transcript archived at the Documentation Center of Cambodia, Phnom Penh.

6. Thim Norm, interviewed by Long Dany, 15 June 2011, transcript archived at the Documentation Center of Cambodia, Phnom Penh.
7. Tuy Sophal, interviewed by Hin Sothearny, 18 June 2011, transcript archived at the Documentation Center of Cambodia, Phnom Penh.
8. My Mao, interviewed by Sok Vannak, 16 June 2011, transcript archived at the Documentation Center of Cambodia, Phnom Penh.
9. Muong Ry, interviewed by Sok Vannak, 16 June 2011, transcript archived at the Documentation Center of Cambodia, Phnom Penh; Nhoun Soeum, interviewed by Vathan Peou Dara, 15 June 2011, transcript archived at the Documentation Center of Cambodia, Phnom Penh.
10. Hermeralopia is an ailment also known as 'day blindness'; it refers to an inability to see during the day time. Those suffering from the disease were not excused from work; rather, they were required to help pass buckets of dirt from the excavation site, much as volunteer fire-brigades once shuttled water. See Thim Norm, interviewed by Long Dany, 15 June 2011, transcript archived at the Documentation Center of Cambodia, Phnom Penh.
11. Nou Chuong and Ko Vann, interviewed by Chhunly Chhay, 16 June 2011, transcript archived at the Documentation Center of Cambodia, Phnom Penh.
12. Phoeu Chun, interviewed by Som Bunthorn and Chan Pronh, 15 June 2011, transcript archived at the Documentation Center of Cambodia, Phnom Penh.
13. Soeu Saut, interviewed by Long Dany, 17 June 2011, transcript archived at the Documentation Center of Cambodia, Phnom Penh.
14. Khor Mean, interviewed by Sok Vannak, 17 June 2011, transcript archived at the Documentation Center of Cambodia, Phnom Penh.
15. Various species of waterfowl and mammals are plentiful but are protected by laws which are enforced by a local conservation team with assistance from the International Crane Foundation and the Wildlife Conservation Society of Cambodia.
16. Vann Teav, interviewed by Hin Sothearny, 17 June 2011, transcript archived at the Documentation Center of Cambodia, Phnom Penh.

REFERENCES

Alberts, H. and H.D. Hazen (2010), 'Maintaining authenticity and integrity at cultural World Heritage sites', *Geographical Review*, **100**, 56–73.

Benzaquen, S. (2014), 'Looking at the Tuol Sleng Museum of Genocide Crimes, Cambodia, on Flickr and YouTube', *Media, Culture & Society*, **36**, 790–809.

Chandler, David P. (1999), *Voices from S-21: Terror and History in Pol Pot's Secret Prison*, Berkeley, CA: University of California Press.

Chhabra, D. (2005), 'Defining authenticity and its determinants: toward an authenticity flow model', *Journal of Travel Research*, **44**, 64–73.

Colls, C.S. (2015), 'Uncovering a painful past: archaeology and the Holocaust', *Conservation and Management of Archaeological Sites*, **17**, 38–55.

Crouch, D. (2010), 'Flirting with space: thinking landscape relationally', *cultural geographies*, **17**, 5–18.

DeLyser, D. (1999), 'Authenticity on the ground: engaging the past in a California Ghost Town', *Annals of the Association of American Geographers*, **89**, 602–32.

DeSilvey, C. (2007), 'Salvage memory: constellating material histories on a hardscrabble homestead', *cultural geographies*, **14**, 401–24.

DeSilvey, C. and T. Edensor (2012), 'Reckoning with ruins', *Progress in Human Geography*, **37**, 465–85.

Doss, Erika (2008), *The Emotional Life of Contemporary Public Memorials: Towards a Theory of Temporary Memorials*, Amsterdam: Amsterdam University Press.

Edensor, T. (2005), 'The ghosts of industrial ruins: ordering and disordering memory in excessive space', *Environment and Planning D: Society and Space*, **23**, 829–49.

Edensor, T. (2008), 'Mundane hauntings: commuting through the phantasmagoric working-class spaces of Manchester, England', *cultural geographies*, **15**, 313–33.

Farmer, David, Leonardo Gueli, Maria Zintl and Rada Kong (2009), *The Potential of Rice Intensification in Paoy char, Banteay Meanchey Province, Western Cambodia: Case Study in Trapeang Thma Khang Tboung and Poay Ta Ong Villages*, SLUSE Report, Faculty of Life Sciences, University of Copenhagen, Denmark.

Guttormsen, T.S. and K. Fageraas (2011), 'The social production of "attractive authenticity" at the World Heritage Site of Røros, Norway', *International Journal of Heritage Studies*, **17**, 442–62.

Hardy, D. (1988), 'Historical geography and heritage studies', *Area*, **20**, 333–8.

Harrison, R. (2009), 'Excavating second life: cyber-archaeologies, heritage and virtual communities', *Journal of Material Culture*, **14**, 75–106.

Harrison, Rodney (2013), *Heritage: Critical Approaches*, New York: Routledge.

Hartig, Kate V. and K.M. Dunn (1998), 'Roadside memorials: interpreting new deathscapes in Newcastle, New South Wales', *Australian Geographical Studies*, **36**, 5–20.

Harvey, D.C. (2001), 'Heritage pasts and heritage presents: temporality, meaning and the scope of heritage studies', *International Journal of Heritage Studies*, **7**, 319–38.

Hughes, R. (2003), 'The abject artefacts of memory: photographs from Cambodia's Genocide', *Media, Culture & Society*, **25**, 23–44.

Hughes, R. (2008), 'Dutiful tourism: encountering the Cambodian genocide', *Asia Pacific Viewpoint*, **49**, 318–30.

Ingold, T. (1993), 'The temporality of the landscape', *World Archaeology*, **25**, 152–74.

Jonker, J. and K.E. Till (2009), 'Mapping and excavating spectral traces in post-Apartheid Cape Town', *Memory Studies*, **2**, 303–35.

Kiernan, Ben (1996), *The Pol Pot Regime: Policies, Race and Genocide in Cambodia under the Khmer Rouge, 1975–1979*, New Haven, CT: Yale University Press.

Lane, R. and G. Waitt (2001), 'Authenticity in tourism and native title: place, time, and spatial politics in the East Kimberly', *Social and Cultural Geography*, **2**, 381–405.

Lazzari, M. and A. Korstanje (2013), 'The past as a lived space: heritage places, re-emergent aesthetics, and hopeful practices in NW Argentina', *Journal of Social Archaeology*, **13**, 394–419.

Ledgerwood, J. (1997), 'The Cambodian Tuol Sleng Museum of Genocidal Crimes: national narrative', *Museum Anthropology*, **21**, 82–98.

Loeung, K., D. Schmidt-Vogt and G.P. Shivokoti (2015), 'Economic value of wild aquatic resources in the Ang Prapeang Thmor Sarus Crane Reserve, North-Western Cambodia', *Wetlands Ecology and Management*, **23**, 467–80.

Long, Colin and Keir Reeves (2009), '"Dig a hole and bury the past in it": reconciliation and the heritage of genocide in Cambodia', in William Logan and Keir Reeves (eds), *Places of Pain and Shame: Dealing with a 'Difficult Heritage'*, New York: Routledge, pp. 68–81.

Lunstrum, E. (2010), 'Reconstructing history, grounding claims to space: history, memory, and displacement in the Great Limpopo Transfrontier Park', *South African Geographical Journal*, **92**, 129–43.

MacCannell, Dean (1976), *The Tourist: A New Theory of the Leisure Class*, Berkeley, Los Angeles and London: University of California Press.

Manning, P. (2015), 'Reconciliation and perpetrator memories in Cambodia', *International Journal of Transitional Justice*, **9**, 386–406.

Norén-Nilsson, A. (2011), 'Children of former Khmer Rouge cadres', *Peace Review*, **23**, 462–8.

OCIJ (Office of the Co-Investigation Judges) (2010), *Closing Order, Case File No.: 002/19-09-2007-ECCC-OCIJ*, Phnom Penh, Cambodia: Extraordinary Chambers in the Courts of Cambodia.

Rickly-Boyd, J.M. (2009), 'Establishing authenticity in a tourist landscape: Spring Mill Pioneer Village', *Material Culture*, **41**, 1–16.

Robertson, I.J. and D. Webster (2017), 'People of the croft: visualising land, heritage and identity', *cultural geographies*, **24**, 311–18.

Sánchez-Carretero, Cristina and Carmin Ortiz (2011), 'Grassroots memorials as sites of heritage creation', in Helmut Anheier and Yudhishthir Raj Isar (eds), *Heritage, Memory & Identity*, London: Sage, pp. 106–13.

Schlund-Vials, Cathy J. (2012), *War, Genocide, and Justice: Cambodian American Memory Work*, Minneapolis, MN: University of Minnesota Press.

Schnell, S.M. (2003), 'The ambiguities of authenticity in Little Sweden, USA', *Journal of Cultural Geography*, **20**, 43–68.

Sion, B. (2011), 'Conflicting sites of memory in post-genocide Cambodia', *Humanity: An International Journal of Human Rights, Humanitarianism, and Development*, **2**, 1–21.

Smith, Laurajane (2006), *Uses of Heritage*, London: Routledge.

Stangl, P. (2008), 'The vernacular and the monumental: memory and landscape in post-war Berlin', *GeoJournal*, **73**, 245–53.

Steinberg, M.K. and M.J. Taylor (2003), 'Public memory and political power in Guatemala's postconflict landscape', *Geographical Review*, **93**, 449–68.

Stoler, A. (2008), 'Imperial debris: reflections on ruins and ruination', *Cultural Anthropology*, **23**, 191–219.

Tegelberg, M. (2010), 'Hidden sights: tourism, representation and Lonely Planet Cambodia', *International Journal of Cultural Studies*, **13**, 491–509.

Till, Karen E. (2005), *The New Berlin: Memory, Politics, Place*, Minneapolis, MN: University of Minnesota Press.

Till, K.E. (2012), 'Wounded cities: memory-work and a place-based ethics of care', *Political Geography*, **31**, 3–14.

Tunbridge, John E. and Gregory J. Ashworth (1996), *Dissonant Heritage: The Management of the Past as a Resource in Conflict*, New York: John Wiley & Sons.

Tyner, James A. (2008), *The Killing of Cambodia: Geography, Genocide and the Unmaking of Space*, Aldershot, UK: Ashgate.

Tyner, James A. (2014), 'Violent erasures and erasing violence: contesting Cambodia's landscapes of violence', in Estela Schindel and Pamela Colombo (eds), *Space and the Memories of Violence: Landscapes of Erasure, Disappearance and Exception*, New York: Palgrave Macmillan, pp. 21–33.

Tyner, James A. (2017a), *Landscape, Memory, and Post-Violence in Cambodia*, London: Rowman & Littlefield International.

Tyner, James A. (2017b), *From Rice Fields to Killing Fields: Nature, Life, and Labor under the Khmer Rouge*, Syracuse, NY: Syracuse University Press.

Tyner, J.A. and S. Rice (2016), 'Cambodia's political economy of violence: space, time, and genocide under the Khmer Rouge, 1975–79', *Genocide Studies International*, **10**, 84–94.

Tyner, J.A. and R. Will (2015), 'Nature and post-conflict violence: water management under the Communist Party of Kampuchea, 1975–1979', *Transactions of the Institute of British Geographers*, **40**, 362–74.

Tyner, J.A., G.B. Alvarez and A. Colucci (2012), 'Memory and the everyday landscape of violence in post-genocide Cambodia', *Social and Cultural Geography*, **13**, 853–71.

Tyner, J.A., S. Sirik and S. Henkin (2014), 'Violence and the dialectics of landscape: memorialization in Cambodia', *Geographical Review*, **104**, 277–93.

Voase, R. (1999), '"Consuming" tourist sites/sights: a note on York', *Leisure Studies*, **18** (4), 289–96.

Watson, S. and E. Waterton (2010), 'Reading the visual: representation and narrative in the construction of heritage', *Material Culture Review*, **71**, 84–97.

Wiesenthal, Simon (1997), *The Sunflower: On the Possibilities and Limits of Forgiveness*, New York: Schocken Books.

Williams, P. (2004), 'Witnessing genocide: vigilance and remembrance at Tuol Sleng and Choeung Ek', *Holocaust and Genocide Studies*, **18**, 234–54.

Winter, T. (2014), 'Heritage studies and the privileging of theory', *International Journal of Heritage Studies*, **20**, 556–72.

3. Motorbikes as 'aspirational' heritage: rethinking past, present and future in Vietnam

Jamie Gillen

INTRODUCTION

Imagine you are a passenger on a motorbike in Vietnam. Disorientation and anxiety overcome you as the world whizzes past. Riders do not seem to be paying attention to the road because they are smoking, chatting on the phone or with a friend on the back of their motorbike, adjusting their helmet or clothing, or trying to pull a hair from their face using one of the side-view mirrors for assistance. All of this feels dangerous. There is an added sense of helplessness that comes from the constant barrage of honking, tropical heat, braking, precipitation and alien smells. You feel stripped of the ability to control or even change the action occurring in front of you. Your hands tighten around the grip controls. Amidst all of this overbearing uncertainty, however, lies a hint of excitement. There is a freedom the motorbike affords. Objects and people are closer to you. The space of the road feels more intimate, more immediate. When you arrive at your destination, you feel as if you accomplished something important. The familiarity of personal mobility so comfortable and predictable in the automobile, taxi, train, plane or bus is rearranged as a set of unknowns in riding a motorbike.

This unsettling depiction of motorized transport is a metaphor for the present chapter: in Vietnam, the motorbike disrupts the order inherent to conventional understandings of heritage. Here, the motorbike is 'aspirational heritage', a term that signals how heritage is a present and future-oriented set of ideas and practices in Vietnam. The supposedly historical nature of heritage has little to do with heritage-making performed through the motorbike, hence this chapter centers on the present and future dimensions of heritage-making in Vietnam. In making these arguments, I follow Laurajane Smith's (2006, p. 84) evocation of the temporal possibilities of heritage when she states, 'What makes certain activities "heritage" are those activities that actively engage with thinking about and acting out not only "where we have come from" in terms of the past, but also "where we are going" in terms of the present and future.' In fact, when the motorbike is used to look backwards in time, heritage becomes a tool to erase the past rather than prompting nostalgia, memory and recuperation. In this sense, my argument takes seriously Winter's (2009, p. 107) point that 'each society . . . develops its own cultural norms and shared ideas of how to negotiate, mediate and delineate the traditional from the modern, the "authentic" from the "inauthentic"'. Relatedly, his claims about the importance of heritage 'stakeholders', 'values' and 'a plurality of voices' drive my interests in the present work. Here, heritage is scrambled among temporalities: the motorbike discredits historical forms of Vietnamese mobility, it restricts its usefulness to the present and marks the future through heritage's imagined march forward.

This chapter has two primary aims. First, I wish to illustrate the ephemerality of past, present and future in the construction of everyday heritage in Vietnam. Modern objects like the motorbike are pointed to as fundamental to being Vietnamese and therefore crucial examples of heritage. However, in ordinary life, such heritage is left unprotected, easily replaceable as a marker of 'Vietnameseness' by something potentially more exciting, more useful and more symbolic of the country's contemporary mobilities, like the automobile. In other words, while the motorbike is a 'better' form of Vietnamese heritage right now, it does not most clearly represent Vietnam as it ought to be. Instead of thinking about how heritage carries the past forward to be commodified and conserved in the present, this chapter asks how heritage is created out of the present in an effort to antiquate past iterations of heritage. After drawing brief attention to the rickshaw and pedicab as outmoded aspects of Vietnamese cultural identity formation, the example of the bicycle is used to illustrate the fleetingness and limited temporality of heritage.

The second aim of this chapter is to favor heritage as an aspirational and future-oriented set of practices. Using and consuming a motorbike in Vietnam is embraced and celebrated even as it is understood to represent a brief moment in society. Outsized, fast, aesthetically pleasing and safe types of motorbike are coveted by my respondents because they are assumed to be precursors to a future Vietnam when they own a car. To purchase and use a motorbike is to be a contributor to the heritage of the country. And despite the ubiquity of the motorbike, Vietnam's people are casting their consumptive eyes to the future when the automobile will replace the motorbike as a new form of national heritage. In what follows, I show how heritage is not so much about something 'local' to be protected but about the provisionality and time-dependency of what is considered culturally unique.

After I address the methodology used in the chapter in the next two paragraphs, the rest of the chapter has three substantive sections and a conclusion. The next section indicates the motorbike's importance in Vietnamese society and the following two sections trace the temporal aspects of heritage-making. In the first temporal section, the motorbike is used as a lens in to the mediocrity of the bicycle, a formerly dominant mode of personal transportation now peripheral to the construction of everyday Vietnamese heritage. In this section, the bicycle's supposed 'flaws' are considered against the contemporary vitality of the motorbike. The second temporal section investigates the motorbike's value in shaping aspirations of the future. It zeros in on four-wheeled transportation to differentiate the automobile's futuristic dimensions from the impending hollowness of the motorbike. These angles do not encompass the richness of the motorbike to Vietnamese society but they do illustrate the ways in which heritage is a lived phenomenon. With a focus on urban high-speed rail currently under construction in Ho Chi Minh City and Hanoi (Vietnam's two largest cities), the conclusion reflects on the future of Vietnamese mobility to drive home the importance of heritage's presence.

The chapter's methodological framework is built on a multi-sited, in-depth qualitative approach to collecting data. I gathered primary data through semi-structured interviews conducted in Hanoi and Ho Chi Minh City and participant observation in the country's now widespread motorbike tourism expeditions (see Gillen 2016). Secondary data was acquired through popular media outlets like *Saigoneer*, *The Word*, *AsiaLife*, newspapers, blogs and Facebook groups. The bulk of my fieldwork for this chapter has been conducted in frequent but short two- or three-week research 'bursts' to both cities from 2015 to the present. Virtually every one of my research participants owns a motorbike and a handful of them own a family car too. Working in cities undoubtedly skews my research findings toward motorbike and automobile owners because it is rare to come upon an urban resident who does not have at least occasional access to a motorbike. Moreover, many urban Vietnamese are familiar with automobiles through their use of taxis or other ride-sharing services. Thus, the narratives about the evolution of transportation in today's Vietnam are based on the experiences of urban rather than rural dwellers. All this said, the motorbike is brought to proverbial 'life' for me when I draw on personal stories from interviews and conversations or through the pages of websites and social media sources.

MOBILIZING VIETNAM: THE UBIQUITIES OF THE MOTORBIKE

Even if you, the reader, have yet to visit Vietnam, you have no doubt been introduced to the country through the motorbike. Youtube videos of the crowded and loud chaos of city intersections are widely shared if not emulated back home. Vietnam is a country famously difficult for pedestrians wishing to cross its roads because swarms of unceasing motorbikes do not pause for anyone on foot, even at stoplights (Wilder 2013). Disorder arises from the pervasiveness of the motorbike in society, where Hondas, Lambrettas, Minsks, Piaggios, SYMs, Yamahas, and their less expensive or 'fake' offshoots move around in an unpredictable, voluminous and amplified dance. These issues are also unique to Vietnam because of lax enforcement of traffic laws, open flouting of laws by people and unclear street 'rules' for foreign pedestrians who are trying to get somewhere (a few tips: walk slowly, steadily and in a straight line so motorbike riders can adjust their speed and direction to accommodate your gait). Hansen (2017, p. 628) describes a typical scene on a Hanoi street like this: 'The two-wheelers are seemingly everywhere, either parked or in motion, and the humming and honking of millions of motorbikes is the soundtrack to the contemporary city'.

While someone unfamiliar with Vietnam may be intrigued by how riders navigate the street under these intimidating conditions, in the country itself, the motorbike is a national treasure and an icon to personal embodiment. In 1996, there were 4 million motorbikes in Vietnam; in 2014, there were 43 million of them, a staggering ten-fold increase for a population of approximately 90 million people (Hansen 2017, p. 629). Vietnam's motorbike market is second only to Indonesia's in Southeast Asia (a country two and a half times its size in population) and fourth in the world behind China, India and Indonesia (Small forthcoming).

Vietnam's *đổi mới* ('renovation') period,[1] which began in 1986, has been a primary trigger for the ocean of motorbikes moving through the country today. The reform era has opened Vietnam to foreign investment, decentralized the political system, deregulated bloated state-owned enterprises and relaxed some of the more onerous laws impeding private businesses (Gainsborough 2010). In other words, Vietnam's single-party Communist government turned to a more fast-paced and potentially less predictable open market economy after over a decade operating a command economy structure. Fast, chaotic, independent, stylish and a little bit funky, the motorbike can therefore arguably stand in for the broader economic changes that have unfolded in Vietnam over the past 30 years. For Truitt (2008, p. 3), motorbikes are 'unexpected "agents" of liberation in . . . Vietnam, liberating not the nation and its people but the individual consumer'. If there is one object to represent the 30-year market reform era in Vietnam it is the motorbike.

The motorbike is a structural representative of Vietnam because it is the outcome of a country where traffic laws are loose, the weather is warm and sunny, infrastructure is basic, population rates and personal wealth are rising, and people need to get to places quickly. As noted above, in the startling rise in motorbike usage rates, it is also an everyday apparatus of transportation. Most consequentially for this chapter, the motorbike is an intensively personal statement on class, identity and status. A high-quality motorbike is an aspirational marker for those who do not own one and a symbol of power for those who do. High quality means foreign-made (particularly Italian, but also some high-end Japanese manufactured models), more powerful (larger engine displacements), automatic transmission, more 'beautiful' or stylish, or 'safer' than other brands and models. Vietnamese people who ride these do so to show off their personal wealth, their aptitude as consumers, and/or their connections (for example, if they should have a rich family or benefactor assisting them in the purchase and upkeep of a motorbike). On the other hand, a run-down, loud, environmentally unfriendly, 'fake' (i.e., Chinese-made, *xe máy Trung Quốc*), or unsafe motorbike is an indication of the rider's poverty, unhygienic disposition and disinterest in his or her safety. The motorbike's spectrum of high- and low-quality types (*chất lượng cao*/*chất lượng thấp*) is no less than a spectrum covering Vietnamese people's identities.

The motorbike is a gendered object too. To cite one example of this from the transforming perspectives on the vehicle's operation, early in the motorbike's entry into Vietnam, males were stereotypically understood to be the ones able to ride them, with women only able to sit pillion/as passengers. Over time, however, women have gained much more operational agency with regard to the motorbike and, in the cities at least, both men and women now ride them. In recent years, it is not only typical for women to own and operate their own motorbikes but, as will be shown below, automobiles as well.

From a utilitarian standpoint, much like the consumption of material heritage objects such as knives in China (Zhang and Crang 2016), or falcons in the Middle East (Koch 2015), the motorbike is embraced, performed and 'aesthetically stylized for consumption' (Winter 2009, p. 110). Protection of something valuable is seen as an underlying force for heritage-making, but this protection is often framed in hierarchically managed ways. For example, material heritage and its intellectual property have historically been viewed as being under the province of a small group of cultural 'owners' who surrender its commodification and management to international groups (most notably UNESCO, see Shepherd 2017). Now, however, the explosion of material heritage claims throughout the world has shifted groups like UNESCO's focus 'to an emphasis on local community interests' (Shepherd 2017, p. 558). With respect to the Vietnamese motorbike, what is suspect about UNESCO's supposed novel inclusion of 'local community interests' is that whatever material objects are understood to be 'heritage'-worthy must also be agreed upon by international managers in consultation with other national stakeholders. Under this line of thinking, there seems to be little interest in keeping an object's propriety among everyday heritage-makers. The recent appearance of a negotiated approach to material heritage-making among stakeholders at different scales (international, regional, national and local) limits material heritage to objects that stakeholders at each of these scales feel warrant attention and protection. Thus, certain material objects, like the motorbike, are considered not credible enough to be elevated to the UNESCO World Heritage List, not community oriented enough to be of broader relevance to society, not stable enough to be conserved, too marginal to build capacity for heritage globally, and incapable of generating a simple and effective message communicating 'local' heritage to the world (Shepherd 2017). The motorbike fulfills none of UNESCO's '5 Cs' (credibility, community, conservation, capacity-building, communication) and yet it holds considerable value as an anchor to Vietnamese culture, society and identity. This anchor, as I illustrate below, is arguably loose and includes an as yet unknown half-life, but it is certainly established . . . for now. What is unique about the motorbike is its functionality as a statement about Vietnam in the world with little long-term imaginative relevance to many people in the country going forward. The brief but powerful elevation of the motorbike to 'aspirational heritage' in Vietnam follows in a long line of other 'aspirational heritage' markers in the mobility field, including the bicycle, pedicab and even walking. The next section highlights the bicycle's use in Vietnam to signpost its temporariness and mark its value as a symbol of a particular future in which it is understood to be largely irrelevant.

BICYCLES IN VIETNAM – SKIPPING NOSTALGIA?

In thinking about what would constitute conventional heritage-making in the transportation industry in Vietnam, precursors to the motorbike, such as the rickshaw, the pedicab and the bicycle, stick out as being particularly 'Vietnamese'. The rickshaw – an apparatus with a bucket seat sitting on two large wheels being pulled using a handle attached to the seat – was popular in the late 1800s and early 1900s during the French colonial era

(Hahn 2013). A common representation of colonial wealth, leisure and exploitation, pullers dragged wealthy French through the cities of Hanoi and Saigon (as it was called at that time) during long, hot and rainy days (and nights). Later in the twentieth century, pedicabs came to replace rickshaws as the leading type of mobility for colonial French residents and, subsequently, by wealthy Americans and Vietnamese alike. Pedicabs, which are also (confusingly) called cyclos/*xích lô* in Vietnamese, are similar to rickshaws in that they have a basket seat for travelers attached to two large wheels but with the added ease of being attached to the front part of a bicycle. Pedicab drivers sit on a seat and pedal as a bicyclist would though with their customers sitting behind them being pulled down the street. These contraptions were not only popular ways to move around cities in Vietnam but throughout Asia during the twentieth century. Rural Vietnamese looking to make a quick buck moved to cities to work as rickshaw pullers and then pedicab drivers.

Vietnam reunified in 1975 after a long period of war and many of those Vietnamese who fought alongside the Americans were sent to reeducation camps for indoctrination into the socialist manner of thought (Hoang 2016). After being sufficiently 'rehabilitated', males from southern Vietnam were encouraged to work as pedicab drivers in cities throughout southern Vietnam. With their strong command of the English language, they are even today thought of as cultural ambassadors for foreigners visiting Vietnam for the first time. Their line of work, however, is precarious, exhausting, wrapped in perpetual financial destitution and increasingly out of date due to more attractive market niches like motorbike taxi riders,[2] taxis and private automobiles. Notwithstanding a strong command of the English language (including slang), today's pedicab drivers in Ho Chi Minh City, Hoi An or Hanoi are understood to be elderly and therefore relics of a distant past. No Vietnamese person I know of would ever willingly ride in a pedicab; they are for foreign tourists and maintained to keep Vietnamese 'uncles' insecurely employed. The pedicab is therefore not so much considered a material object of heritage for Vietnam as it is a dinosaur that is slowly if methodically dissolving in relevance to society. Because it is a weaker cousin to the motorbike, the only merit the pedicab seems to have in society is to glorify the motorbike through its feebleness. In this way, we can think of pedicabs not as 'invented tradition' (Hobsbawm and Ranger 1983) but 'invented irrelevance' or the willful transformation of something important to society into something inconsequential. This is the unmaking of heritage, a neglected move in the more conventional heritage literature because it is not in keeping with the idea of production, commodification and collaborative preservation.

Then there is the bicycle, a classic object of personalized mobility throughout Asia and Vietnam, imaginatively associated as material herit-age by the state but also through images of the 'Orient' (Said 1978). In design and usage, it compares favorably to the motorbike. It has two wheels, it is individualized because it is designed for one rider and (sometimes) a passenger, it does not take up a lot of space, it can be used on many different kinds of roads and paths and, relative to most other types of vehicle, it is an extremely efficient and economical means of getting around. It also exposes both rider and passenger to the elements, to other riders, and to road conditions in a way unimaginable to those in a car. The Vietnamese government is fond of feminizing the bicycle in its representations of Vietnamese society because its tourism industry slogans and taglines regularly depict a group of Vietnamese women donning *áo dài* (traditional Vietnamese clothing) and serenely clutching or riding their bicycles.[3] The bicycle is a commonplace indicator of the supposed simplicity, elegance, efficiency and relaxed attitude prevalent in Vietnam.

As much as they pervade Vietnam, the conventional narratives sur-rounding the bicycle are contested. Much as the state and some parts of society would like the bicycle to be eternally representative of Vietnamese identity, its triviality in the contemporary period is conveyed in at least three ways. First, state officials cannot stand by the bicycle as a marker of identity because they would not use one. The conveniences of modern wealth accompany them through their lives: state officials are harangued by the public because they are understood to work in air-conditioned offices (*phòng máy lạnh*) with easy access to private cars and personal drivers, and garden villas. They will use a motorbike when they need to go somewhere quickly, or more frequently at night and on weekends. The motorbike is, like the bicycle, more 'fun' to operate than a car but impracti-cal given the 'demands' placed on state officials. This also goes for those in private industry who are closely if opaquely linked to state wealth and connections (Harms 2013).

Second, the bicycle in modern Vietnam occupies 'foreigner' status. This categorization is complex because 'foreigner' includes foreign tourists and 'foreign' Vietnamese overseas (*Việt kiều*) people. In the first instance, bicycles are an object for tourist consumption. Tourists (*khách du lịch*) use them in tourist towns like Hoi An, Sapa and throughout the Mekong Delta. Vietnamese believe they are 'easier' to use for foreigners than motor-bikes and relegated to this group of people as such. The collective certainty is reinforced by the many bicycle tours of Vietnam that are expensive, time-consuming and attractive to those types of people who have an abundance of both time and money at their disposal (i.e., foreign tourists). In the second instance, bicycles are 'foreign' because the Vietnamese overseas market has captured them as objects of the Vietnamese experience. This point may be provocative and contentious for Vietnamese overseas but, in everyday conversation among Vietnamese living in Vietnam, it is not. Numerous examples exist in writing and film. An early case comes from Andrew X. Pham, a Vietnamese-American who chose to rediscover the country of his origin by bicycling through it. Along the way he encountered unhygienic circumstances, chaos, solidarity, isolation, odd characters and experiences, and a Vietnam unrecognizable to that of his childhood (Pham 1999). If you want to visit the country and you have the financial ability and time available, many Vietnamese would ask, why would anyone choose a bicycle when a faster, easier/less taxing and a potentially safer option is available? Though Pham's book, *Catfish and the Mandala*, is popular in backpacker areas throughout Vietnam, among the Vietnamese overseas community, and with the travel-writing literati, it is a curiosity among Vietnamese who have lived through the changes described by Pham. In making this point, I do not wish to uphold the supposed accuracy of what constitutes 'Vietnam' among Vietnamese citizens by lionizing local realities over Pham's experiences. Rather, I am using this argument to build the point that the bicycle is an indication of foreignness, pastness and thus an implausible marker of Vietnamese heritage.

The film *Cyclo* (1995) occupies a like-minded position for Vietnamese nationals. The movie, a kaleidoscope of mystery and intrigue set among an ensemble cast in 1990s Saigon, is the work of Vietnamese-French director Trần Anh Hùng (Trần 1999). The film focuses on the consequences of rising inequality, the allure of immoral dealings in the face of limited employment opportunities and the social reconfiguration of the family in a rapidly urbanizing country. As implied by the film's title, the cyclo is arguably the central character in the film. It is the sole means of income for a poor Saigon family before it is stolen, which robs them of earnings and forces its members into lives of prostitution, theft and drug peddling. The juxtaposition between the 'past' (the cyclo) and the present (immorality or 'social evils', in Vietnamese *tệ nạn xã hội*) presented in the film is, for many Vietnamese, an extreme if not irrelevant binary framing the post-war Vietnamese city. For many, it caricaturizes and exoticizes Ho Chi Minh City, a city that has many faults but includes a dynamism ill-fitted to a movie like *Cyclo*. Once again, the movie is popular on the backpacker tourist circuit and among overseas film aficionados but, in the eyes of everyday Vietnamese, it is an overzealous depiction of Ho Chi Minh City.

The provocations presented above set the stage for a critique of nostalgia, a key element seeding the beginning stages of heritage-making. Writing an anthropological critique of the movie *Cyclo*, Robert (2012, p. 407) argues that nostalgia 'works on the principle of melancholic recollection and . . . involuntary memory'. The sometimes ruthless pragmatism of Vietnamese society prevents a 'melancholic recollection' of the pedicab and especially the bicycle. If the pedicab is effectively finished in Vietnamese society, then the bicycle is only worthwhile for children and old people in today's Vietnam (it is cheaper, easier to train on, more easily replaceable and fixable in a way a motorbike is not). Bicycles are also used in exercise classes at gyms throughout the country, reconfiguring them from invaluable household possessions to markers of a new urban middle class (see Leshkowich 2008). Here my argument on the equivocality and fleetingness of heritage returns: if a piece of transportation equipment becomes unconnected to the needs of the people, it becomes limited along with memories of it, replaced by something bigger, stronger, faster and more useful (like the motorbike). This is not to say that an object like the bicycle is forgotten, however; only that its importance is ephemeral and its value constantly shifting as society moves forward.

In May 2017, I was having a conversation with a Vietnamese woman named Mai who had recently returned to Ho Chi Minh City after spending a year studying film making in London. She asked me what I had been working on and I described the process of writing this chapter on two-wheeled transportation in Vietnam. She laughed and told me that a persistent question framed her conversations with Vietnamese friends, neighbors and family after she arrived at her destinations on a motorbike: 'Wow, you remember how to ride a motorbike?' Leaving aside my friend's motorbike aptitude (which is strong), the question implies that anyone outside of Vietnam is incapable of operating a motorbike, or that once a Vietnamese person leaves the country, he or she forgets how to ride a motorbike, or it assumes that those who leave the country lose their 'Vietnameseness' by forgetting how to ride a motorbike. In the latter instance, the question presumes that the act of returning to Vietnam does not necessarily mean that someone can reestablish his or her Vietnamese identity.

Another respondent named Bich, traveling through western Europe on a tourism road show for her work, highlighted in a recent interview with me that the length of time she spent overseas meant that she would lose her cognitive ability to ride a motorbike. Though she appreciated how civilized the European streets were, without loud noises incessantly emanating from motorbikes (such as backfiring, braking, accelerating and omnipresent honking), she laughingly commented on her imagined confusion when she sat on a motorbike for the first time after returning to Ho Chi Minh City. 'I have lost my roots!', she lightheartedly explained to me. Most important in Mai and Bich's comments for this chapter's main argument is that their experiences in Europe illustrate how the motorbike is a marker of the Vietnamese 'here and now'. That is, the motorbike is a representation of the current era, embedded in a predetermined territory recognized as

Vietnam and which is unique to a particular group of people known as the Vietnamese.

What is it about Vietnamese identity that associates the motorbike with the borders of the country in the present moment? The idea of 'aspirational heritage', of something forward looking in its meanings, is possibly a valuable heuristic to go about answering this question in the section that follows. Additionally, the concept of 'aspirational heritage' assumes that there is a transience to heritage; in the case of Vietnam, the motorbike marks an automotive future in Vietnam as much as it represents the heritage of today.

FROM PRESENCE TO ERASURE: THE FLEETINGNESS OF MOTORBIKE HERITAGE

Vietnam treats the motorbike as both a community and individual vehicle. With respect to the community aspects of the vehicle, a common feature of the motorbike is its overcrowding of people and goods. Witnessing death-defying feats of motorbike balance and weight is common in the streets of Vietnam. Vietnam's reputation is staked on its ability to safely if perilously transport any kind of consumer good (e.g., chickens, televisions, rebar, bricks, goats, water, fabric, furniture) from point A to point B.[4] Furthermore, it is not uncommon for entire families to ride together on a motorbike just as it is not uncommon to see riders transporting large objects in acrobatic and dangerous juggling acts. In Vietnam, the motorbike holds meaning as a family vehicle in much the same way that North America treats the household car. Its safety, reliability and comfort are seen as representative of a family's stability. A common rite of passage in Vietnam is for parents to hand down a family motorbike to youngsters in a similar way that the family car is transferred to a teenager in the United States when he or she reaches driving age. Families often pile on to motorbikes to relax and kill a few hours in parallel to the fabled 'Sunday drive' routine prevalent in America.

Vietnamese families park their motorbikes inside their homes at night and when they are not being used, most often in their living rooms on the ground floor of their residences. The official justification for this decision is to mitigate the risk of theft and keep the vehicle out of poor weather conditions. Symbolically, however, it adds two important facets to the presentist status of the motorbike in Vietnamese society. First, it illustrates a family's protective and preservationist tendencies toward the vehicle. Much as the garage's official use is to protect the car from thievery and weather, it also serves to bring the vehicle into the welcoming embrace of the family home in countries like the United States, Canada, the United Kingdom and Australia. These multifaceted meanings are mimicked in the Vietnamese living room. The second point relates to the first and suggests that the routinized protection of a motorbike at home forges a bond between household and vehicle. 'Don't forget to bring the motorbike in!' is a common refrain parents exclaim as they try to build a sense of personal ownership and responsibility in their children. The motorbike is the only member of the family that can drip oil, belch exhaust and make loud honking noises in the house without reprimand.

Thus, the motorbike's 'heritage from below' status is heterogeneous because every Vietnamese family's relationship to the motorbike is unique. And yet these relationships are produced within a set of shared social norms that elevate the importance of the motorbike beyond the family unit and embed it into the fabric of the nation. The difference between this type of material heritage and others is that the motorbike has no experts to vet its importance or shepherds to claim definitional parameters over its meaning in society. The motorbike's processual nature – what Smith (2006, p. 44) explains as 'a cultural process that engages with acts of remembering that work to create ways to understand and engage with the present' – is exemplified in its ability to bounce between and among scales, moving from the embodied to the domestic unit, the street to the neighborhood, the neighborhood to the city, the city to the nation, in a way that makes it distinctive to Vietnamese society. In 'top-down' processes of heritage-making, the 'realization of a cultural practice' (Salemnik 2016, p. 322) is often followed by orders to control, protect and commodify habits. Outsiders and Vietnamese experts are incapable of intervening in the heritagization of the motorbike because they cannot capture the range of practices and meanings attached to it, nor effectively timetable its future role in society. While I have argued throughout this chapter that the motorbike's 'aspirational heritage' status is marked by its fleetingness and uncertainty, this statement does not mean its role is dampened in society today. Rather the point showcases the urgency and malleability of heritage-making 'from below'.

Although it conveys a sense of community in Vietnam, the motorbike's heritage status is also, as Waterton (2014, p. 824) argues, centered on 'affective and emotive values' that make it a deeply personal type of motorized vehicle. Said slightly differently, alongside its security as a family vehicle and a marker of the nation, the motorbike provides people with an opportunity to generate a customized relationship between their bodies, their city and other people. Because it can only reasonably hold two adults, the motorbike is an important tool to achieve some measure of privacy and intimacy with another person. Young adults borrow the family motorbike to impress and gain some affection with their beaus outside of the prying eyes of their families. In the evening, parks throughout Vietnam are peppered with young and in love couples idling away the hours sharing bubble tea and looking at each other's smart phones on their motorbikes. If they grow restless from sitting around, Vietnamese often describe the sense of freedom they feel when they can *đi chơi* (go for fun) or *đi vòng vòng* (ride in circles) on the back of a motorbike (Small forthcoming). Lovers of all ages demonstrate their trust and care for their significant others by surrendering their motorbikes to them to borrow or to transport them around. The quality of someone's motorbike forms the basis for deeply held beliefs about who he or she is and who he or she wants to be, which connects to a belief that heritage-making can 'help us make sense of and understand not only who "we" are, but also who we want to be' (Smith 2006, p. 2).

Individuals spend beyond their means to acquire a 'safe', 'beautiful' or 'powerful' motorbike that accurately represents their true and/or imagined identity. A respondent named Nhung (personal communication, 22 May 2017) recently arrived to meet me at a coffee shop driving a brand new Vespa motorbike. After shedding layers of clothing, a hat and large sunglasses that protected her from the unrelenting Vietnamese sun, we began discussing her recent purchase. As a single mom, Nhung explained to me, she has to transport her daughter to and from school, and to her extracurricular activities with close attention for her safety. She continued by saying that the traffic in Ho Chi Minh City is so heavy she needs the securest motorbike on the market to guard her and her daughter from an accident. In previous meetings, Nhung bemoaned her low salary and corresponding inability to purchase a high-quality motorbike. So I asked her why she spent so much on an Italian Vespa. With some measure of indignation, she admitted that she borrowed money from her relatives to be able to buy the motorbike of her choice. Additionally, she said that her job as a yoga instructor at a posh studio in District One means that her students are driving some of the best motorbikes on the market. What Nhung implied in making this point is that her motorbike must convey material prestige equal to her students. Her identity rests on her capacity to meet the expectations of her clientele beyond her skills as a yoga teacher.

When Truitt (2008, p. 4) posits that the motorbike is a 'constant source of expenditure' in Vietnam, she is maintaining that there are substantial financial investments required of a motorbike owner in purchasing and maintaining the bike. But, as demonstrated in the brief vignette about Nhung above, motorbike spending can be character-driven too. In a review of the more-than-representational aspects of heritage-making, Waterton (2014, p. 824) states that there is a 'turn toward "practice", which, when thinking about the spaces of heritage, means shifting from static "site" or "artefact" to questions of engagement, experience, and performance'. The performance of and on the motorbike constitutes an important dimension of the heritage-making of the motorbike. A clean and undented motorbike communicates a high level of owner self-respect, but a new and/ or expensive model expresses material wealth and accomplishment. That so many urban Vietnamese cobble together money from many disparate sources (banks, family, friends and acquaintances) in order to purchase a high-quality motorbike – often despite the precarity of their income and their modest capacity to repay loans – illustrates the multiple, entangled relationalities between people and motorbikes throughout a city like Ho Chi Minh City. But more than this, it demonstrates the intensities between bodies, infrastructure, encounters, experiences and the motorized two-wheeler. Tracking mundane engagements between the material and the experiential reflects a shift in what comprises heritage-making from a single-minded focus on 'the grander setting of large museum spaces' to a broader interest in 'the ways in which people interact – routinely and creatively – with heritage . . . in everyday life' (Waterton 2014, p. 829).

When placed under an analytic microscope, the motorbike's temporal worth rests more generally on the short-lived nature of heritage-making 'from below' in Vietnam. To more clearly articulate this point, the last part of this section reflects on the presumed disappearance of the motorbike as it makes way for the future universality of the automobile. The motorbike represents a sense of 'hereness and newness' in Vietnam and illustrates how 'aspirational heritage' forecasts erasure as much as it indexes presence and futurity. To contextualize this point, Hansen (2016, p. 554) has recently written about the motorbike's 'diminished' value to Vietnamese society of late. Concentrating on the ambitious plans at work in the country's urban transportation sector, he points out that the Vietnamese state wishes for 'public transport . . . to satisfy 15–25% of demand in major cities' by 2020 (Hansen 2016, p. 554). While motorbikes continue to be the dominant means of getting around in Vietnam's rural areas, the motorbike is a 'necessary evil' among 'many people and policy makers' in Hanoi and 'does not seem to hold a central position in the national vision of industrialization and modernization' (Hansen 2016, p. 554). If the motorbike market has reached its 'saturation point', we are, as Hansen (2016, p. 554) puts it, 'left with the car' as one of Vietnam's 'spearhead industries' driving development in the country. To those of us who spend a lot of time in the cities of Vietnam, urban governance's plans stretch the limits of credibility. After all, Vietnam's cities are strained to the limit with motorbike traffic, and these vehicles take up a fraction of the street space of cars. Additionally, in Ho Chi Minh City the alley (*hẻm*) is the place of residence for a significant portion of the population. These thoroughfares place dramatic limits on city resident mobility. In Hanoi, the streets are very narrow and clogged with motorbike and foot traffic. What is more, these two cities are constantly criticized for having far too much air and noise pollution, largely as a result of the overwhelming numbers of motorbikes criss-crossing urban areas spewing exhaust and honking at one another (Atkinson 2015; Schramm 2016). These cities would seemingly be the last places in the world to be able to reasonably accommodate four-wheeled vehicles now or in the future.

And yet state officials view the automobile as a growth industry for a number of reasons. With respect to export-led growth, it has strong potential for high profit margins in a region where personal wealth is rising and a budding middle class is emerging. Being a leader in automobile manufacturing will drive a more sophisticated form of industrialization for a country hungry to be considered 'developed' by the global economy (Hansen 2016). When concentrating on the arguments in this chapter, local state officials believe the automobile is a symbol of personal strength, power, and forges for them a place in the highest ranks of society. It also signals the emergence of a modern society. If the infrastructure can be properly developed, Vietnam's leaders seem to think, a rising flow of automobiles entering the market will follow.

Interviews with respondents in the tourism industry in Ho Chi Minh City and Hanoi generally concur with the authorities' trust in the automobile as a marker of modernity. While the content of my research in Vietnam is not explicitly centered on transportation, motorbikes and automobiles are an inevitable aspect of most conversations in Vietnam because everyone seems to want to move rapidly through cities while grappling with traffic and pollution of various sorts. As I have argued elsewhere, four-wheeled personal vehicles are 'safer' for its occupants, 'cleaner' for the environment, 'more comfortable', and generate a wealthy and highly sophisticated identity in its drivers and passengers (Gillen 2018). Travels to Vietnam's closest competitor cities, such as Singapore, Bangkok, Kuala Lumpur, Manila, Jakarta and even Phnom Penh, confirm that plans necessary for national development in countries throughout Southeast Asia must more clearly incorporate the automobile (Lee 2015).

And yet, in contrast to the official rhetoric of state officials, the vast majority of Vietnamese people will neither have the capital or space to own a car, nor the training needed to operate one. However, this does not stop people from imagining that the motorbike's current heritage status will be soon be tossed aside by the automobile when the latter more fully penetrates the market. This point was articulated to me again in May 2017, when I spoke with a respondent named Trinh about why she no longer rides a motorbike in Ho Chi Minh City where she lives. She explained to me that she has recently replaced the precariousness of the motorbike with the stability of automobiles by selling her motorbike and choosing to take taxis, Uber and Grab cars. 'Motos are dirty', she confirmed, 'and they are not safe'. To this I mentioned that Grab and Uber motorbike riders are considered to be of better and safer quality than the 'traditional' motorbike taxis of the 1990s and 2000s. 'No!', she proclaimed, quickly adding, 'there are many fake (*giả*) Uber and Grab moto riders who make replica uniforms and ride very dirty and old motorbikes'. In response to this, I raised the point that many Vietnamese blame the increasing number of automobiles on city roads for raising the already contemptible amount of time sitting in traffic to a higher level of intensity. 'In the future, the road conditions will be better', she replied, and reminded me of the rapid infrastructure development in wealthy districts like District Two and District Seven as evidence supporting her point (Harms 2016).

For Trinh, the idea of preserving the motorbike as a symbol of the unique urban characteristics of present-day Vietnam does not make sense. While it may adequately channel the collective identity of Vietnamese society today, in Trinh's eyes, the motorbike's conspicuous weaknesses make it easily expendable in the future. For her, heritagization fluctuates according to particular times and spaces and if heritage-making takes time, so too does its unmaking. In the broadest sense, the process of heritage's unmaking relates to Vietnam's economic growth, but in an everyday sense Trinh is willing to discard the motorbike as a heritage object because of her shifting demands for a cleaner and more securitized vehicle. There seems to be no nostalgic sentiment when thinking about the automobile's role in the demise of the motorbike. For Trinh, today's urban conditions are fraught with risk and require an appropriate personal decision to use automobiles to get around.

In December 2016, another confidante who resides in Hanoi named Ha proudly showed off a new Toyota sedan he had purchased for his family. 'There are new roads now,' he effusively shared with me, 'so I can use the new highway to visit Sapa in four hours.' Sapa – a well-known mountainous ethnic minority area north of Hanoi on the border with China – has long been a notoriously difficult region to access. Indeed, it is long thought that only foreign tourists who place enough confidence and patience in the overnight train make the trip to Sapa from Hanoi. Ha invited me to join his family on their next road trip to Sapa, which he claims they all take once a month in his new car. Though he continues to use his motorbike to navigate Hanoi's narrow and crowded streets, he told me that he is at his happiest and most relaxed on his excursions to the mountain border.

One of the classic critiques of conventional heritage-making is how 'experts' purportedly go to great pains to recognize the cultural values of local communities yet ultimately lose sight of the ongoing 'living heritage' of people engaging with sites on an everyday basis (Winter 2004). This critique presumes that there is an original essence to an object or set of practices that is capable of being transferred to other shepherds for safekeeping no matter what global forces emerge in the future. But what if heritage-making in a country like Vietnam assumes that there will always be global forces at play in the future and that these should not be considered threats to the transformative dimensions of heritage? What if a future-oriented global force like the automobile is always going to be a loose and unwieldy factor of the present for local communities who are only willing to believe in the heritage of an object such as the motorbike if they alone can determine how global forces like the automobile influence it? For Ha and his family, the instrumentality and status of the car outshines any infrastructural road constraints or utilitarian value of the motorbike. Much as it would seem obvious to prop up the motorbike as an exemplary and everlasting component of Vietnamese society, thus making it subject to established heritage norms, someone like Ha is only willing to entertain the heritage of the motorbike if the aspirational and future-oriented aspects of the automobile are taken into account too. For him, this is a fundamental aspect of 'aspirational heritage': just as it materializes and is omnipresent, it can also just as easily disappear as the horizon comes into closer focus.

CONCLUSION

The extent to which Vietnamese people trust and rely on the motorbike today implies that it is a candidate for heritage status in the country. And yet many ordinary Vietnamese would likely dispute the implementation of such a concretized initiative. Yes, the motorbike is a solid representation of what has been possible over the past three decades: utilizing a mix of street smarts, industriousness, creativity and passion, there have been few limits to what the motorbike has recently accomplished. The motorbike, however, is not a textbook example of what is imaginable in Vietnam going forward. That designation is more fitting for something like the automobile, a vehicle seen by many as a significant, multifaceted improvement over the motorbike.

The impermanent nature of the present and the optimistic dimensions of the future underpin the conceptual backbone of 'aspirational heritage' used in this chapter. 'Aspirational heritage' is object-focused (e.g., motorbike and automobile) and process-oriented. It follows Smith (2006, p. 4) when she writes: 'Heritage is not necessarily about the stasis of cultural values and meanings, but may equally be about cultural change.' This chapter has deliberately chosen to focus on how changing values and meanings reflect the impermanence and future orientation of heritage rather than the foundational and historical dimensions of much of the heritage canon. 'Aspirational heritage' is not concerned with the rediscovery of the past so much as it is an acknowledgement that heritage must account for an uncertain now and prospective yet unpredictable futures. Under these conditions the only type of heritage that is possible is the one that is provisional.

The idea of 'aspirational heritage' is a small move toward the restoration of the public's unsettled voice in the active reimagining of heritage. In ways common to heritage-making 'from below', the motorbike is a connective tissue in Vietnam, bringing disparate types of people and places together. Rather than looking to any sort of expert for guidance on what constitutes Vietnamese heritage, this chapter wishes to impress upon the reader the need to look to the streets and in people's homes for what constitutes heritage. In this chapter, heritage is presented as processual and executed through activities conducted on the motorbike, like snogging at the park, driving around doing nothing, moving large numbers of people and goods, and aesthetic improvements to the style of the bike. In essence, the work of heritage leans on quotidian and learned behaviors and its importance lies in its embodied rather than sanctified nature. Heritage-making also involves the unmaking of something 'old' or 'unproductive', a moment the motorbike is now experiencing in Vietnam. For those people interested in the permanency, preservation and protection of objects and practices considered consequential to the world, the transitory nature of 'bottom-up' heritage-making in Vietnam is probably not the best place to look.

NOTES

1. Called *đổi mới* or 'new change' in Vietnamese.
2. *Xe Ôm*, or 'hug' drivers.
3. A quick Google search for 'Vietnam travel' yields a website for a Vietnamese state-owned company advertising bicycle tourism. Its opening photograph depicts a large group of Vietnamese women riding bicycles in traditional hats and conical hats. See Vietnam Travel, 'Bicycle tourism in Vietnam', accessed 21 September 2017 at https://vietnam-travel.services/featured/bicycle-tourism-in-vietnam.html.
4. YouTube is the best option for viewing homemade videos of overloaded motorbikes and chaotic congestion in action. Hans Kemp created a photo essay of items carried on motorbikes for Slate that can be viewed here, 'Vietnamese motorbikes and the amazing things they carry', accessed 21 September 2017 at http://www.slate.com/blogs/behold/2014/05/08/hans_kemp_photographs_motorbike_drivers_in_his_book_bikes_of_burden.html, Slate.com, Behold Photo Blog, 8 May 2014. A popular Facebook group called 'Another Side of Vietnam' is well known for collecting moments of overburdened

motorbikes on camera. See 'Another Side of Vietnam Facebook Group', accessed 21 September 2017 at https://www.facebook.com/groups/21346846424/.

REFERENCES

Atkinson, A. (2015), 'Asian urbanization: the final dash seen through the case of Ho Chi Minh City', *CITY*, **19** (6), 857–74.

Gainsborough, Martin (2010), *Vietnam: Rethinking the State*, London: Zed Books.

Gillen, J. (2016), 'Urbanizing existential authenticity: motorbike tourism in Ho Chi Minh City, Vietnam', *Tourist Studies*, **16** (3), 258–75.

Gillen, Jamie (2018), 'Rural aspirations in urban Vietnam: the city as a means to an end', in Tim Bunnell and Daniel Goh (eds), *Urban Asias: Essays on Futurity Past and Present*, Berlin: Jovis, pp. 77–85.

Hahn, H.H. (2013), 'The rickshaw trade in colonial Vietnam, 1883–1940', *Journal of Vietnamese Studies*, **8** (4), 47–85.

Hansen, A. (2016), 'Driving development? The problems and promises of the car in Vietnam', *Journal of Contemporary Asia*, **46** (4), 551–69.

Hansen, A. (2017), 'Hanoi on wheels: emerging automobility in the land of the motorbike', *Mobilities*, **12** (5), 628–45.

Harms, E. (2013), 'The boss: conspicuous invisibility in Ho Chi Minh City', *City and Society*, **25** (2), 195–215.

Harms, Erik (2016), *Luxury and Rubble: Civility and Dispossession in the New Saigon*, Berkeley, CA: University of California Press.

Hoang, T. (2016), 'From reeducation camps to Little Saigons: historicizing Vietnamese diasporic anticommunism', *Journal of Vietnamese Studies*, **11** (2), 43–95.

Hobsbawm, Eric and Terence Ranger (1983), *The Invention of Tradition*, Cambridge: Cambridge University Press.

Koch, N. (2015), 'Gulf nationalism and the geopolitics of constructing falconry as a "heritage sport"', *Studies in Ethnicity and Nationalism*, **15** (3), 522–39.

Lee, D. (2015), 'Absolute traffic: infrastructural aptitude in urban Indonesia', *International Journal of Urban and Regional Research*, **39** (2), 234–50.

Leshkowich, A.M. (2008), 'Working out culture: gender, body, and commodification in a Ho Chi Minh City health club', *Urban Anthropology and Studies of Cultural Systems & World Economic Development*, **37** (1), 49–87.

Pham, Andrew X. (1999), *Catfish and the Mandala: A Two-Wheeled Voyage Through the Landscape and Memory of Vietnam*, New York: St. Martin's Press.

Robert, C. (2012), 'The return of the repressed: uncanny spaces of nostalgia and loss in Trần Anh Hùng's Cyclo', *Positions: East Asia Critique*, **20** (1), 389–415.

Said, Edward (1978), *Orientalism*, New York: Patheon Books.

Salemnik, Oscar (2016), 'Described, inscribed, written off: heritigisation as (dis) connection', in Philip Taylor (ed.), *Connected and Disconnected in Vietnam: Remaking Social Relations in a Post-Socialist Nation*, Canberra: Australian National University Press, pp. 311–346.

Schramm, S. (2016), 'Flooding the sanitary city: planning discourse and the materiality of urban sanitation in Hanoi', *CITY*, **20** (1), 32–51.

Shepherd, R. (2017), 'UNESCO's tangled web of preservation: community, heritage, and development in China', *Journal of Contemporary Asia*, **47** (4), 557–74.

Small, I. (forthcoming), 'Affecting mobility: consuming driving and driving consumption in Southeast Asian emerging markets', *Journal of Consumer Culture*.

Smith, Laurajanne (2006), *Uses of Heritage*, London: Routledge.

Trần Anh Hùng (director) (1995), *Cyclo*, Paris: Canal+.

Truitt, A. (2008), 'On the back of a motorbike: middle-class mobility in Ho Chi Minh City, Vietnam', *American Ethnologist*, **35** (1), 3–19.

Waterton, E. (2014), 'A more-than-representational understanding of heritage? The "past" and the politics of affect', *Geography Compass*, **8** (11), 823–33.

Wilder, Carol (2013), *Crossing the Street in Hanoi: Teaching and Learning about Vietnam*, Bristol, UK: Intellect Books.

Winter, T. (2004), 'Landscape, memory, and heritage: New Year celebrations at Angkor, Cambodia', *Current Issues in Tourism*, **7** (4–5), 330–45.

Winter, T. (2009), 'The modernities of heritage and tourism: interpretations of an Asian future', *Journal of Heritage Tourism*, **4** (2), 105–15.

Zhang, J.J. and M. Crang (2016), 'Making material memories: Kinmen's bridging objects and fractured places between China and Taiwan', *cultural geographies*, **23** (3), 421–39.

4.   The Bruce Lee statue in Mostar: 'heritage from below' experiments in a divided city

Ana Aceska and Claudio Minca

INTRODUCTION

> Today when kids bring guns to school and look up to criminals, this monument will be a reminder to dream of a better world. (Raspudic in *Enter the Dragon* 2006, min: 7.50)

Mostar, Bosnia-Herzegovina, May 2013: the Bruce Lee statue is back in Zrinjski Park, golden and shiny, a controversial and somewhat surprising presence in the urban landscape of a 'wounded city' at the heart of Bosnia-Herzegovina (on wounded cities see, among others, Till 2012) (Figure 4.1). Bruce Lee's statue, with its proud and defiant pose, is supposedly there to support an anti-nationalist narrative in a city still torn apart by nationalist forces in the long aftermath of the so-called Bosnian Wars (1992–95). Bruce Lee, a global movie hero who used to fight on the silver screen against 'bad guys' in the name of universal justice, is there to help Mostarians recall past moments of unity and shared cultural practices in one of the most devastated post-Yugoslavian urban fabrics. This chapter is focused on this rather unique initiative, the realization in November 2005, in the city of Mostar, of the first monument ever dedicated to this Hong Kong martial arts movie star, who apparently was very popular across all generations in the former Socialist Republic of Yugoslavia, of which Bosnia-Herzegovina and Mostar were part until the explosion of the several conflicts that, in the early 1990s, led to its dissolution as a state entity. In particular, we discuss the realization of the Bruce Lee statue by sculptor Ivan Fijolić as an attempt – on the part of the Mostar Urban Movement (MUM), a group of influential Mostar-based intellectuals – to inspire a form of 'heritage from below' narrative capable of resisting and rejecting the extremely divisive claims made by separate nationalist political movements over every historical aspect of the city. Interestingly, this is a narrative that is also critical of, and

Source: A. Aceska.

Figure 4.1   Bruce Lee statue in Mostar

crafted as an alternative to, the interpretations proposed by international organizations, such as the European Union Administration of Mostar and UNESCO, of the shared heritage of this beautiful city embracing the Neretva River. While these two dominant narratives have opposite objectives in mind (a nationalist and radical partition of the city, in one case, an appeal to a universal and multicultural heritage, in the other), what they have in common, according to the Mostar Urban Movement, is the fact that they seem to impose on the city and its identity a heritage fundamentally formulated 'from above'.

For Iain Robertson (2012), who coined the term 'heritage from below' (hereafter, HFB), heritage should not be conceived merely as a reconstruction of the past that is commercialized or celebrated for political purpose. Heritage, in his understanding, may also be invisible, or something limited to the sphere of the personal, 'a sense of inheritance that does not seek to attract an audience' (Robertson 2012, p. 2). In proposing this alternative reading of heritage, he therefore highlights the need to recognize the existence of multiple forms of popular heritage that take expression at the most diverse scales. HFB is thus heritage incorporated via a set of specific practices by 'ordinary people', less aimed at visitors and tourists, and more inclined instead to appreciate the specificity of historical interpretations as experienced by selected collectives or even individuals. By recognizing the existence and even the value of these alternative forms of heritage experience and interpretation, it also becomes possible to resist and, at times, subvert existing unified narratives about the past imposed 'from above' by the state and other powerful agents of the cultural industry – what Laurajanne Smith (2006) has famously described as Authorized Heritage Discourse (AHD). In this chapter, therefore, we engage with the idea that, while heritage, especially in the form of AHD, may be a tool to pursue specific political objectives on the part of elites entitled to define what 'proper' past should be celebrated and preserved, and also a way to incentivize the commodification of a sanitized and selected version of history, it may at the same time be used as a form of resistance to official qualifications of heritage and of how it should be experienced. Indeed, even as AHD is frequently advanced by national or international elites (including national governments and supranational organizations such as UNESCO) as stemming out of the need to save the past from the transformative power of aggressive modernization, uncontrolled urban developments, massive tourism impacts and the devastating consequences of war, it is also a powerful force capable of naturalizing the practices (and products) of *certain* interpretations of the past (and not others), in this way implicitly obscuring the selective 'work' behind such practices which tends to marginalize and neglect (Smith 2006, p. 11).

The Mostar Urban Movement representatives, in illustrating the motivations behind the realization of the Bruce Lee statue, explain the desperate need in Mostar of truly unifying narratives, of cultural events capable of reminding people how they used to live together in Yugoslavia before the Bosnian Wars, and how they can still do it in the name of many shared past and present cultural practices. At the same time, they suggest that these forms of shared heritage should come from the people, 'from below', since they wish to resist both the divisive narratives proposed – and largely imposed – by the post-war nationalist movements, and by the AHD proposed by the international organizations involved in the reconstruction and the reconciliations of Mostar after the devastating conflict.

Monuments to foreign popular celebrities in the post-Yugoslav territories have often made international headlines in the past decades. Bob Marley, for example, got his first statue on European soil in 2008, in the tiny village of Banatski Sokolac in Vojvodina, Serbia, where the local 'Rockvillage Festival' is annually held. A year earlier, in another small Serbian village called Zitiste, a statue of Rocky Balboa (the eponymous hero from the famous boxing movies starring Sylvester Stallone) was revealed to the public. To celebrate the statue's unveiling, the village, located not very far from Belgrade, even held a ceremony dedicating the statue to the fictional boxing star. Samantha Fox almost made it on this list: again, in Serbia, the people of Cacak raised money to build a statue of the British celebrity when she visited their town in 2007. The statue was never built but the intention remains meaningful. This list should perhaps also include the unfinished statue of Tarzan in Medja, Serbia, and the plans to erect a statue of the hip-hop artist Tupac Shakur in Belgrade (on this, see Steflja 2015). There are also statues of Bill Clinton in Kosovo and George W. Bush in Albania, possibly related to the perceived benefits derived from those two Presidents to the Albanians living in this region (in both cases supporting the independence of Kosovo). But why Samantha Fox, Tarzan or Rocky at the time when all the monuments dedicated to the Yugoslav period are instead falling apart all around the region?

While one can certainly find many insightful blog-texts devoted to these phenomena (see among others Zaitchik 2006; Dawson 2014), academic work focused on the realization of monuments dedicated to foreign celebrities in the post-Yugoslav territories in general, and to the Bruce Lee statue in Mostar in particular, is relatively limited. An important contribution is Steflja's (2015) comparative analyses of the monuments dedicated to foreign celebrities in the region, where she suggests that these monuments represent radical political statements on the part of emerging civil societies in the lengthy process of transition from socialism to the insurgence of nationalism in the 1990s – at the origin of the violent partition of the former federation – and to the foreign-led economic liberalization and democratization of the political systems born out of the collapse of Yugoslavia. Jakiša (2016), however, takes a different view. She discusses Bruce Lee's symbolic presence in this urban context as a form of artistic narrative concerned with the transition of former Yugoslavia from a socialist regime to a free market regime and its violent dissolution as a unified political entity, and explores in particular the ways in which the failure of 'post-war urban management' is presented via artistic interpretations. She accordingly links this argument to the analysis of the novel *Vuk* written by Veselin Gatalo, the film *Odbrana i zastita* ('A Stranger') directed by Bobo Jelcič, and the installation of the Bruce Lee statue. Bolton and Muzurovič (2010), instead, read the monument dedicated to Bruce Lee in opposition to the many new post-war divisive religious symbols present in the city. Together with the activities of the Abrasevic Youth Center and of the United World College, they see the statue as a remarkable initiative that is attempting to develop new civic spaces in a deeply wounded urban landscape (Bolton and Muzurovič 2010, p. 195). All these examples seem to suggest that, in the divisive political context of ex-Yugoslavia, the recourse to shared expressions of popular culture is seen as a way to aestheticize urban landscapes and bring people together, especially if compared to attempts at imposing unified historical memories 'from above' often at the origin of ever-new disputes between the different factions. If it is the case that, in this post-war atmosphere, political memory tends to divide while popular culture may help to unite, then we would like to argue that such use of popular culture should be considered as a form of HFB, since it is around the visible and invisible presence of elements of shared popular culture – in particular when referring to the times of unity under Yugoslavia – that processes of identity-making and affective affiliation emerge and become new and important ways to practice the memory of the past.

We thus propose to critically reflect on this unique initiative as an attempt to solicit, among the broader population in Mostar, new manifestations of HFB, that is, discourses and practices that may supposedly emerge thanks to the presence of this statue and the embodied forms of memories and values that it is supposed to inspire. At the same time, we suggest that this initiative is not only limited in scope – at least in terms of reaching out to targeted audiences – but also driven by a rather specific agenda promoted by a group of highly educated individuals (led mainly by an academic and a writer) who, with their cosmopolitan narrative about Mostar and its daily life, explicitly use public art, and a figure like Bruce Lee, to gather momentum around alternative projects for the future of the capital of Herzegovina. This seems to speak to the different levels of HFB and to the related critique of certain forms of HFB as inherently associated with the conception of heritage normally endorsed by the institutions pursuing forms of AHD. As noted by Smith (2006), it is not only AHD that is politically driven; even its contestation, whether in the form of HFB or other forms of critique, is always inherently political in nature. In other words, the materialization of any interpretation of the past in the form of heritage always contains a political element, although, according to Lehrer (2010), even this realization may help in using heritage for conciliatory purposes.

In the case of Mostar, while the project behind the Bruce Lee statue may be commended for its progressive and inclusive nature, especially when compared to the heritage 'from above' initiatives (associated with AHD) dominating the ways in which the urban landscape of Mostar has been reconstructed after the war, the specific language used by the promoters and their claim to speak for the people in Mostar raises questions on whether artistic initiatives aimed at soliciting HFB practices may remain nonetheless relatively exclusive.

In order to analyse these tensions with the conceptual lenses adopted by this book, we thus engage with the statements of the initiators as expressed in public speeches and in the dedicated documentary meaningfully entitled *Enter the Dragon* (original title: 'U zmajevom gnijezdu', directed by Milharčič 2006) – like Bruce Lee's last movie – and we briefly discuss the reactions of the local and international press to the installation of the statue in November 2005 to its almost immediate vandalization, and to its 'second life' when it was re-installed after being restored in 2013. We conclude with a few considerations about the ambivalent nature of initiatives like this one, which, on the one hand, are conceived in order to promote heritage practices that should be more inclusive and diverse and possibly establish a pacified coexistence of parallel stories about the past, but, on the other, often reproduce new elitist readings of the local cultural identity and tend to have, accordingly, just a limited impact on how people's everyday practices incorporate these new alternative versions of urban and national heritage.

MOSTAR, A WOUNDED CITY

The statue of Bruce Lee in Mostar is in many ways the product of an extremely complex social, economic and political urban context. The Bosnian Wars (1992–95) that have torn apart Bosnia-Herzegovina – one of the six republics of the Federal People's Republic of Yugoslavia – have also contributed in a decisive way to the dissolution of the federation and the emergence of new independent state entities based on nationalist claims. The conflict among the three major ethnic components of Bosnia-

Herzegovina – the Bosniaks (Bosnian Muslims), the Serbs and the Croats – exploded after a referendum, neglected by the Serbian component, that brought about a unilateral and internally contested declaration of independence in March 1992 (Banac 1984; Donia and Fine 1994; Malkolm 1994; Velikonja 2003; Ramet 2005). In the aftermath of the Bosnian Wars, the city of Mostar was sharply divided into the East side and the West side, respectively dominated by residents commonly identified as Bosniaks (Muslims) and Bosnian Croats (Catholics) (see Aceska 2016).

The Bosnian Wars have also significantly affected the demographic, administrative and territorial structure of Mostar. The city population, which counts today around 110,000 residents, was, prior to the conflict, roughly one-third Muslim, one-third Croatian, one-fifth Serbian, but with a portion of the population that declared itself as 'Yugoslav', with no ethno-religious identity (Grodach 2002, p. 61). Nowadays, the Serbs of Bosnia-Herzegovina live mainly in the 'Republika Srpska', one of the two constitutional and administrative entities currently composing the post-war Bosnia-Herzegovinian state. The other entity, the 'Federation of Bosnia and Herzegovina', of which Mostar is part, is largely inhabited by Croats and Bosniaks. Several linked processes have contributed to produce the current demographic partitions: while many residents have either died in the war, were 'internally displaced', or have left Bosnia-Herzegovina altogether, others, mainly from the surrounding villages, have in the same period moved to the city (Grodach 2002, p. 62). The geography of the city has accordingly changed. Mostar was traditionally considered as one of the architectural pearls of the region, the result of a combination of diverse past planning strategies, but also of buildings and infrastructures developed under Ottoman rule, Austro-Hungarian rule and socialist Yugoslavia (Vego 2006). While most of the residential and institutional buildings were destroyed during the war, the reconstruction phase has been seriously influenced by the conflicting social and political context – largely dominated by ethnic division in all aspects of public life – that has marked the city in the aftermath of the civil war in a decisive way. It is in this context that the story of Bruce Lee in Mostar must be located.

The way in which the city was rebuilt after the war is seen by many as the result of complex – and often controversial – peace agreements. The Dayton Peace Agreement of November 1995 formally sanctioned the end of the war. However, in Mostar, it was the ceasefire that followed the Washington Agreement of March 1994 that ended the actual armed conflict between the Bosnian and Croatian armed forces in the city and the surrounding territories (Yarwood 1999). The institutional body called the European Union Administration of Mostar (EUAM) was established soon after the Washington Agreement, and has served as a project of political and administrative rule of the divided city. The aim of EUAM was to develop strategies of conflict management and resolution, but also to reconstruct the main buildings and infrastructures, while trying to facilitate the freedom of movement across the front line established during the conflict, de facto sanctioning the radical division of the city into two parts. The EUAM also had a key role in organizing a unified police force, managing the new urban and housing planning, and providing public services to all residents, including electricity and water (Yarwood 1999, p. 7).

Such political and administrative interventions aimed at peace-building in the post-war years, however, have paradoxically contributed to generate, in Bosnia-Herzegovina generally, and in Mostar in particular, a state of permanent low-key conflict between the different factions. According to some commentators (see Bollens 2007, 2008), in Mostar, the EUAM mandate has in many ways facilitated the de facto partition of the city. In 1996, in fact, seven municipal districts were formed under the command of EUAM: three with a Croat majority in the West side of Mostar, three with a Bosniak majority in the East side and a smaller jointly controlled Central Zone – giving origin in this way to the very specific (and fragmented) spatial and administrative division of the city that has developed since. For the residents, the dividing line separating the Bosniak-dominated from the Croat-dominated districts was the street commonly called *Bulevar* (the boulevard). The three municipal districts on each side had separate Mayors and municipal governments, and their respective urban planning institutions worked in parallel and in relative isolation until 2004 (Bollens 2007, 2008). The Interim Statute established in 1996 under the guidance of EUAM has governed the city until the implementation of a new Statute in 2004. Supervised by the Office of the High Representative (OHR), the new Statute united the two city administrations, marking the end of the formal division of the city.

These interventions 'from above' have also opened the space for questionable planning and place-making strategies that have allowed the emergence of a situation in which political, economic and religious actors from both sides have used architecture, monumentality and spatial design to implement further separation in the city (Wimmen 2004; Bollens 2007, 2008; Makas 2007). Bollens (2007, p. 247), in his scholarly analyses of urban governance in divided cities, argues that urbanism and urban governance in post-war Mostar have been the primary means through which 'war profiteers' have reinforced existing ethnic divisions. One of these projects included, for example, the two landmarks marking the skyline of the Croatian/Catholic side: the bell tower of the Franciscan Church of Ss. Peter and Paul is now three times taller compared to its pre-war predecessor and the Jubilee Cross on Hum Hill was placed on a spot associated with the war-time shootings. The names and the signage of the streets were changed in the post-war times too. The new street names on the Croatian side of the city are almost exclusively inspired by the official history of Croatia and the blue background of street signs characterizing all parts of the pre-war city is now changed to red. Pre-war monuments were also replaced with versions that refer only to one of the ethno-religious groups of contemporary Mostar. The city has now two central squares, two central bus stops, two universities and two main promenades.

All these examples show how the post-war administrative interventions produced a context in which places could be planned and constructed as only *ours* or *theirs*. One of the top-down attempts to escape this dichotomy was the post-war reconstruction of the Old Bridge, the *Stari Most*. The most important landmark of the *Stari Grad*, Mostar's historical centre, the Old Bridge was the main architectural symbol of the Ottoman times, not only in Mostar, but in the wider region. The bridge, a UNESCO cultural heritage site, was purposely destroyed in 1993, in the middle of the war, by the Croatian military. The post-war reconstruction of the bridge, financed by regional and international donors, was based on a specific narrative that presented it not only as a masterpiece of Ottoman architecture, but also a symbol of unity for the whole city, manifested in the highly emphasized opening ceremony of the reconstructed bridge on 23 July 2004 (for more on the (New) Old Bridge, see Grodach 2002) (Figure 4.2). In a way, the

Source: A. Aceska.

*Figure 4.2   The New 'Old Bridge' (*Stari Most*)*

advocates of the (New) Old Bridge as a unifying architectural element in post-war Mostar and the initiators of the statue of Bruce Lee had a similar aim: to realize a material presence with which all Mostarians may identify with in an otherwise highly divided and deeply wounded urban fabric.

BRUCE LEE: A COMMON HERO

The statue to the Chinese-American kung fu star Bruce Lee in Mostar, despite its immediate symbolic associations, deserves an introduction. The year was 2005, exactly one decade after the end of the Bosnian Wars, and the initiators, as mentioned above, were members of the local non-profit MUM, a multiethnic and antinationalist group of activists composed of (mostly young) people from both sides of the city. The statue was part of a larger project called 'De/Construction of Monument' organized by the Sarajevo Centre for Contemporary Art that included a conference and many art installations, and was financed by a German foundation (for more, see Raspudic in *Enter the Dragon* 2006, min: 33.30). And yet, despite the fact that the statue was welcomed by many residents from both sides, it had a very short fate at that time – a few days after being erected, the monument was vandalized and consequently removed. However, the statue returned in 2013 to its original location, the central Zrinjski Park, where it now still stands.

With its position, orientation, design and timing, the original statue intended to deliver several straightforward messages to the post-war divided city. Both the time and the location were carefully chosen. The statue was inaugurated on 26 November 2005, a day before what would have been Bruce Lee's sixty-fifth birthday. It was purposely unveiled on that day since the city of Hong Kong was itself planning to inaugurate its own memorial dedicated to Bruce Lee the following day. In this way Mostar became the first city in the world to have a statue of the famous star (see Makas 2007). The inscription on the monument said *Tvoj Mostar* ('Your Mostar') with no reference to any city division, ethnicity or religion. The pose and orientation of the statue was meaningful as well, depicting Bruce Lee's 'defensive kung fu pose' – since his famous 'attacking pose' was thought inappropriate for such a post-conflict urban context. In addition, it was strategically oriented towards the north, as if positioning it towards the east or west might have been understood as picturing Bruce Lee defending one side from the other. As Raspudic in *Enter the Dragon* (2006, min: 19.05) put it:

> We had to deal with all kinds of problems along the way because everything here is hyper-politicized. We even had to think about which side Bruce Lee will

face. If he faces East they will say that he is Croat Bruce Lee threatening eastern
Mostar where Muslims live. If he faces West they will say he is a Muslim Bruce
Lee against Croat people. So, we decided he will face North. How to interpret
that? Perhaps as Herzegovian Bruce Lee against Sarajevo, Zagreb, Belgrade,
Brussels, Washington etc. Important decisions were always made in the North
(*sic*), so let it be North.

On top of these rather straightforward messages, the statue was also conceived to operate on several other symbolic scales, including the initiators'
claim to facilitate manifestations of cultural identification/affiliation on
the part of residents that were not imposed from above, but incorporated
into their daily practices and shared interest in the past for the pop culture
represented by the figure of Bruce Lee. Accordingly, we would like to argue
that this statue became an attempt on the part of non-institutional – and
in this case also non-economic and non-religious – agents to construct a
narrative about the existence of common values and a joint past among
Mostarians, values and past commonalities somewhat materialized in the
figure of the Hong Kong actor. Indeed, many other post-war Bosnian
symbols have been constructed in a similar way: the Bosnian anthem
has no lyrics in order to avoid (mis)representing any national/religious
component, while the design of the post-war Bosnian flag was chosen by
European Union representatives involved in the reconstruction phase as
the Bosnian Parliament was unable to agree on it.

In a post-war context in which every cultural initiative may have
appeared controversial, despite the foreign donations and the particular
institutional setting of MUM, Bruce Lee's presence was conceived as a
form of HFB. This emerges quite clearly, we argue, from the statements of
the initiators as expressed in their public speeches and in the documentary
Enter the Dragon, as well as in the local and international press devoted
to the statue. The two main initiators of the project, Nino Raspudic and
Veselin Gatalo, were active members of MUM. Both born and raised in
Mostar, they claimed that their narrative concerning the role of Bruce
Lee in Mostar stemmed from their positions of insiders – as Mostarians
expressing their opinions and stances about the future of the city in a
peculiar but at the same time entirely embedded way. Today, Raspudic, a
Croat Mostarian, no longer lives in Mostar. He has moved to Zagreb and
works as a professor of philosophy at the University of Zagreb, Croatia.
He is also a commentator and a columnist for the local and regional
press, in addition to acting as editor, translator and writer. Gatalo, a Serb
Mostarian, is a local and regional public commentator, columnist and a
writer for political TV debates, political magazines and Internet portals
and a poet. He still lives in Mostar.

In a speech in Halle, Germany, Raspudic (2004), explained why and how they envisioned Bruce Lee as a symbol of common values and joint past for all the youth despite the different ethnic and religious backgrounds in Mostar and, as such, as a symbol of togetherness in a divided city:

> [I]n the city where everything is divided, we would like to remind that, outside of the vicious circle of national conflict, there still exist numerous things that are common to all citizens of Mostar. For example, everybody is fond of Bruce Lee: Bosniaks, Croats and Serbs, left and right political options.

He also spoke of Lee's values and the ways in which they are relevant to Mostar today:

> The value of Bruce Lee's figure lays in its universal character and in its concreteness, capable of provoking concrete emotions, first of all a sense of necessity to fight for justice. Therefore, in Mostar it is not the actor or the character played by him that the monument is being built to, but it is the very idea of justice, represented in a plastic and universally acceptable way, that is also able to awake some positive vibrations through the figure of the famous kung-fu hero we have loved so much during our childhood. (Raspudic 2004)

Similarly, in the documentary film *Enter the Dragon*, the two protagonists comment on their choice to present Bruce Lee as a symbol of common values and a shared past in Mostar. They both argue that the statue of the Chinese-American Hollywood star, precisely because it is devoid of any reference to the Bosnian past, should not be understood as a joke, but rather as 'an attempt at an intervention in public space by placing in a strong symbol that means something to my generation and many other generations' (Raspudic in *Enter the Dragon* 2006, min: 4.40). Gatalo explains that Bruce Lee 'was equally close to all of us and equally distant from all of us, so we don't have to think what his family did in World War I, World War II, under the Ottomans, or the Austrians. After all the man was an athlete, non-smoker. He fought for justice all of his life' (Gatalo in *Enter the Dragon* 2006, min: 6.00). Other statements envisage quite explicitly Lee as a response to the socio-political context in which it is placed:

> If this statue was made in any other part of the world, it would be interpreted as an act of local kung-fu fanatics. But a symbol gets a meaning within a context and the context of Mostar is of a hyper-politicized town where everything is divided. The statue wants to say that big parts of our lives have nothing to do with war and ideology and this is common to all people. (Raspudic in *Enter the Dragon* 2006, min: 5.05)

This reference to 'what is common to all people' clearly hints at the idea of soliciting feelings and a sense of belonging among ordinary citizens, in a context normally hyper-politicized and therefore unable to give space to cultural expressions that may differ from the grand narratives imposed by nationalism or, alternatively, by the persuasive power of the funding provided by the international organizations led by the EUAM and involved in the reconstruction.

However, Dawson (2014) has identified further symbolic elements of the statue compared to the ones expressed by the initiators, and has argued that the historical epoch associated with the figures of most of the statues to foreign celebrities in the post-Yugoslav territories is crucial to understanding their contemporary cultural role. The zenith of Bob Marley, Rocky Balboa and Bruce Lee was the 1970s–1980s, and their popularity in Yugoslavia at that time was linked to the emergence of a large local reggae scene, boxing clubs and vast interest in the martial arts. Dawson (2014) emphasizes the importance of the fact that religiosity was not central to any of these characters' identities and, in addition, that they all embodied nonnationalist and perhaps even antinationalist figures, since they all originated from places outside of the territory of former-Yugoslavia and all have 'mixed' ethnic identities attached to their public personas: Balboa was an ItalianAmerican, Lee a ChineseAmerican and Marley a political PanAfricanist, active in mediating the violent political tensions of the early 1970s in Jamaica.

The local press, however, often did not envisage the symbolic presence of Bruce Lee in line with how the initiators had imagined it. For Makas (2007), the overall project was in fact received at different levels by different local audiences pertaining to the public sphere: reactions therefore varied from supportive comments to ironic remarks about how Bruce Lee was polluting the cityscape since it is entirely out of context. And yet, while some journalists entirely missed the presumed value of a symbolic figure like Bruce Lee for the future of a wounded and divided city like Mostar, others were able to recognize the interest in Bruce Lee on the part of many residents as a form of common heritage. For example, Jergović, one of the country's best known journalists and commentators, supported the idea of foreign charismatic figures being called upon as symbols of the city and the state, especially since no pre-war local heroes were acceptable to all groups in Bosnia-Herzegovina (Makas 2007). What is more, the link between popular culture in former Yugoslavia and the potential of a unifying narrative about the present based on this shared heritage ('from below') is presented as inherently depoliticized, non-bipartisan, foreign and, for this reason, not associated with local politics, but nonetheless symbolically meaningful for the ordinary people of Mostar.

The vandalism and the consequent removal of the original statue have also been interpreted in multiple and diverse ways. While it remains unclear whether the vandals were politically motivated, several analysts have recognized that both their actions and the related removal of the vandalized statue on the part of the initiators were a by-product of the radically divisive atmosphere of post-war Mostar (see Makas 2007; Steflja 2015). Raspudic has even suggested that the vandalization of the statue may be connected to Bruce Lee's desire to become a victim too, much like the people of Mostar feel they have been the victims of the violent recent history of the city (Dawson 2014). However, Dawson (2014) reports how a few Mostarians have described the vandalism of the statue as motivated by the desire of the perpetrators to keep the conflict among the different ethnically divided political factions in the city alive, and concludes that it was destroyed precisely because it celebrated the recognition of common values and shared pasts among those same communities separated by the Bosnian Wars. According to his analysis, therefore, the demolition of the statue was a way of 'vandalizing the urban, secular and nonnational' (Dawson 2014, p. 8).

Interestingly, this did not come as a surprise for Gatalo who, during an interview prior to the installation of the statue, did hint at possible negative reactions:

> Who knows? Maybe some vandals will destroy the monument the next day. Maybe it will last a few generations. But that is not the point. It is about this moment and people with ruined childhoods and youths. And it is important that Mostar became famous for something that is not destruction, division, ethnic conflict and so on . . . (Gatalo in *Enter the Dragon* 2006, min: 8.13)

His response the day after the statue was vandalized is equally interesting, since it was based on a call for people not to feel ashamed, implicitly claiming to represent with his voice the Mostarians who did not commit vandalism, and those who putatively make the silent majority keen to engage with a brighter future:

> I don't know why I should talk about it [the act of vandalism of the statue the day after the opening]. I did what was needed and it is up to the authorities to take care of it. The Mayor spoke today and he strongly disapproved the act. First, I call upon people not to feel ashamed of what was done as they didn't do it. I also decided not to feel ashamed for those without shame. (Gatalo in *Enter the Dragon* 2006, min: 39.15)

In many ways, the vandalization of the statue has become, in his words, an opportunity for people to embrace a form of heritage – their common interest for Bruce Lee and the universal values that he incorporated – and to resist those who prefer to live in permanent conflict and destroy any attempt to build new manifestations of heritage born 'from below'. In this sense, HFB proves to be, in the Mostar context, potentially both divisive as much as it is integrative, with nationalist groups in particular resisting any possible alternative interpretation of the past – and inherently of the future – of Mostar and of its public life/space. When interviewed on the national radio and asked whether he expected the statue to be vandalized, Gatalo responded:

> That hurts me the most. It is not about a piece of bronze, it is about the way we comply to things like that. The way we got used to such things is horrible, the way it became normal. (Gatalo in *Enter the Dragon* 2006, min: 42.15)

This comment reflects in many ways Whelan's (2002) considerations on the role of British monuments in Dublin, and on the importance of understanding how, when a monument is destroyed, also the meanings/symbols behind it may be destroyed. Such deletion of memory and of its material presence in public space is not only inherently violent, but also tends to imply a form of normalization of violence.

Raspudic similarly has used this opportunity to speak for the people of Mostar and their sentiments for the recent events:

> I don't know. It was strange. People had a new hope on that 26th. During that one hour in the park you could feel Zen in the air. It was powerful. You could see a new hope being born after years of grim life. But after what happened, that hope turned into disappointment. So, on the 27th people were sadder than they were on the 25th. I asked myself if we spent two years to sadden people even more. (Raspudic in *Enter the Dragon* 2006, min: 40.52)

The statue, in his rhetoric, has thus become the embodiment of something that people in Mostar have been waiting for a long time, that is, a pacified, shared and popular form of common HFB, in this case emerging from their feelings for and memories of a shared passion for Bruce Lee, a commonly admired hero, a pop culture icon of the Yugoslavian days, whose statue had presumably the power to reinvigorate and affirm an urban narrative void of nationalism and ethnic rivalry. The appropriation of such heritage on the part of the people attending the inauguration seemed, in the words of the promoters, to open the door to a possible common future, a brighter horizon for a city constantly faced with the divisive remnants of a brutal war experience. As Gatalo in *Enter the Dragon* (2006, min: 46.52) put it:

> First, they damaged him, broke the nun-chuck. Then he was spray-painted with black spray. Someone wrote something too. Some good people tried to wash it,

as it usually happens here. Anyway, there is much more good than evil in the world, but the evil is more visible.

The events around the installations of the statue has then translated, in the narrative of the leading figures of MUM, into an opportunity to refer to the universal battle between good and evil, particularly in Mostar, and to claim that the 'good people', for example, those who tried to wash the vandalized statue, are the majority despite being less visible compared to those pursuing divisive agendas. In any case, the brief and controversial history of this monument has made it immediately part of the material heritage of the city, part of the shared cultural practices and sentiments that, if recognized and valorized, can help 'Mostar' to hope for a better and unified future: 'Although the Bruce Lee monument was damaged and desecrated in Mostar, it shouldn't be forgotten that the first Bruce Lee monument was erected here in Mostar' (Gatalo in *Enter the Dragon* 2006, min: 47.25).

The return of the statue in 2013 has provoked diverse reactions on the part of the local audiences. Even though many newspapers and Internet portals reported the event, most of them covered it only factually,[1] with not many comments, including the official website of the city.[2] The temporal interlude of seven and a half years since the removal might have been too long for the initial ideas around the statue to be remembered. Yet, some media outlets commented that the return of the statue might bring new hope for the citizens of Mostar[3] and new opportunities for tourism development.[4] For example, the local newspaper *Republika* reported: 'Maybe it will give hope to the people in Mostar as well as to the members of the MUM, who have different lives today, somewhere far away from Bruce Lee, their childhood hero.'[5] Some media have adopted the language of the promoters and referred to Bruce Lee as 'one more Mostarian that returned to his Mostar home', implicitly comparing him to the residents who returned to the city after having fled the war.[6] Others, however, reminded their readers that 'Mostar hasn't even had local elections yet and the city will soon see demonstrations of trade unions because there is no money to pay people's salaries.'[7]

FOR WHOM IS BRUCE LEE ACTUALLY SPEAKING? HFB AS AN ELITIST PROJECT

The Bruce Lee initiative in Mostar, like many other similar initiatives across the territories of former Yugoslavia, may seem an odd initiative to many readers. The very idea that Bruce Lee may be seen as a vehicle for a specific narrative 'from below' about the past and the present of this severely wounded city is indeed difficult to accept for many, and it is difficult if not impossible to assess the actual impact that this initiative has had among the Mostarians. However, what we were particularly interested in highlighting (and possibly problematizing) here is the ways in which the Bruce Lee statue project was conceived as a way to solicit and give voice to (presumed) common feelings about the past and the present among the Mostarians who have been repressed and silenced by the heavily politicized cultural atmosphere of the post-war period. In particular, the initiators have argued that the statue has affected people more directly and deeply than any other monument in the city. For Raspudic in *Enter the Dragon* (2006, min: 8.40):

> ... monuments like this one have deeper meanings radiated in space. For instance, when you get depressed in Mostar, it is enough to remember that near you stands the bronze Bruce Lee statue with the text 'Bruce Lee Tvoj Mostar' and it gives you some strength and some relief. It tells people to keep on fighting for what they think is good. It will be a source of positive energy that won't chase people away from Mostar. It will attract people to Mostar.

Despite the rhetoric of the Bruce Lee advocates constantly making references to universal values and the cosmic battle between good and evil, their main objective remains that of voicing people's 'true' feelings and thoughts, of creating a space and an opportunity for the emergence of people's hope for a less divisive future. However, in the ways in which the whole Bruce Lee episode was presented and performed – in the narratives, but also in the square, in the documentary, in the press and, of course, in the material presence of the statue – what became apparent was also a tension between the initiators' explicit aim to let people express themselves via Bruce Lee *and* their desire to send a message to these very people, a message that has often taken the form of an ambivalent political statement. From the statue initiative – and the reactions to the related vandalism – what emerges is in fact the initiators' intention to reflect on the city's peaceful coexistence in the past and, at the same time, propose a new project for the future of Mostar. We believe this tension between telling people what to think and feel *and* giving voice to their 'true' thoughts and feelings is present in many HFB initiatives. This is particularly evident when the agenda of the initiators, like in the case of the MUM, is not so much focused on how the people incorporate elements of heritage in their daily practices, but rather on the grand (alternative) narratives dear to those who claim to be speaking precisely in the name of some supposedly unexpressed but very real popular sentiments.

> People have made money, flats, houses . . . Some of them by collecting money from our people who worked abroad even before the war, some from refugees,

some from selling this story to the media and all sorts of humanitarian organizations. In fact, behind all this lies money. And, in the park, will stand a monument to something that has nothing to do with money. (Gatalo in *Enter the Dragon* 2006, min: 12.50)

We want people to stop for a moment and think about the idea of universal justice. About a man from the other side of the planet, a man of different race (*sic*), who lived in Hong Kong, than (*sic*) in the USA. (Gatalo in *Enter the Dragon* 2006, min: 13.15)

A second, related element emerging from this agenda is a deep critique to the mainstream narratives on the post-war reconstruction of the city pursued by non-governmental organizations (NGOs), humanitarian organizations and other international political institutions. According to the initiators, since these international interventions simply did not understand the everyday post-war experience of most residents in Mostar, they thus operated according to abstract categories which missed the fundamental political and cultural forces shaping the life of this divided city:

The problem here is that people didn't get the instruction booklet along with new democracy. It has been sent to us afterwards, through NGO organizations where young people are paid as much as three doctors or three professors. They don't know what to change nor how to do it. And why would they change anything, with all the privileges they have? (Gatalo in *Enter the Dragon* 2006, min: 18.13)

Unlike the heritage 'from above' spirit pervading most initiatives promoted by these international actors, the Bruce Lee project is different from any other previous project; while both international interventions and the nationalistic rewriting of the urban landscape tend to celebrate a certain monumentality imposed formally, Bruce Lee and its related symbolism go against the divisive and/or empty narratives of such monuments, since they speak of a united past and of a possible shared future:

The demarcation line used to be here. Can you imagine a dividing line just 10–15 meters wide? People could hear and see each other. They used to attend the same schools, loved the same girls, ate the same food, wore the same clothes, watched the same TV, listened to the same radio but, in the end, they were forced to shoot at each other. I say forced because it wasn't their choice. (Gatalo in *Enter the Dragon* 2016, min: 16.43)

For this reason, Bruce Lee comes forth, in their interpretations, as a unifying force, a way to incorporate a real or imagined common heritage of the ordinary people in the Yugoslavian days, a form of heritage apt to resist and contrast the main post-war interpretations imposed on the Mostarians via the reconstruction projects. However, as in many individual artistic endeavours, the Bruce Lee project also runs the risk of remaining merely an elitist project infused with universal rhetoric and an implicit political agenda; a missed opportunity to open actual new spaces for reconciliation.

And this brings us to our last point. The Bruce Lee project was also about putting Mostar on the world map thanks to the visibility given to this initiative by some international media and by the fact that Mostar could claim to be the first city with a monument dedicated to the Hong Kong movie star. Among many other international media reports, the *Guardian* has given particular relevance to the event, underlying its sensitive nature in such a divisive political context:[8]

> The city of Mostar, torn apart by inter-ethnic fighting during Bosnia's civil war in the 1990s, has inaugurated a statue of martial arts star Bruce Lee as a symbol of reconciliation. The life-size 5.5ft bronze statue, situated in Mostar's central park, shows the Chinese-American actor in a typical defensive fighting position. Lee was a hero to teenagers all over the country in the 1970s and 1980s, said Veselin Gatalo, one of the initiators of the project. 'This does not mean that Bruce Lee will unite us, because people are different and cannot be united and we will always be Muslims, Serbs or Croats', he said. 'But one thing we all have in common is Bruce Lee'. Mr Gatalo added that Lee epitomised justice, mastery and honesty, virtues the town had badly missed.

While the BBC, tellingly, reported the event in the section 'Entertainment':[9]

> The Mostar unveiling was attended by the ambassadors of China and Germany, both of whom assisted the project. The city witnessed fierce fighting between rival ethnic factions in the 1992–95 war. It remains split with Bosnian Muslims, Croats and Serbs still deeply divided. Lee was chosen by organizers as a symbol of the fight against ethnic divisions. 'We will always be Muslims, Serbs or Croats', said Veselin Gatalo of the youth group Urban Movement Mostar. But one thing we all have in common is Bruce Lee.

International intervention and the related funding were much appreciated by the initiators. Perhaps a confirmation that this initiative was not so much about the emergence of a new form of popular cultural affiliation around the figure of Bruce Lee, or of ordinary everyday practices among the people of Mostar, but rather another elitist narrative in disguise, even as the unifying aims and the popular values behind the revival of this cinema hero must be commended. One may even go further to argue that, since the Mostar monument was funded by external actors, it cannot really be seen as a manifestation of local heritage or as a form of HFB, despite the claim of the proponent to speak for the silent majority of Mostar.

We are approaching the big moment. The eyes of the whole world are watching our town. Today we are not a hole in the ground, today we are the Dragon's nest. (Raspudic in *Enter the Dragon* 2006, min: 35.55)

The celebratory tones pervading a large part of the commentary that has accompanied the appearance of Bruce Lee in Mostar quite certainly do not belong to the daily talk of ordinary Mostarians, but rather to the desire to leave a mark in the remaking of this tormented city, in the name of its cosmopolitan past, but also in the name of the eloquent and imaginative initiators of this unique cultural event. This case reveals, we would like to argue, the inherent tensions possibly pervading all HFB initiatives similar to the one discussed here. The Bruce Lee statue in Mostar, despite being an initiative tightly linked to elements of past popular culture, shows to be just as selective as some other narratives concerning the heritage of the city; while it seeks to speak for the many, it actually originates from a few (however well-intentioned few) who have used the discourse of public art (the statue in the park) and popular culture (Bruce Lee) to build a unifying cosmopolitan counter-narrative for this deeply wounded city. This case also illustrates how the monumentalization of public spaces, despite being aimed at reaching out to a popular sentiment related to past everyday practices (for instance, the common interest for Bruce Lee's movies), has proven to be perhaps a missed opportunity to promote more participatory elements in the ways in which the past and the future of the city may be conceived and possibly built on popular consensus. A statue is still a statue, with all its fixity and its inherent reference to more conventional forms of heritage-making. Hence, notwithstanding the intentions of the initiators to speak for the silent majority of Mostarians, the statue has not managed to become a kind of 'living' monument, a true opportunity for reconciliation and the mutual acceptance of divergent albeit coexistent understandings of the past.

NOTES

1. See, for example: http://www.jutarnji.hr/kultura/art/nakon-punih-sedam-godina-bruce-lee-se-vratio-u-mostar-majstor-borilackih-vjestina-postavljen-u-park-zrinjevac/1150295/; http://bportal.ba/statua-ponovo-postavljena-bruce-lee-se-vratio-u-mostar/; http://www.mojportal.ba/novost/159976/Bruce-Lee-se-vratio-u-Mostar; http://www.nezavisne.com/novosti/gradovi/Brus-Li-se-vraca-u-Zrinjevac/140417 (accessed 28 September 2017).
2. https://www.mostar.ba/vijesti_citanje/brucee-lee-se-vratio-u-park-zrinjevac.html (accessed 28 September 2017).
3. See, for example: http://www.6yka.com/novost/39117/bruce-lee-se-vratio-u-mostar; http://depo.ba/clanak/93441/bruce-lee-se-vratio-u-mostar; http://republikainfo.com/index.php/vijesti/9065-bruce-lee-se-vratio-u-mostar; http://www.nkp.ba/mostarac-bruce-lee-se-vratio-u-park-zrinjevac/ (accessed 14 November 2017).
4. See, for example: http://www.index.hr/black/clanak/u-mostar-se-ponovno-vratio-bruce-

lee/680952.aspx; http://www.scena.ba/clanak/3763/u-mostar-se-ponovno-vratio-bruce-lee (accessed 14 November 2017).
5. http://republikainfo.com/index.php/vijesti/9065-bruce-lee-se-vratio-u-mostar (accessed 14 November 2017).
6. http://www.nkp.ba/mostarac-bruce-lee-se-vratio-u-park-zrinjevac/ (accessed 14 November 2017).
7. http://www.6yka.com/novost/39117/bruce-lee-se-vratio-u-mostar (accessed 14 November 2017).
8. https://www.theguardian.com/film/2005/nov/29/news1 (accessed 14 November 2017). See also the *Telegraph*: 'Bruce Lee beats Pope to be peace symbol of Mostar' at http://www.telegraph.co.uk/news/worldnews/europe/bosnia/1471575/Bruce-Lee-beats-Pope-to-be-peace-symbol-of-Mostar.html (accessed 14 November 2017).
9. http://news.bbc.co.uk/2/hi/entertainment/4474316.stm (accessed 14 November 2017).

REFERENCES

Aceska, Ana (2016), 'Our side, their side and all those places in-between: neutrality and place in a divided city', in Eamonn O. Ciardha and Gabriela Vojvoda (eds), *Politics of Identity in Post-Conflict States: The Bosnian and Irish Experience*, London: Routledge, pp. 107–17.

Banac, Ivo (1984), *The National Question in Yugoslavia: Origins, History, Politics*, Ithaca, NY: Cornell University Press.

Bollens, S.A. (2007), 'Urban governance at the nationalist divide: coping with group based claims', *Journal of Urban Affairs*, **29** (3), 229–53.

Bollens, S.A. (2008), 'Urbanism, political uncertainty and democratisation', *Urban Studies*, **45**, 1255–89.

Bolton, Grace and Nerina Muzurovič (2010), 'Globalizing memory in a divided city: Bruce Lee in Mostar', in Aleina Assmann and Sebastian Conrad (eds), *Memory in a Global Age*, London: Palgrave Macmillan, pp. 181–98.

Dawson, A. (2014), 'Domicide and struggle over the material reconstruction of post-war Bosnia: the case of Bruce Lee', *Integraph – Journal of Dialogic Anthropology*, **4** (1), 1–10.

Donia, J. Robert and V.A. John Fine (1994), *Bosnia and Hercegovina: A Tradition Betrayed*, New York: Columbia University Press.

Grodach, C. (2002), 'Reconstituting identity and history in post-war Mostar, Bosnia-Herzegovina', *City*, **6** (1), 61–82.

Jakiša, Miranda (2016), 'A funeral, a wolf and Bruce Lee in Mostar: revised urban contract and the intersection of time and space', in Eamonn O. Ciardha and Gabriela Vojvoda (eds), *Politics of Identity in Post-Conflict States: The Bosnian and Irish Experience*, London: Routledge, pp. 233–44.

Lehrer, E. (2010), 'Can there be a conciliatory heritage?', *International Journal of Heritage Studies*, **16** (4–5), 269–88.

Makas, Emily Gunzburger (2007), 'Representing competing identities: building and rebuilding in postwar Mostar, Bosnia-Hercegovina', Doctoral Dissertation, Department of Architecture, Cornell University, Ithaca, NY, http://emilymakas.com/ (accessed 2 February 2017).

Malkolm, Noel (1994), *Bosnia – A Short History*, New York: New York University Press.

Milharčič, Ozren (2006), *Enter the Dragon*, Mostar: Vagabundo Productions.

Ramet, S. Petra (2005), *Thinking about Yugoslavia: Scholarly Debates about the Yugoslav Breakup and the Wars in Bosnia and Kosovo*, Cambridge: Cambridge University Press.

Raspudic, Nino (2004), 'The monument to Bruce Lee – yes and why?', http://www.projekt-relations.de/en/download/273Raspudic_BruceLee_NJEMACKA_en.DOC (accessed 5 November 2017).

Robertson, Iain J. (2012), 'Introduction: heritage from below', in Iain J. Robertson (ed.), *Heritage from Below*, London: Ashgate, pp. 1–27.

Smith, Laurajane (2006), *Uses of Heritage*, London: Routledge.

Steflja, I. (2015), 'To history or to Hollywood? Monuments to foreign celebrities in twenty-first century Balkans', *Europe-Asia Studies*, **67** (8), 1302–27.

Till, K.E. (2012), 'Wounded cities: memory-work and a place-based ethics of care', *Political Geography*, **31** (1), 3–14.

Vego, Jaroslav (2006), 'Das Architektonische Erbe Mostars aus der Zeit der Oesterreichisch-Ungarischen Verwaltung', Doctoral Dissertation, Technischen Universitaet, Graz.

Velikonja, Mijta (2003), *Religious Separation and Political Intolerance in Bosnia-Herzegovina*, Austin, TX: Texas University Press.

Whelan, Y. (2002), 'The construction and destruction of a colonial landscape: monuments to British monarchs in Dublin before and after independence', *Journal of Historical Geography*, **28** (4), 508–33.

Wimmen, Heiko (2004), 'New nations, imagined borders: engineering public space in post-war Mostar/Bosnia & Herzegovina', Paper presented at the Conference for Public Spheres, Beirut.

Yarwood, John (1999), *Rebuilding Mostar Urban Reconstruction in a War Zone*, Liverpool, UK: Liverpool University Press.

Zaitchik, Alexander (2006), 'Mostar's little dragon: how Bruce Lee came to be a symbol of peace in the Balkans', http://reason.com/archives/2006/04/01/mostars-little-dragon (accessed 5 November 2017).

5. Death camp heritage 'from below'? Instagram and the (re)mediation of Holocaust heritage

Richard Carter-White

INTRODUCTION

It is increasingly acknowledged that digital media has a role to play in facilitating user engagement with heritage (Giaccardi and Palen 2008). Beyond offering promotion for heritage sites, digital media has helped facilitate the emergence of a 'participatory culture' in which non-elite actors are free to share user-generated content in spontaneous and creative ways (Giaccardi 2012). This valorization of interactive, autonomous and democratic meaning-making converges with the analytic shift enacted by the term 'heritage from below' (Robertson 2012), away from studies related to overt contestations of state- and institution-led heritage narratives, towards a co-construction that blurs the distinction between 'ordinary' users and 'elite' curators (Muzaini 2017).

The active participation enabled by digital media would seem to complement the contemporary remit of heritage institutions. Framing museums as 'stewards of cultural heritage', Wong (2011, p. 106) describes the ethics of New Museology as concerned with 'the inclusion of diverse human experiences and the democratization of their appeal, access, and construction of knowledge' (see also Tunbridge et al. 2000; Muzaini 2014; Kreps 2015; Pocock et al. 2015). However, while an ethics of open collaboration can cause tensions with equally fundamental museological principles of accuracy and trust in any heritage site (Wong 2011), it also raises particular questions when considered in relation to sites of 'difficult' heritage (Morgan and Pallascio 2015). The sensitive histories of violent and disastrous events, and the related sense of ownership and protection towards the historical legacy of such events among victim groups, may clash with a participatory culture in which all are free to contribute regardless of expertise or status, leading to questions over censorship, respectful remembrance, and interactions between diverse communities (Morgan and Pallascio 2015; see also Wong 2011).

These questions are of particular sensitivity in relation to sites of Holocaust heritage. The historical distinctiveness of these places has been framed by survivors in terms of a stark experiential gap between themselves and outsiders (see Wiesel 2006), leading to a protective sense of authority among survivors that has been translated into a series of prohibitions within cultural criticism regarding 'appropriate' means of representing the Holocaust (Boswell 2012). In turn, Boswell (2012, p. 6) highlights the parallel emergence of works of Holocaust 'impiety' within popular culture, which are overtly guided by 'outsider' perspectives and tend to deliberately flout these prohibitions. While these works have been criticized for violating and lessening the unique and knowable status of the Holocaust, Boswell (2012, p. 10) argues that the deliberate transgression of hegemonic representational norms in fact may 'induce a deeper ethical engagement with their subject matter', not least by undermining 'the totalitarian impulse towards the suppression of undesirable attitudes and practices that is evidenced in Holocaust piety'. With the rise of digital media, debates over the ethics, historical value and ownership of Holocaust representation must therefore be extended beyond popular culture to address the abundant quantity of user-generated content produced and shared by visitors to sites of Holocaust heritage.

In recent years, digital media platforms have emerged as a popular means for visitors to Holocaust landscapes to share their original content, particularly photographs and, in doing so, interact with audiences distributed well beyond the reach of the physical site itself. Building on studies of visitor motivations for taking photographs at and of death camp sites (see Dalziel 2016), this chapter offers an analysis of social media as itself constitutive of a heritage object. Specifically, it focuses on the online photograph-sharing platform, Instagram, and its particular construction of the Auschwitz-Birkenau Memorial and Museum (hereafter ABMM). On Instagram, photographs of this site are incorporated into contexts well beyond the control of museum authorities, suggesting that the encounter between Holocaust heritage and social media offers an exemplary enactment of a particular 'heritage from below'. However, the prevalence of Instagram's own highly ritualized conventions of content and interaction also renders it questionable whether digital heritage necessarily equates with active, imaginative or meaningful democratization of heritage resources. Instead, I suggest that the capacity of social media to host unexpected and often surreal juxtapositions exceeds any static binary of heritage from above or below, resulting in a highly ambivalent 'democratization' of heritage.

DEATH CAMPS AS HERITAGE SITES

The emergence of Auschwitz as the pre-eminent site of Holocaust heritage appears to exemplify the image of heritage management as 'a field of practice that has heavily emphasized materiality' (Pocock et al. 2015, p. 962). The ABMM is the most prominent site of Holocaust heritage, having been designated as a UNESCO World Heritage site in 1979 (Thurnell-Read 2009), with over a million visitors each year since 2007 and a record number of 2,053,000 in 2016 (Auschwitz-Birkenau State Museum 2017). This is partly due to the centrality of Auschwitz in Holocaust historiography and its iconic place in the history of the twentieth century. More than that, however, compared to other former death camp sites, such as Sobibor and Treblinka, a key 'advantage' of Auschwitz is that a significant part of the architecture of the camp is still standing, albeit supplemented by reconstruction (see Charlesworth and Addis 2002). The dominance of the ABMM within Holocaust heritage would therefore seem to fit a top-down, institutionally driven view of cultural heritage. Yet, the question of how this site should function as heritage has been addressed in ways that converge with the recent emphasis on intangible and non-elite heritage processes.

Visits to Holocaust landscapes, particularly the ABMM, are often cited as a key example of dark tourism (Stone and Sharpley 2008), a form of tourist activity based around places of macabre historical significance. Reflecting the theoretical eclecticism of the label (see Stone 2006), motivations for visiting Auschwitz have been theorized variously as, to name a few, the search for education and cultural capital (Poria 2013), a voyeuristic fascination with disaster (Lisle 2004), and/or a confrontation with ontological anxieties over death (Stone and Sharpley 2008). Dark tourism thus entails a blurring of education, entertainment and commemoration, and it is in this context that organizations such as the ABMM face the dilemma of how to pursue their curatorial goals.

As Keil (2005, p. 485) observes, one strategy used by the museum authorities to manage these varied motivations and expectations is the scripting of visitor behaviour through the arrangement of materials and physical surroundings such that 'brick barracks and electrified barbed wire form corridors down which guided tours are led', with key structures and objects illustrated and narrated with photographs, captions and testimonial extracts. This channelling of visitor movement and framing of interpretation is reinforced by ground rules forbidding certain activities within the museum and setting the tone for particular behavioural norms around the camp space (Mitschke 2016). Effective as these strategies may be for communicating a singular, coherent and authoritative historical narrative of the camp, the downside of structuring, ordering and standardizing visitor movement, interpretation and behaviour in a space of prescription is that a distance is imposed between visitor and location leading to 'a visitor-role which is semi-passive' and 'the assignment of more or less fixed and retrievable roles and meanings' (Keil 2005, p. 486; see also Murdoch 1998). The enforced passivity of visitors is thus reminiscent of the highly regulated representational space of Holocaust piety (Boswell 2012). Against this tendency, Biran et al. (2011, p. 838) have recommended, in their study of visitor experiences and motivations at the ABMM, that the agency of heterogeneous audiences be better incorporated into the management of the site. In this regard, new types of heritage media have been central to recent attempts to construct a more participatory heritage experience at Holocaust sites.

HOLOCAUST LANDSCAPES AND VISITOR AGENCY

According to Cooke and Frieze (2015), the remit of Holocaust heritage is not simply to provide basic comprehension of the facts of the Holocaust; the conservation rationale for such sites is also to offer a transformative experience of heightened moral reflection and insight. Towards this end, the use of survivor testimony on Holocaust heritage sites is seen as an effective means of unlocking the potential of these landscapes as genuinely dialogic heritage resources. While the physical ABMM site remains a carefully prescribed experience, the museum has drawn on another mediating platform, its official website, as a locus for visitor interactivity. As Krisjanous (2016, p. 345) observes, dark tourism websites have 'the capacity to communicate meaning on multiple levels through multimodal sensory communication', in a way which, following Biran et al. (2011), is customizable to diverse tourist interactions. In the case of the ABMM, the focus has been on developing virtual tours of the site, with two currently available, on remember.org and, more recently, at panorama.auschwitz. org. The latter uses hundreds of high-quality photographs to provide interactive 360-degree panoramic landscapes, with users able to explore various locations of the site, guided by an optional 'hotspots' interface visually highlighting areas of particular historical significance. Some of these locations are inaccessible at the physical site itself, and photographic imagery is further augmented by textual information, maps and social media-sharing options. The website also offers extensive photo galleries, again including physically inaccessible areas. The various possible modes of interaction offered by these virtual tours afford online visitors a certain degree of agency in their engagement with the site, although the enforced limitation of users' sensorial engagement to the visual 'circumscribe[s] the appropriation of the depicted spaces significantly' (Kaelber 2007, p. 29). Equally significant is the reliance of these virtual tours on the decision-making of museum authorities: ultimately, visitors' movements around the camp are determined by the sites and categories deemed significant at the institutional level, a limitation shared with the photo galleries.

The prominence of iconic photographs of Auschwitz may, however, have indirectly prompted a more meaningful form of visitor agency, through the way it has affected the photographic practices of visitors to the physical site. Dalziel (2016) uncovers a wide range of motivations for visitor photography at the ABMM, from a compulsion to replicate iconic imagery (such as that distributed on the official website) as proof of having visited, to a repositioning of the camp as an abstract site of aesthetically 'good' photography; from the production of a visual reminder that can be shared with distant audiences, to personal expressions of empathy. Dalziel (2016, p. 203) concludes that, whatever the motive, visitors are not taking photographs 'mindlessly' but are instead cognitively engaged to the extent that they use 'photography to shape their own experience of their visit to the Museum and highlight the aspects of their visit that will stay with them'. Reynolds (2016) goes further in suggesting that photographs at Holocaust sites are not merely the expression of an objectifying 'tourist gaze' but can instead provoke self-reflection among visitors, whether through encounters with the 'reverse gaze' of fellow tourists, or through the reminder provided by exhibitions throughout the camp that the same photographic technology was used for surveillance and propaganda pur-poses by the perpetrators in the process of genocide. For Reynolds (2016, pp. 341–2), the latter 'disquieting sense of complicity' deprives tourist photographs of any triumphant quality and induces in the photographer 'an ethically engaged subjectivity'. Such transformations in the subjectivity of visitors seem to correspond with that promised by museum authorities, but they do not derive in any simple way from the top-down scripting and imposition of meaning, instead emerging from actions that are independ-ent of institutional prescriptions.

This discussion of Holocaust heritage and visitor agency illustrates the point that heritage is never simply or solely about material objects; heritage 'logically refers to the interpretations, indeed usually plural, which are ascribed to the manifold resources derived from – or alluding to – the past' (Tunbridge et al. 2000, p. 367), resources which might be tangible or intangible. Visitor photography helps facilitate interpretations of tangible heritage resources at sites such as Auschwitz. Consequently, scholars have conceptualized the act of taking photographs as an important heritage process for individuals physically present at the site, allowing them to diverge from the institutional scriptings of the site. This chapter extends that logic by focusing on the sharing of visitor photographs on digital media as itself constituting a Holocaust heritage object, one that can further destabilize 'heritage from above'.

SOCIAL MEDIA AND HERITAGE

Digital media is an increasingly influential driving force in the study of memory (Garde-Hansen et al. 2009), with contemporary technology actively reshaping how society relates to the past (Recuber 2012). Hoskins (2009, pp. 29, 31) describes this as a new type of 'mediatisation of memory', whereby 'everyday and individual memory is "imbricated" . . . in the recording technologies and media that afford memory its strength through our mediatised connection with others'. The burgeoning use of social media sites as a kind of 'archive' has profound implications for memory as an essentially networked phenomenon (Acker and Brubaker 2014), according to a model of 'the social' that is peer-to-peer rather than top-down in the manner of traditional broadcast media (see also Hoskins 2009). Crucially, this 'social network memory' (Hoskins 2009, p. 30) entails a new, hybrid form of public/private memory, whereby 'the "personal" in personal archives can no longer be individuated', instead becoming 'dependent upon networked relationships in online and distributed platforms' (Acker and Brubacker 2014, p. 7).

The peer-to-peer 'participatory culture' of social media (Giaccardi 2012), whereby producer and consumer are blurred into a flat network of 'prosumers' (Recuber 2012), has profound implications for theories and practices of heritage. The accessibility of Web 2.0 platforms has 'facilitat[ed] more participatory and inclusionary allowances for learning about . . . and recollecting the past' (Muzaini and Yeoh 2015, p. 54), providing visibility to non-elite and disenfranchised actors such that they can contribute to or contest established top-down historical narratives. The democratization of heritage is complemented by a greater diversity in the type of heritage being shared, with the instantaneity of media platforms such as the video-sharing site YouTube enabling the conservation of deeply personal and experiential forms of heritage (Pietrobruno 2013). The extent of this putative democratization of heritage is limited, however, by the ordering function present in any archive (Derrida 1995 [1998]). As Garde-Hansen (2009) observes, the particular technical structure of digital archives scripts and directs digital memory practice even as it seemingly offers transparent and equitable access. Through digital interfaces, algorithms and templates, memory becomes embedded in a specific media logic (Hoskins 2009), providing profitable content to media conglomerates that ultimate retain the capacity to form heterogeneous communities of visibility and prominence in a top-down manner (Garde-Hansen 2009). From the opposite angle, a different limit to any digital democratization of memory is revealed in the absence of curatorial direction (Garde-Hansen et al. 2009, p. 7), and thus the unlikeli-hood of this vast heritage archive being drawn upon towards the formation of a new collective politics (Recuber 2012).

In many ways, the ABMM is an archetypal digital media object, and therefore an effective case through which to explore these issues. At the same time that the site is so carefully ordered, its iconic imagery has experienced several decades' worth of 'remediation' (Bolter and Grusin 2001) – reworked, reformulated, recontextualized and recycled in various media that continually reference and influence one another (Garde-Hansen et al. 2009). The collision of these worlds has become notorious, with the rise of 'Auschwitz selfies' culminating in the recent 'Yolocaust' controversy (Gunter 2017). In this chapter, the presence of the ABMM on the prominent Web 2.0 photo-sharing app Instagram is analysed in order to consider how the 'prosumption' of the ABMM might productively complement or counter the excessive institutional scripting of the physical site, and what scope there is for the democratization of such a remediated space of memory.

Whereas research on heritage, photography and social media has used digital archives as an entry point or supplement for investigating the motivations and creative processes of photographers (see Dalziel 2016), here I am solely concerned with the point of encounter with digital archives as a heritage object in itself (see Mylonas 2017). Given the role that photography plays in facilitating the active engagement of visitors to the physical site of Auschwitz, I am interested in how the 'digitalisation of Holocaust memory' (Dalziel 2016, p. 187) constitutes a distinctive heritage resource that, for many, might provide the sole form of contact with the museum. By focusing on the user-end experience, the research aims to avoid the 'misappropriat[ion of] social media data as indicators rather than proxies of human activity' that can occur when attributing meaning or intentionality to the often mundane material contributed to social media platforms (Leszcynski 2017, p. 9). Even so, this approach also has its own limitations which are later discussed in the conclusion.

INSTAGRAM AS A HOLOCAUST HERITAGE OBJECT

With 600 million active users, the pre-eminent photo-sharing service Instagram was selected for this research. The widespread use of smartphones – and thus the ready availability of high-quality cameras – has played a key role in facilitating the use of photography as a means of documenting tourist visits to the ABMM. Instagram, which allows users to quickly and conveniently upload, edit and share smartphone photos, is therefore an appropriate medium for following the digital lives of such images. The official ABMM account on Instagram (tagline: 'Like=Remember') has posted 655 photographs as of January 2017, with over 22,000 followers, while searching Instagram with the hashtag #auschwitz yields over 180,000 results. Even with the large number of historical or unrelated photographs tagged in this way, this minimal search produces a vast archive of publicly available visitor photography of the ABMM.

Instagram photos can be found by searching for hashtags or geotags, or by browsing the profiles of individual users. When searching by hashtag or geotag, as in this study, search results are organized in reverse chronological order of upload date. Due to the impossibility of ordering search results in any other way, this research was limited to analysis of photographs that had been shared relatively recently. While this restricted the research in some ways, it also provided a realistic replication of how the 'writeable collective memory' (Recuber 2012, p. 539) of Instagram is typically encountered by users, in the spirit of Light et al.'s (2016) 'walkthrough method' of app analysis. Thus, during November and December 2016, 650 photographs were collected and analysed, not in view of providing a representative sample but to provide a sense of how the ABMM is enacted on Instagram during a limited period in time. Images yielded by these search methods which did not feature the ABMM were not analysed, although the contribution of such material to a 'new media ecology' (Hoskins 2009, p. 32) is discussed. Several clear themes emerged, related to the content of the images, the interactions generated by the particular logic of Instagram and the 'personal media assemblages' (Morgan and Pallascio 2015, p. 266) of individual user photo feeds.

Content and Conventions

Notable differences were observed between images uploaded at different times during the research period: on one day in mid-November, for example, several images featured visitors displaying Israeli flags at the ABMM, while in December fewer images featured people in general. Naturally the content of ABMM-related imagery depends to some extent on the vagaries of individuals and groups visiting the site, with seasonal differences also likely to influence, for example, the willingness of people to pose outside. Despite these differences, however, a clear picture emerges of an ambivalent digital heritage object that is caught between the iconography of the ABMM and the ordering conventions of digital media.

By far the most common features of the ABMM site to be depicted were the entrance gate to Auschwitz I, with the notorious 'Arbeit macht frei' sign written over it, and the iconic view of railway tracks leading into the Birkenau gatehouse. These images can in turn be divided into two categories, those with human subjects and those without. Photographs that did not feature people as an explicit focus of the composition occasionally used unconventional angles or colour alterations but generally adhered to a composition that replicated the iconic imagery of the camp. This seems to be an effect of remediation, with visitor photographs acting to perpetuate the dominant imagery established in traditional print and broadcast media (Hoskins 2009; see also Hirsch 2001). These photographs also reproduce the institutional scripting of the museum, where emphasis is placed on the topological significance of gates and entrances as indicating a threshold beyond which some transformative experience becomes available (Keil 2005).

By contrast, photographs that prominently featured people diverged from the institutional scriptings of the site, with iconic imagery subverted by the cheerful expressions and disposition of visitors. Such cases flout the 'Holocaust etiquette' whereby visitors '[fulfil] their expected role' as having entered a sacred site by 'manifesting expressions of sorrow, pity, anger, disbelief, and so on' (Mitschke 2016, p. 238). The ABMM is instead presented like a conventional tourist site at which such poses are commonplace. However, as one set of heritage scriptings is undermined, another emerges, with visitors to the camp adhering to a remarkably repetitive set of poses. Particularly noticeable is the prevalence of selfie-style photos. Many of these images feature smiling individuals, hand-holding couples and groups, although occasional concessions are made towards the traditional etiquette of visiting such a place by adopting more sober expressions.

Much as they potentially challenge excessive institutional scriptings, it is arguable that these photographs undermine the integrity of Holocaust heritage. No doubt there are a wide range of motivations for taking and sharing photographs in which one has posed playfully at the site of systematic torture and mass murder, but the immediate impression is that the heritage resources of Auschwitz, and the horror it stands for, are being instrumentalized as a prop for the 'curation of the self' (Ibrahim 2015, p. 217). As the chronological photo feed unfurls, the relentless repetition of these cheerful images suggests that the ABMM has arguably simply failed in its mission to communicate the grave and momentous reality of the Holocaust. However, as Paul Frosh (2015) argues, for all that selfies are typically associated with narcissism, these images unavoidably draw on the power of indexicality; it is in the fundamental nature of their composition to draw attention to the fact of being physically present in a particular place, and to therefore insist on the significance of that place. This effect too is amplified on Instagram by its repetition, to the extent that one could argue for the emergence of a distinct reverence for the site, albeit expressed in unfamiliar terms in the context of Holocaust representation. Moreover, if people-less visitor photographs tend towards the reproduction of documentary-style iconic imagery of the camp, then the embodied quality of selfies and the imperfect compositions that result from the bodily contortions involved in their production can provide unusual, defamiliarizing perspectives on iconic symbols of the Holocaust – the 'Arbeit macht frei' sign from almost directly below, for example. This derided genre of amateur photography thus has a potentially important role to play in reminding audiences that the ABMM is a three-dimensional site, the contours and topography of which (see Charlesworth 2004) are not exhausted by the mythologizing symbols of Holocaust iconography, a theme to which we will return in the next sub-section. Muzaini and Yeoh (2015) argue that digital heritage does not replace the tangible appeal of physical sites, but imagery that is more expressive of a site's materiality might have a complementary role to play in providing greater visibility to the living context in which heritage sites dwell. In the case of such infamous sites as Auschwitz, unusual, demy-thologizing perspectives, if curated effectively, might be able to provide greater awareness of multiple local and competing claims on the site (see Charlesworth et al. 2006), itself a vital stage in peacebuilding processes (see Flynn 2011). As such, the embodied agency of selfies and the unlikely combination of site reverence and defamiliarization that it provides renders a form of heritage that is more complex than the rampant narcissism with which these photos are commonly associated.

The emergent digital media scripting of Holocaust heritage is even more conspicuous in photographs taken by third parties. While these images often adhere to the conventions of amateur travel photography (see Robinson and Picard 2016), particularly those taken by the Auschwitz I entrance, visitors posing in front of the Birkenau gatehouse do so in two specific ways: either standing with one foot placed upon the railway track while looking away from the camera into the middle distance, or sat upon the track with the exact same gaze. This affected performance of thought-ful reflection repeats itself with a striking regularity and standardization, and whether or not the decision to adopt these poses was influenced by exposure to the Instagram photographs of previous visitors to the camp, the narrow conventions and apparent self-referentiality of these images gives the impression of a distinctive social media remediation of Auschwitz.

Despite this, institutional scripting makes its presence felt again in photographs that feature other, less iconic areas of the camp. While these photos displayed a diversity of content from various locations, the tendency remained to focus on features highlighted by the museum authorities, particularly corridors of barbed wire that channel the movement of visitors through the site and which are depicted by visitors in highly repetitive and conventional ways, with the corridors forming a vanishing point into the distance. Warning signs, exhibitions of prisoner uniforms and belongings, memorials, and, in particular, an inscription on one of the barracks in Auschwitz I of George Santayana's famous quotation 'those who cannot remember the past are condemned to repeat it' make up the majority of photographic content, and serve to transmit the scripting of visitor experiences described by Keil (2005). Few images disturb this institutional mediation of the past, with the exception of an image of the Oświęcim[1] train station that contrasts with the absolute separation between inside and outside Auschwitz implied by the obsession with entrances in visitor photographs and the management decisions of the museum authorities alike.

Based on the content of these images, it is difficult to draw a line between the top-down narrative of the ABMM institutional authorities and any 'heritage from below' expressed by social media remediation, at least in terms of expressing participatory forms of heritage. Whether replicating the dominant iconography and narrative of the camp, or composing a raucous group selfie according to the conventions of social media, the authority, script and rituals might differ but the semi-passive behaviour of the visitor appears to be comparable. However, the content of these images is only one dimension of their functioning as heritage. To understand Instagram as a unique heritage object, it is necessary to look more closely at the ways in which personal memories are constituted and deindividuated in digital media networks (Acker and Brubaker 2014). As Frosh (2015, p. 1621) reminds us, an integral element of the selfie is its inherently communicative, social dimension: the prominence of the self, enacted through the centrality of the face, is a 'gestural invitation to distant others' (see also Levinas 1969 [2001]).

Interactions

Viewed in isolation, the content of visitor photographs offers an online heritage encounter with Auschwitz that seems no less prescribed than that of the physical museum, even if this prescription threatens at times to subvert the sanctity with which the Holocaust is typically treated in institutions like the ABMM. Of course, in practice these images do not exist in isolation, and so the aim of this sub-section is to respond to Weilenmann et al.'s (2013, p. 1844) call for academic studies focusing on 'the particulars of Instagram as a medium'. This sub-section is especially concerned with how images of the ABMM are remediated on Instagram and incorporated into diverse, networked interactions, and again the impression is one of ambivalence: a heritage object by turns anarchic and puerile, yet potentially generative of critical perspectives.

The two methods used to search for images of the ABMM on Instagram, the hashtag #auschwitz and the geotag Auschwitz-Birkenau, produced significant overlaps in terms of photographic content, as described earlier. There were some noticeable differences, however, which appear to be born of the kind of interactions sought by the user, and which have important effects on the performance of these images as heritage objects. One significant difference is that almost all of the images found via a geotag search were photographs actually taken at the ABMM.[2] As such, the overall impression when viewing these images is of a virtual tour of the camp. This set of images provides a useful contrast with images searched via the #auschwitz hashtag.

The #auschwitz hashtag produces an anarchic range of materials, from visitor photos of the ABMM and archival images related to Nazism and the Third Reich, to unrelated imagery tagged under #auschwitz for humour or provocation. Space limitations preclude analysis of the latter, but the chaotic juxtaposition of this material with visitor photography of iconic ABMM imagery is an important element of how the latter functions as heritage. Provocative material tagged with #auschwitz generates its intended effect by drawing on the infamy of Auschwitz and deliberately breaching the taboo that prohibits its frivolous representation and, indeed, it is disturbing to be confronted with these images when searching for photographs of the ABMM. However, as with smiling Auschwitz selfies, what initially appears to be a wholly negative side-effect of digital Holocaust heritage can be understood more ambivalently. The rationale for maintaining limits on representations of the Holocaust is partly to avoid its normalization and trivialization. Yet, as Mitschke (2016, p. 233) argues, the circulation and recycling of 'internationally recognized' symbols of the Holocaust, of which Instagram images of the ABMM are such an exemplar, end in a similar result: 'It is precisely because of the fact that these symbols have become so widely associated with and representative of the Holocaust that their original power and dreadfulness has diminished' (see also Boswell 2012). For Mitschke, it is through representation that violates Holocaust taboo that spectators are shocked into remembering the original basis for this taboo. I am not suggesting that the act of attaching #auschwitz to unrelated material necessarily has any thoughtful or critical rationale behind it, but that through the juxtapositions enabled by the architecture of Instagram, overly-familiar Holocaust iconography might become charged with a disturbing quality that it would otherwise no longer possess. Perhaps a sense of digital Holocaust heritage from below emerges here: not in the self-conscious replication of heritage and social media scripts by individuals, nor trashy internet humour, but in the juxtapositions enabled by digital media. If so, the agency of ABMM visitors dwells not in the content of their photographs, which seem so scripted and uncritical, but in the act of deciding whether to align their photographs with the hashtag or the geotag network, an enrolment that is subsequently beyond individual control (Murdoch 1998).

These juxtapositions are characteristic of social media (Garde-Hansen et al. 2009), and there are numerous other ways in which the ABMM is absorbed into the participatory culture of Instagram. In addition to using hashtags and geotags that explicitly connect images to Holocaust heritage (#exterminationcamp, #ww2, #holocaust and #atrocities), ABMM visitors frequently share their photographs by associating them with more general tags, such as #peace, #humanity and #memories. These more general hashtags offer an alternative, affective form of captioning, one that reflects the brevity of expression characteristic of the 'attention economy' (Davenport and Beck 2013). But more distinctive to the logic of social media, these more general hashtags connect images of this very specific cultural heritage to a wider, if ephemeral and ad hoc, audience (Bruns and Burgess 2015). Each hashtag enrols the photograph into a coordinated network through which it can be discovered, and while the sheer quantity of enrolled images render some hashtags effectively useless for this purpose,[3] the combination with other, less general but still non-Holocaust-related hashtags (other examples observed in this study included #letsgosomewhere, #picoftheday, #learnfromthepast and #instatraveling) improves the possibility of camp photographs being noticed by communities beyond those specifically seeking Holocaust-related images (see Bruns and Burgess 2015). Thus, an Instagram user's selection of hashtags enacts multiple unpredictable recontextualizations of the ABMM, amounting to the mirror effect of tagging unrelated material with #auschwitz. In effect, Holocaust heritage is inserted into all manner of everyday and conventionally touristic contexts, appearing randomly alongside drunken selfies and idyllic beach sunsets.

In each of these strategies designed to improve the 'findability' of digital uploads (Pietrobruno 2013, p. 1264), the imbrication of personal memory into new media logic (Hoskins 2009) becomes evident, with users seeking to utilize the particular architecture of the Instagram archive in order to maximize the possibility of their own photo appearing prominently on the app. This could be considered a rebuttal to critiques of the digital democratization of memory. While the media conglomerates profiting from digital media platforms may utilize personal memories in exploitative and discriminatory ways (Garde-Hansen 2009), users seem to be adept and self-aware in finding effective ways of manipulating the ordering structure of the digital archive. But if this amounts to a 'democratized' form of heritage, it is one that has little to do with the agency of individuals. While the repetitive content of visitor photographs may find itself decontextualized in unusual and interesting, albeit often disturbing, juxtapositions, this is largely due to the metadata of the archive rather than any deliberate act of user intervention.

The digital recontextualization of the ABMM is infinitely extended by the responses of other users. In rare cases, this is manifest in confrontational viewer comments, accompanied by the frankness of expression redolent of social media. One image, a carefully composed landscape shot of a watchtower accompanied by a respectful quotation, was met with the response: 'Why r u in a fucking death camp at Christmas'. To this, the user replied: 'why not' and the exchange ended. Without overstating the insight offered by this conversation, the transformation of a commemorative photograph into a terrain for contestation demonstrates an accessibility for commentary by fellow users that might provoke reflection upon the nature of dark tourism, among audiences if not among the participants themselves (Giaccardi and Palen 2008). Furthermore, and reminiscent of the previous discussion of ABMM selfies, the raw potential is here for social media platforms to function as a venue for reconciliation and peacebuilding. Why, indeed, did this person visit a death camp at Christmas? What are the assumptions held by the commenter that rendered this act so provocative? When is a 'good' time to visit a death camp? But, in the absence of curation, the potential for meaningful debate, personal reflections, and any associated political vision that might bring something new to the ABMM narrative disintegrates (Recuber 2012). Besides, the exchange has long since disappeared into the remote reaches of the hashtag feed. For this reason, a more illustrative example of the tension inherent to social media heritage is how, in many cases, the grim content and emotional captions of camp visitors are simply ignored by other users, who instead complement the user's appearance or photographic skill, through smiley face emojis, heart icons and yet more hashtags.

A more indirect form of user response – one that emphasizes the blurring of producer/consumer into 'prosumer' in digital culture – is the emergence of ABMM-visiting Instagram users who refuse to embed their images so thoroughly and strategically in Instagram's media logic. These users label their photographs with minimal Holocaust-related tags and a traditional photographic caption. In such cases the institutional scripting of the camp experience again makes its presence felt, with such captions often consisting entirely of a commemorative quotation from a camp memorial. Very occasionally, a photograph is captioned with the personal reflections of the visitor and again these comments tend to adhere to the institutional narrative of the camp as a tragic but ultimately transformative space. This suggests that the appearance of a crass image does not tell the whole story of social media heritage. Whether or not these more traditional images are shared in 'shocked' reaction to the digital construction of the ABMM on Instagram, they attain a type of power from being placed in proximity to such images. On Instagram, the assemblage of heterogeneous materials is the novel heritage object, a record of Holocaust memory's own dynamic and contested nature.

Viewed through the prism of interactions generated by the participatory culture of social media, digital Holocaust heritage assumes another layer of ambivalence. The bizarre and often offensive juxtaposition of camp imagery with unrelated material, and the introduction of Holocaust iconography into banal contexts, might well possess a critical potential. Yet, as with all heritage encounters, the value of such criticality competes with a range of other imperatives, not least respectful commemoration. The ABMM's status as a space of prescription certainly weakens in the face of Instagram's distinctive architecture of sharing and interaction – a weakening which cannot therefore be attributed to the agency of individual visitors – but in the absence of deliberate and coordinated curation, the heritage value of this is far from guaranteed. Auschwitz as a digital heritage object implies a very different relation with the present to the isolated topology of the museum, and this is most clearly manifest in the final means by which visitor photographs of the ABMM can be found on Instagram, the biographies of individual users.

Biographies

At the same time that images of the ABMM are enrolled and recontextualized in myriad networks, they are also retained in the one archive over which users have some degree of control: the chronological feed of uploaded photos associated with a user's account. Here the bizarre and incongruous juxtapositions of digital Holocaust heritage are given full expression, and the implications for Holocaust heritage are once again deeply ambivalent.

User profile feeds were analysed by first searching for images as previously described, and then following the recontextualization of individual images in the photo feed of the uploading user. As with the selection and composition of photographic content, the Instagram feeds of visitors to the ABMM are remarkably consistent. Individual visitors tend to share only one or two photographs of their visit, supporting Dalziel's (2016) point that visitors do not take photographs of the camp mindlessly. While the motives of individuals for limiting their uploads undoubtedly vary, in light of the previous discussion on the strategic use of hashtags, it is worth noting that consistently uploading 'high-quality' images rather than sharing large numbers is considered an effective method of maintaining and expanding an Instagram 'brand' (see Marwick 2015). Due to the chronological ordering of uploads, feeds begin with one or two photographs from the ABMM, usually capturing one of the two iconic sights. A photograph of Krakow follows, either a selfie or a landscape shot, reminding us that part of the success of Auschwitz as a heritage site can be attributed to its incorporation into the city's tourist network (Thurnell-Read 2009). Finally, the rest of the photo feed largely consists of the basic currency of Instagram: conventional tourist destinations and outdoor activities, food, social events, individual and group selfies, fashion and technology. Auschwitz is thus recontextualized from a unique and isolated site at which individuals undergo fundamental transformation to a component in the narration of an online persona.

Once again, it is tempting to view this recontextualization of Auschwitz as an indicator of a deeply superficial engagement with the memory of the Holocaust, Instagram providing a mechanism for visitors to the camp to place a distance between themselves and the horror of Auschwitz (Thurnell-Read 2009; Dalziel 2016), and thus to utilize it for voyeuristic and narcissistic purposes (Ibrahim 2015). Yet, distance is an inevitable and meaningful dimension of difficult heritage. It is inevitable, because temporal distance is fundamental to the conception of the past as heritage, as an object distinct from and threatened by the present, and so in need of conscious preservation. The means of delivering that preservation – whether through architectural reconstruction (Charlesworth and Addis 2002), the rearrangement of objects (Keil 2005), the establishment of narrative devices and representation of the past *as* past (Krisjanous 2016) or any other common practices of heritage management – also serves to acknowledge and consolidate that distance (Reynolds 2016). If heritage is always, to some degree, a process of mediation, then on Instagram visitors exercise their agency in (re)mediating the ABMM experience in a way that is meaningful to them. There are of course clear differences of insight and historical value between the distance inherent to the juxtaposition of Auschwitz with banal photographs and the distance imposed by the expert interpretation offered by an exhibit in the material site of the camp. However, it is precisely in its incongruity that the juxtapositions

of Instagram possess their own value as a form of heritage, as an inces-
sant reminder of the strange and unsettling presence of the ABMM
within mainstream European tourism networks, itself a potentially potent
metaphor for the position of the Holocaust within western history and
philosophy.

One of the dilemmas of Holocaust historiography and education is how,
given the extreme nature of the Holocaust, to avoid representing it as an
aberrant event, absolutely separate and isolated from modern civilization
(Carter-White 2012, 2016). If the preservation of Auschwitz has any value
as heritage, it is surely to combat this notion of the Holocaust as *over* and
therefore *other*; to try to communicate a sense of the disaster as that which
does not pass (Lyotard 1983 [1988]), will not be reduced to an 'insert facticity' (Clarke et al. 1996, p. 482), but instead continues to haunt the present.

The insertion of user-generated Holocaust iconography into personal
photographic biographies does not in any way fulfil this imperative, but
the casual placement of symbols of genocide along with the banal trivia
of everyday life functions as a heritage object by offering a corrective to
the isolated topography of the physical site of the ABMM. It is disturbing
because it attempts to incorporate into a smooth narrative that which
has been rendered isolated and aberrant. This fundamental tension of
Holocaust heritage management is made explicit by the flattening quality
of social media.

CONCLUSION

Throughout this study, the distinctive dimension of Instagram's construction of the ABMM has dwelt not in the isolated content of visitor
photographs, which in many cases reflect the institutional narrative of
the museum authorities, but in the juxtapositions of content enabled
by the architecture of the app. Whether in the contrast between iconic
photographs and badly composed selfies of the Birkenau gatehouse,
or the insertion of death camp imagery into everyday banality, these
juxtapositions offer potentially interesting ways of looking at both the
museum site and the norms and prohibitions of Holocaust representation
more generally. How this amounts to a 'democratization' of Holocaust
heritage, though, is unclear: it is true that once these photographs are put
into circulation online they are entirely beyond any direct efforts among
heritage authorities to standardize and control the practice of heritage,
and so new meanings can emerge, but this process owes as much to the
algorithmic technology of Instagram and the continuous remediation it
facilitates as the critical participation of non-elites. Perhaps this amounts

to a 'deindividuated democratization', where personal memories 'from below' are incorporated into a structuring archive established by media conglomerates 'from above' and put into conversation with media, images and comments from all possible directions in time and space, including those of traditional heritage discourses. If so, the democratization of heritage heralded by digital media appears to be more complicated than simply giving voice to hitherto under-represented groups, and requires further consideration as to the meaning of 'democratization' it portends.

The issue of curation has been a recurring theme, leading us back to the opening questions of authority and ownership over Holocaust heritage. The unexpected and potentially interesting collisions of content witnessed on Instagram are made possible by the absence of gatekeepers, which allows almost anything to join the digital 'cacophony of commemoration' (Recuber 2012, p. 545). However, this also means that such moments of connection and tension, as highlighted in this chapter, that might have amounted to some kind of reflection or deeper conversation about heritage remain uncultivated and quickly lost. This ephemerality is particularly pronounced on Instagram, with its constantly receding timeline. Whether this is considered a wasted opportunity to develop a truly meaningful new form of heritage depends again upon what value is accorded to the peculiar form of democratization enabled by the instantaneity and accessibility of digital media. In order to address this issue, future research needs to more fully incorporate the 'prosumer' concept into methodology. The approach of this study has to some extent maintained a dichotomy between 'uploaders' and 'viewers', but a more triangulated form of digital methods (Leszczynski 2017) accounting for the use of social media before, during and after visits to sites of difficult heritage is necessary in order to investigate the heritage value for individuals of the transient and anarchic (re)mediations offered by Instagram.

NOTES

1. The Polish town in which the ABMM is located.
2. This is perhaps predictable because most contemporary smartphones and cameras automatically geotag photographs through GPS data, so users uploading their photographs from the actual site of the ABMM will simply need to acknowledge their geotag to be associated with the location.
3. As of January 2017, searching via the hashtag #memories generated over 46 million random images arranged in reverse chronological order. A photograph of the ABMM would quickly disappear into this constantly updating photo feed.

REFERENCES

Acker, A. and J. Brubaker (2014), 'Death, memorialization, and social media: a platform perspective for personal archives', *Archivaria*, **77**, 1–23.

Auschwitz-Birkenau State Museum (2017), 'Over 2 million visitors at the Auschwitz Memorial in 2016', accessed 5 January 2017 at auschwitz.org/en/museum/news/over-2-million-visitors-at-the-auschwitz-memorial-in-2016,1232.html.

Biran, A., Y. Poria and G. Oren (2011), 'Sought experiences at (dark) heritage sites', *Annals of Tourism Research*, **38** (3), 820–41.

Bolter, Jay D. and Richard Grusin (2001), *Remediation: Understanding New Media*, London and Cambridge, MA: MIT Press.

Boswell, Matthew (2012), *Holocaust Impiety in Literature, Popular Music and Film*, Hampshire, UK: Palgrave Macmillan.

Bruns, Axel and Jean Burgess (2015), 'Twitter hashtags from ad hoc to calculated politics', in Nathan Rambukkana (ed.), *Hashtag Publics: The Power and Politics of Discursive Networks*, New York: Peter Lang, pp. 13–28.

Carter-White, R. (2012), 'Primo Levi and the genre of testimony', *Transactions of the Institute of British Geographers*, **37** (2), 287–300.

Carter-White, Richard (2016), 'The interruption of witnessing: relations of distance and proximity in Claude Lanzmann's *Shoah*', in Paolo Giaccaria and Claudio Minca (eds), *Hitler's Geographies: The Spatialities of the Third Reich*, London and Chicago, IL: University of Chicago Press, pp. 313–28.

Charlesworth, Andrew (2004), 'The topography of genocide', in Dan Stone (ed.), *The Historiography of the Holocaust*, Hampshire, UK and New York: Palgrave Macmillan, pp. 216–52.

Charlesworth, A. and M. Addis (2002), 'Memorialization and the ecological landscapes of Holocaust sites: the cases of Plaszow and Auschwitz-Birkenau', *Landscape Research*, **27** (3), 229–51.

Charlesworth, A., A. Stenning, R. Guzik and M. Paszkowski (2006), '"Out of place" in Auschwitz? Contested development in post-war and post-socialist Oswiecim', *Ethics, Place & Environment*, **9** (2), 149–72.

Clarke, D., M. Doel and F. McDonough (1996), 'Holocaust topologies: singularity, politics, space', *Political Geography*, **15** (6), 457–89.

Cooke, S. and D.L. Frieze (2015), 'Imagination, performance and affect: a critical pedagogy of the Holocaust?', *Holocaust Studies: A Journal of Culture and History*, **21** (3), 157–71.

Dalziel, I. (2016), '"Romantic Auschwitz": examples and perceptions of contemporary visitor photography at the Auschwitz-Birkenau State Museum', *Holocaust Studies*, **22** (2–3), 185–207.

Davenport, Thomas A. and John C. Beck (2013), *The Attention Economy: Understanding the New Currency of Business*, Boston, MA: Harvard Business Press.

Derrida, Jacques (1995), *Archive Fever: A Freudian Impression*, trans. E. Prenowitz (1998), London and Chicago, IL: University of Chicago Press.

Flynn, M. (2011), 'Decision-making and contested heritage in Northern Ireland: the former Maze Prison/Long Kesh', *Irish Political Studies*, **26** (3), 383–401.

Frosh, P. (2015), 'The gestural image: the selfie, photography theory, and kinaesthetic sociability', *International Journal of Communication*, **9**, 1607–28.

Garde-Hansen, Joanne (2009), 'My Memories?': personal digital archive fever and Facebook', in Joanne Garde-Hansen, Andrew Hoskins and Anna Reading (eds), *Save As . . . Digital Memories*, Hampshire, UK and New York: Palgrave Macmillan, pp. 135–50.

Garde-Hansen, Joanne, Andrew Hoskins and Anna Reading (eds) (2009), *Save As . . . Digital Memories*, Hampshire, UK and New York: Palgrave Macmillan.

Giaccardi, Elisa (2012), *Heritage and Social Media: Understanding Heritage in a Participatory Culture*, Oxon, UK and New York: Routledge.

Giaccardi, E. and L. Palen (2008), 'The social production of heritage through cross-media interaction: making place for place-making', *International Journal of Heritage Studies*, **14** (3), 281–97.

Gunter, J. (2017), '"Yolocaust": how should you behave at a Holocaust memorial?', BBC, 20 January, accessed 20 May 2017 at http://www.bbc.com/news/world-europe-38675835.

Hirsch, M. (2001), 'Surviving images: Holocaust photographs and the work of postmemory', *The Yale Journal of Criticism*, **14** (1), 5–37.

Hoskins, Andrew (2009), 'The mediatisation of memory', in Joanne Garde-Hansen, Andrew Hoskins and Anna Reading (eds), *Save As. . . Digital Memories*, Hampshire, UK and New York: Palgrave Macmillan, pp. 27–43.

Ibrahim, Y. (2015), 'Self-representation and the disaster event: self-imaging, morality and immortality', *Journal of Media Practice*, **16** (3), 211–27.

Kaelber, L. (2007), 'A memorial as virtual traumascape: darkest tourism in 3D and cyber-space to the gas chambers of Auschwitz', *e-Review of Tourism Research*, **5** (2), 24–33.

Keil, C. (2005), 'Sightseeing in the mansions of the dead', *Social & Cultural Geography*, **6** (4), 479–94.

Kreps, C. (2015), 'Appropriate museology and the "new museum ethics": honoring diversity', *Nordisk Museologi*, **2** (8), 4–16.

Krisjanous, J. (2016), 'An exploratory multimodal discourse analysis of dark tourism websites: communicating issues around contested sites', *Journal of Destination Marketing & Management*, **5** (4), 341–50.

Leszczynski, A. (2017), 'Digital methods I: wicked tensions', *Progress in Human Geography*, doi: 10.1177/0309132517711779 (online first).

Levinas, Emmanuel (1969), *Totality and Infinity: An Essay on Exteriority*, trans. A. Lingis (2001), Pittsburgh, PA: Duquesne University Press.

Light, B., J. Burgess and S. Duguay (2016), 'The walkthrough method: an approach to the study of apps', *New Media & Society*, **20** (3), 881–900.

Lisle, D. (2004), 'Gazing at ground zero: tourism, voyeurism and spectacle', *Journal for Cultural Research*, **8** (1), 3–21.

Lyotard, Jean-François (1983), *The Differend: Phrases in Dispute*, trans. G. Van Den Abbeele (1988), Minneapolis, MN: University of Minnesota Press.

Marwick, A. (2015), 'Instafame: luxury selfies in the attention economy', *Public Culture*, **27** (1), 137–60.

Mitschke, S. (2016), 'The sacred, the profane, and the space in between: site-specific performance at Auschwitz', *Holocaust Studies*, **22** (2–3), 228–43.

Morgan, C. and P.M. Pallascio (2015), 'Digital media, participatory culture, and difficult heritage: online remediation and the trans-Atlantic slave trade', *Journal of African Diaspora Archaeology & Heritage*, **4** (3), 260–77.

Murdoch, J. (1998), 'The spaces of actor-network theory', *Geoforum*, **29** (4), 357–74.

Muzaini, H. (2014), '(In)formal memoryscapes and the unma(s)king of a Malaysian war heroine', *Singapore Journal of Tropical Geography*, **35**, 382–96.

Muzaini, H. (2017), 'Informal heritage-making at the Sarawak Cultural Village, East Malaysia', *Tourism Geographies*, **19** (2), 244–64.

Muzaini, H. and B.S.A. Yeoh (2015), 'An exploration of memory-making in the digital era: remembering the FEPOW story online', *Tijdschrift voor Economische en Sociale Geografie*, **106** (1), 53–64.

Mylonas, Y. (2017), 'Witnessing absences: social media as archives and public spheres', *Social Identities*, **23** (3), 271–88.

Pietrobruno, S. (2013), 'YouTube and the social archiving of intangible heritage', *New Media & Society*, **15** (8), 1259–76.

Pocock, C., D. Collett and L. Baulch (2015), 'Assessing stories before sites: identifying the tangible from the intangible', *International Journal of Heritage Studies*, **21** (10), 962–82.

Poria, Y. (2013), 'The four musts: see, learn, feel, and evolve', *Journal of Heritage Tourism*, **8** (4), 347–51.

Recuber, T. (2012), 'The prosumption of commemoration: disasters, digital memory banks, and online collective memory', *American Behavioral Scientist*, **56** (4), 531–49.

Reynolds, D. (2016), 'Consumers or witnesses? Holocaust tourists and the problem of authenticity', *Journal of Consumer Culture*, **16** (2), 334–53.

Robertson, Iain J.M. (ed.) (2012), *Heritage from Below*, Farnham, UK and Burlington, VT: Ashgate.

Robinson, Mike and David Picard (eds) (2016), *The Framed World: Tourism, Tourists and Photography*, London and New York: Routledge.

Stone, P. (2006), 'A dark tourism spectrum: towards a typology of death and macabre related tourist sites, attractions and exhibitions', *Tourism: An Interdisciplinary International Journal*, **52**, 145–60.

Stone, P. and R. Sharpley (2008), 'Consuming dark tourism: a thanatological perspective', *Annals of Tourism Research*, **35** (2), 574–95.

Thurnell-Read, T. (2009), 'Engaging Auschwitz: an analysis of young travellers' experiences of Holocaust tourism', *Journal of Tourism Consumption and Practice*, **1** (1), 26–52.

Tunbridge, J.E., G.J. Ashworth and B.J. Graham (2000), 'Decennial reflections on A Geography of Heritage', *International Journal of Heritage Studies*, **19** (4), 365–72.

Weilenmann, Alexandra, Thomas Hillman and Beata Jungselius (2013), 'Instagram at the museum: communicating the museum experience through social photo sharing', in Stephen Brewster and Susanne Bødker (eds), *Proceedings of the SIGCHI Conference on Human Factors in Computing Systems*, New York: ACM, pp. 1843–52.

Wiesel, Elie (2006), *Night*, London and New York: Penguin Books.

Wong, A. (2011), 'Ethical issues of social media in museums: a case study', *Museum Management and Curatorship*, **26** (2), 97–112.

6. Unfinished geographies: women's roles in shaping Black historical counter narratives

Matthew R. Cook and Amy E. Potter

The African American Spiritual 'Hard Trials'[1] has a largely untraceable history dating back to the era of chattel slavery in the United States, when enslaved communities created and sang 'plantation songs' spontaneously, usually with deeply religious feeling (Burleigh 1919). Among the earliest published editions of the song is one arranged for a solo singer by H.T. Burleigh published in 1919. American composer Craig Hella Johnson recently arranged a version of the piece for female soloist with choir and piano accompaniment, substituting the original third verse with a text that delves deep into the trials of hundreds of thousands of enslaved Black women in the seventeenth through nineteenth centuries, describing the experiences of being on the auction block, poked and pushed and tried. The piece concludes with the soloist singing of the only escape from the hard trials described in the spiritual being through the inevitability of death.

'Hard Trials' seems to echo the work of Katherine McKittrick (2011) who argues that much of the extant scholarly analysis of racial violence paradoxically fixates on the suffering of and violence against Black bodies while it simultaneously denies a Black sense of place. The representative woman on the auction block in 'Hard Trials' faces all the violence of being chattel for sale, and even while the soloist mimics scripture by singing of the foxes having holes and the birds having nests, she laments that poor sinners – the enslaved – 'ain't got nowhere'. Structures that attempt to destroy a Black sense of place can be seen reflected in the final stanza of 'Hard Trials', as the singer admonishes the listener to be wary of going anywhere without the good Lord in their souls, lest trouble or 'the devil' harken their way.

INTRODUCTION

In this chapter, we write about women working within and beyond the plantation – the 'centre of modernity' – who fight against contemporary racist structures that attempt to keep Black culture and heritage in their place and 'situate black people and places outside modernity' (McKittrick 2011, p. 949).[2] We draw attention to powerful ways in which women – particularly, though not exclusively, Black women – may shape public memory and historical interpretation of Black History in the United States. As a study of 'heritage from below,' our research highlights women's endeavours to challenge dominant narratives – part of what Smith (2006) calls the Authorized Heritage Discourse (AHD) – of slavery through activism, employment and media portrayals. Drawing upon McKittrick's classic text *Demonic Grounds* and other critical race and Black Geographies literature, we seek to feature many voices that are answering one of her major questions: 'What kinds of new and possible spaces are made available through our past geographic epochs?' (McKittrick 2006, p. 123).

Applying this question to public memory and historical interpretation of the chattel slavery system, the voices in this chapter empirically span a variety of sources, from women in filmic and media portrayals of slavery, to a high-profile Twitter user and Southern plantation tourism guides striving to denaturalize sanitized plantation spaces and the predominantly White and male narratives that have been integral to Southern iconography, identity and cultural narratives (Alderman et al. 2016). In the midst of contemporary, ongoing resistance to racial injustice and the need to combat widespread ignorance of the foundational role of slavery in the development of the US political economy, these women occupy what McKittrick (2006, p. 37) calls 'the last place they thought of' – in other words, society's margins. From within the margins, the women in this chapter who work or have previously worked as Southern plantation tour guides labour toward the creation of new spaces and Black senses of place, or what we refer to here as 'unfinished geographies,' by presenting counter narratives of chattel slavery – as 'heritage from below' – that call into question normative geographic orders driven by patriarchy, racism and class. The conceptualization of geographies – spaces and places – as being *unfinished* comes from the work of Sylvia Wynter (Wynter and Scott 2000, p. 164, quoted in McKittrick 2006, p. 123, emphasis added) who argues that there is 'always something else besides the dominant cultural logic going on, and that something else constituted another – *but also transgressive* – ground of understanding . . . not simply a sociodemographic location but the site *both of a form of life and of possible critical intervention*'. After tracing examples of heritage from below as part of their critical interventions, we argue that these women operate as what Dwyer and Alderman (2008) call memorial entrepreneurs: on the *frontlines* of providing education about slavery and expanding compassion and empathetic identification with the enslaved. The work of these women as memorial entrepreneurs is particularly powerful in light of our claim that Black women's histories and geographies are doubly silenced – first by the White supremacist, masculinist cultural importance placed upon White and male narratives, and second because mainstream historical revisionism has tended to focus less on marginalized groups like women, children and people of colour.

In keeping with our belief in a feminist understanding of the situated nature of knowledge creation (Cope 2002), we begin by acknowledging the potentially uncomfortable tension in this chapter stemming from the fact that, while writing about Black women, both authors identify as White individuals who have the privilege of working in academic positions at American universities. Matt is male, and Amy is female. Amy has experience working as a tour guide at a plantation in Southern Louisiana. We state this to point out our particular, intersecting privileged positions that make it possible to feel 'comfortable' or 'safe' researching these topics. In undertaking this research, our political project is to give weight to the voices and positions of others over our own, while situating their work, words and activism in a theoretical framework informed by the study of heritage from below, Critical Race Theory (CRT) and Black Geographies.

It is to these strands of literature that we turn next. Then we describe the methods used to observe and collect information. Following these two brief sections, we examine two case studies to call attention to the women informing this chapter. We start first with social media as a tool to uncover heritage from below through an exploration of tweets and an interview with a former historic plantation guide who operates the Twitter account @AfAmHistFail (the username stands for 'African American History Fail') and shift then to an examination of the recent YouTube series portrayal of slavery in *Ask a Slave*. Both of these examples feature women who challenge stereotypes and racist tropes found in the AHD of slavery and demonstrate the usefulness of social media to studying heritage from below. In the second case study, we dive into the deeply emotional work of Black women tour guides (Tyson 2013), showing how the theoretical threads woven by McKittrick (2006, p. 7) and others can be seen in the work of women in 'the last place they thought of'. Ultimately, however, through our research we find that heritage from below is a powerful – though limited – framework with which scholars can study marginalized groups' efforts to promote counter narratives of their own histories and geographies.

THEORETICAL FRAMEWORK

Heritage from Below

As discussed throughout this edited volume, Robertson's (2012) concept of 'heritage from below' builds upon recognition that the ability to define, use and benefit from heritage is often thought of as being the abode of elites (that is, 'heritage from above'). Smith (2006, p. 29) usefully frames the notion of heritage from above through the lens of the AHD, which 'focuses attention on aesthetically pleasing material objects, sites, places and/or landscapes that current generations "must" care for, protect and revere . . . One of the consequences of the AHD is that it defines who the legitimate spokespersons for the past are'. Heritage from below, in stark contrast, '[embodies] a nexus of interconnections between identity, collective memory and sense of place . . . a sense of inheritance that does not seek to attract an audience. Rather, it is an expression of, and draws on the ordinary and quotidian that, furthermore, is underscored by embodied practice' (Robertson 2012, p. 2). Succinctly summarizing why heritage from below matters, Hall (2005, p. 34) reminds us 'those who cannot see themselves reflected in its [heritage's] mirror cannot properly belong'.

This tension between AHD and heritage from below is played out on a daily basis at plantation museums in the US South. The Southern ante-bellum plantation museum typically presents a romanticized version of Southern history to its audiences, emphasizing the great wealth of Southern planters, the grandeur of their plantations (most clearly demonstrated through high style architecture and ornate gardens), their importance to US history, and generally downplaying the role of chattel slavery in that history (Butler 2001; Eichstedt and Small 2002; Modlin 2008; Buzinde and Osagie 2011; Alderman et al. 2016). Eichstedt and Small's (2002) pioneering, in-depth study of plantation tours across three states concluded that many sites engage in 'symbolic annihilation', or intentional expunging of the enslaved from their spaces of work and everyday life. Symbolic annihilation and Eichstedt and Small's related category of minimalizing slavery, based on the number of times slavery and related terms are mentioned on tours, can be seen as the effectual blotting out of entire enslaved populations' contributions to individual plantation's economies and the larger US political economy *and* heritage. Most, though importantly *not* all, Southern tourism plantation operations could be considered as actively promoting the AHD, particularly in promoting themselves as aesthetically pleasing and in constant need of protection or reverence. In contrast, there are some plantations and other educational sites that actively engage with historical counter narratives, including an emphasis on the role of the enslaved in creating wealth for the plantation owners, describing what life was like for the enslaved, and their contributions to the development of the United States (Carter et al. 2014; Cook 2016).

Black Feminist Geographies

The second body of literature informing our framework for this chapter comes from Black Geographies, Black feminism and Critical Race Theory (CRT). Black women are typically not ascribed much agency in wide swaths of scholarly literature. This echoes fairly common tropes and stereotypes assigned to Black women by White-dominated American society for much of US history. McElya (2007, p. 4), for example, traces the history of the Black mammy stereotype and points out that while mammies bore 'little resemblance to actual enslaved women', they were nonetheless useful stereotyped figures found first in Southern pro-slavery fiction novels before spreading to other commercial products like the Aunt Jemima trademark and films such as *Gone with the Wind*. Angela Davis (1981, p. 5) argues that the popular conceptualization of the matriarchal Black woman is a 'cruel misnomer'. Under slavery, enslaved Black women did not often have the stable kinship relationships or the power structures in place to be matriarchal, according to Davis. However, she (1981, p. 5) contends that 'it should not be inferred that she therefore played no significant role in the community of slaves . . . by virtue of the brutal force of circumstances, the Black woman was assigned the mission of promoting the consciousness and practice of resistance'. And further, 'Even as she was suffering under her unique oppression as female she was thrust . . . into the centre of the slave community. She was, therefore, essential to the *survival* of the community' (Davis 1981, p. 7, emphasis in original).

McKittrick (2006, p. x), in her 'interdisciplinary analysis of black women's geographies in the black diaspora', provides much of the framework for thinking through the ways in which Black women challenge White/European/masculine mappings of historical-geographic America that have, by and large, profited from, erased and oppressed Black bodies. McKittrick incorporates various aspects of American chattel slavery into her analysis, and although she does not focus on specific historical arrangements, she instead emphasizes the memory, writing, theory and geography of slavery to reveal how 'locations of captivity initiate a different sense of place through which black women can manipulate the categories and sites that constrain them' (McKittrick 2006, pp. xvi–xvii). The Transatlantic Slave Trade has deep impacts on the present, a 'recycled displacement of difference' from the slavery era to the present (McKittrick 2006, p. xvii). Most directly, our analysis of the work of women as memorial entrepreneurs, challenging the dominant societal narratives of slavery, is inspired by McKittrick's (2006, p. xxxi) argument that:

> Places and spaces of blackness and black femininity are employed to uncover otherwise concealed or expendable human geographies. Because these geographic stories are predicated on struggle, and examine the interplay between geographies of domination and black women's geographies, they are not conclusive or finished.

Black women's geographies, according to McKittrick, are difficult to trace, find or recognize specifically because 'traditional' (that is, Anglo-American, colonial) geographies, aided by capitalism and sociospatial denial, have worked *quite hard* to make these geographies invisible. By foregrounding narrative in this chapter, we work to more widely circulate and make visible these suppressed geographies. On the importance of narrative to CRT and other Black studies, Hartman (2008) reminds us that there are no surviving autobiographical accounts of the Middle Passage written by an enslaved woman. In this 'silence in the archive', Hartman (2008, pp. 3–4, emphasis added) writes that 'it would not be far-fetched to consider stories *as a form of compensation or even as reparations*, perhaps the only kind we will ever receive'. Price (2010, p. 158) also argues that narratives are of utmost importance to critical race theory/studies movements because narratives have the power to challenge social understandings of race as a fixed and given category through the use of counter-storytelling to 'frame and probe the status quo.'

METHODOLOGY

This chapter is informed by a feminist methodology emphasizing the 'situatedness' of knowledge production. The information presented here is drawn from our own research and the research of others, along with personal interpretations of social media. The chapter includes the perspectives of women tour guides interviewed by a team of researchers on a National Science Foundation (NSF)-funded project[3] investigating the remembrance of slavery at Southern plantation museums. This team, working under the auspices of the multi-university RESET (Race, Ethnicity and Social Equity in Tourism) Initiative since 2012, has conducted research including surveying and interviewing tourists, participant observations of house, grounds and slavery-focused plantation tours and interviews with owners, managers and guides at 15 plantations in Louisiana's River Road region, Charleston, South Carolina and Virginia's James River region. From this research, we draw upon three interviews with Black women guides and visitor survey data.[4] Our work also includes a semi-structured inter-view with the woman who runs the Twitter account @AfAmHistFail. As Potter (2016) describes, the research instrument used for the NSF team's interviews with guides is semi-structured and has three major goals: to identify the guides' demographic information and backgrounds; to better understand the skills and training associated with their position, and to learn more about their typical approach to tours – including level of com-fort with discussing slavery – and experiences that stand out as particularly good, bad or challenging.

As mentioned above, the use of narrative in CRT and Black Geographies is a source of inspiration for the political counter-storytelling that we employ in this chapter. We next turn to case studies to present the memorial entrepreneurs' stories and voices. First, we examine the use of social media as a tool for uncovering heritage from below, looking at @ AfAmHistFail and *Ask a Slave*. We then use the remainder of the chapter to foreground Black women 'in the last place they thought of': working as plantation tour guides.

AFRICAN AMERICAN 'HISTORY FAILS': USING SOCIAL MEDIA TO VOICE DISSENT

Alderman et al. (2016), commenting on the NSF team's research at planta-tion tourism sites, observed, 'the traditional plantation museum is not the only site where the South's pasts are (re)worked'. In keeping with this point, our first case study highlights the efforts of women using social media – the Twitter account @AfAmHistFail and the YouTube web series *Ask a Slave* (Dungey 2013) – as a form of heritage from below. These women's public voices on social media remind us that slavery is not only discussed in academic books or in classroom settings: slavery has increasingly been brought before the nation's conscience more recently through multiple public platforms. Slavery is found in popular media and public discourse, ranging from Michelle Obama's acknowledgement of waking up every day in a house built by enslaved people to films like *Django Unchained*, *12 Years a Slave*, *Lincoln* and TV and Web series like *Ask a Slave*, *Underground*, the *Roots* reboot and *TURN: Washington's Spies*.

The Twitter account @AfAmHistFail appeared in the midst of this surge in public discussion and debate surrounding the historical legacy and social memory of slavery in June 2014. As of July 2017, the account has more than 1,500 tweets and approximately 20,400 followers.[5] The account owner, who is a White woman, worked for about six years in historic interpretation at a museum site in Virginia, where she was specifically hired as an interpreter of African American history. She purposefully does not reveal the name of the museum site because she was still employed there when she first started using the account though she later quit the position. Her Twitter posts reveal actual quotes from visiting tourists concerning Black history, with the majority of tweets focusing on the ridiculous, racist or ahistorical statements said on plantation tours. This social justice-oriented approach to making public the commonly held myths (cf. Modlin 2008) from plantation tourists mimics the approach taken by Dungey (2013) in *Ask a Slave*. In both cases, the two women were former employees of plantation sites who took to different social media platforms (Twitter and YouTube, respectively) to shed light and stimulate public debate on people's unawareness and/or indifference to the history of slavery.

The earliest tweets from @AfAmHistFail highlight plantation visitors' indignation or outright anger at a plantation tour emphasizing slavery:

@AfAmHistFail, 2014-06-22 18:38:29	In my first week of work: 'You're real young, so you don't realize that dragging all this back up is bringing down America'. #firsttweet.
@AfAmHistFail, 2014-06-22 18:39:14	Me: This tour will be about slavery. Visitor: Slavery? We're from Charleston. We hear enough of that already (snorts angrily and storms off).

Many tweets from the user over the first two years also reveal visitors' anger, confusion or disinterest on slavery-themed tours at her workplace. @AfAmHistFail also frequently offers related thoughts on how public history of slavery should be interpreted. For example,

@AfAmHistFail, 2015-01-15 19:56:56	Let's stop using the phrase 'treated well' re: slavery & use 'less starved' 'beaten less frequently' & 'nonetheless still in bondage' instead.

@AfAmHistFail eventually left the position to start a graduate degree, and her pace of tweeting has slowed since 2016.

In a semi-structured interviewed, @AfAmHistFail was asked if there were certain events or happenings that would shape how she presented the tour (Interview, 13 August 2015). Her response echoes Potter's (2016) findings that plantation tours are highly unpredictable and greatly dependent on visitors' questions, body language, age and other demographic factors.

@AfAmHistFail:	When I first started out, of course, it was very 'by the book' because I was new and I wasn't completely, you know, (pause) comfortable with the information yet, as I was learning. And yeah, I began to notice people going cold, occasionally, at certain points, just sort of – their body language would just change a little bit. And, like over time, it became clear like when and why that was happening. . . . I definitely crafted parts of my tours and interpretations with potential contradictory feedback in mind. Um, it definitely influenced the way I would say something, um (pause). I think when I first started – and this was years ago, so I'm really trying to drag it out of my memory – when I first started, people would sometimes ask me if 'household slavery' was easier or better than 'field slavery'. I think – at first – I think I used to say, um, 'Well it was better in some ways, because you get . . .' And then, as time went on, and I realized that folks occasionally were using that question to sort of (pause) suggest that some forms of slavery were benign . . .
Interviewer:	Right.
@AfAmHistFail:	. . . or were not so bad, that altered the way I would respond. And that would be based on the person's body language, you know, it would be tailored to the situation.

Pressed further regarding the nature of the circumstances in which tourists would resist being told about slavery, @AfAmHistFail said (Interview, 13 August 2015):

@AfAmHistFail:	As a side note to that, it seemed to me that people said more ridiculous things on very, very small tours, where it was just their family or one couple, even. Again, that might just be because you have to interact more in a smaller group, by necessity.
Interviewer:	Right.
@AfAmHistFail:	Um, it might be because they felt more free to speak their mind with just one person. They felt they were being less rude by talking, perhaps. I don't really know.
Interviewer:	Yeah. And also, I like how in the *Vox* article, you do sorta make this comparison – that maybe they are more, at sorta face value, comfortable with talking about these issues with you, as compared to some of your colleagues who are African American.
@AfAmHistFail:	I do think so, yeah . . . my African American colleagues definitely received pushback. And much of it, the same or similar to what I describe, and I do talk about some of their experiences, you know, here and there, I think, on Twitter . . .

With these statements, @AfAmHistFail begins to describe the racial tensions that are frequently present when a predominantly White plantation tourism audience that expects to be presented with the AHD instead find themselves on a tour that emphasizes slavery – the 'tough stuff of American Memory', as Horton and Horton (2006) have described it. Visitors may also not be prepared or quite sure how to respond to encounters with first-person interpreters at certain sites like Mount Vernon, where Azie Dungey worked before eventually quitting and creating the *Ask a Slave* YouTube series. The series, composed of videos that average only four minutes in length, centres slavery counter-narratives through the use of satire and humour to challenge actual tourists' questions posed to Dungey, a Black actress, when she worked at Mount Vernon in character as 'Lizzie Mae' the personal housemaid to Lady Washington.[6]

Although the medium of film is frequently considered the domain of large multinational media corporations and/or wealthy elites and used to sell entertaining and often ahistorical versions of heritage, Dungey's project operates like other forms of heritage from below found on social media, poking fun at visitors' historical ignorance and ludicrous questions posed to Dungey while in character. As described by Cook and Alderman (2017), Dungey's work can also be seen as challenging stereotyped images and tropes of the enslaved mammy. The videos give Dungey an outlet to respond to the absurdity of the visitors' questions and racist or insulting statements in a way that she never would have been allowed to do (at least, if she wanted to keep her job). Dungey's response utilizing sarcasm, hyperbole and satire is a natural fit for the ways in which she uses social media as a space for promoting heritage from below through the form of Black historical counter narratives. Similar to @AfAmHistFail, Dungey is able to productively vent her frustrations by channelling 'Lizzie Mae' in a way that prompts discussion and debate – and hopefully, critical reflection – upon the history of slavery and its relevance to contemporary race relations in the United States. When viewed through the theoretical lenses offered by Black feminism, especially those espoused by McKittrick (2006), these women offer a glimpse into the question driving this research regarding what kinds of new and possible spaces can be made through attention to Black Geographies.

While at first glance, visitors' negative reactions to encountering the brutal truths about slavery at plantation sites may seem at odds with the actual history of plantations, in reality the plantation has largely taken on the façade of the AHD as part of a romanticized, mythical past (Modlin 2008). According to Bright and Carter's (2016) analysis of exit surveys of visitors to plantations in the River Road region, for example, visitors are interested in a wide range of topics such as culture, history, architecture and original owners. The history of slavery is among the top categories of interests that visitors report at many of the plantations in our study. Responses of anger, disinterest or confusion over the history of slavery presented on plantation tours as reported by @AfAmHistFail and Azie Dungey are unsurprising reactions for some plantation goers who may only be touring the site for entertainment, rather than educational, purposes.

Examples of ways that social media platforms like Twitter and YouTube have played large roles in progressive social movements abound, but what can they tell us about the use of social media as a form of heritage from below that oppose the AHD? We find relatively apparent benefits and challenges to using social media as a form of heritage from below. Benefits include the free use of social media as a platform for dissemination and providing voice to actors that otherwise would have limited forms of distribution for their message, and relatedly, high accessibility for the public to read and consume these messages. As mentioned earlier, @AfAmHistFail has over 20,000 followers, and with many tweets being retweeted anywhere from one to more than 2,000 times, the number of potential viewers for any given tweet is substantial. Similarly, the YouTube viewership for individual episodes of *Ask a Slave* as of July 2017 ranges from 55,601 to 810,472. Regardless of how viewers feel about the content from these women, their counter narrative messages are being heard and spread.

Challenges, on the other hand, always include the potential that people who advocate for heritage from below can be biased and partial just like the forms of AHD they attempt to confront. Another challenge is the inherent inability for social media users to control how their messages are accepted (or not) and the reactions that social media users may have in response. Take, for example, some of the comments left on the YouTube page for the first *Ask a Slave* episode.[7] While many of the 972 comments are positive and supportive of Dungey's series, other viewers respond with racist or vitriolic comments such as 'Do white irish (*sic*) slaves next', 'Ok. [thumbs up emoji] if you love it keep being slave my love', and 'Christ, I'm bored of all this white guilt crap . . .'. These comments demonstrate that, for these particular users (and many more whose responses to the series we have omitted for lack of space), some attempts to use heritage from below to challenge dominant historical narratives will in fact serve to reinforce the AHD for some observers while pushing others further away from being open to alternative interpretations of history that conflicts with their particular worldview or beliefs.

We support the work of these women and other social media users who challenge widespread ignorance of slavery and Black history and, like Carney (2016), find that social media greatly shapes national discourses about race. However, we must caution that social media and virtual platforms – much like heritage from below more generally – are ultimately not a panacea that can completely overturn the AHD and carry out the difficult work of anti-racist projects. Next, we turn to a case study focusing on three Black women who work as guides at two historic plantations in the 'Deep South' States of Louisiana and South Carolina.

NEW DISCOURSES ON HERITAGE FROM BELOW: BLACK WOMEN AS MEMORIAL ENTREPRENEURS

As Tyler et al. (2009) point out, the United States has a long history of women playing leading roles in historic preservation and interpretation particularly at house museums, which aligns with the perception that domestic space is considered a female domain (see also Domosh 1998). For example, Tyler et al. (2009) discuss the role of the Mount Vernon Ladies Association of the Union – believed to be the first preservation group in the United States – in saving the degraded structure of Mount Vernon from further destruction in the 1850s. The actions of these women established a pattern for private organizations to intervene in saving landmarks prior to national historic preservation legislation. However, it is important to note that these efforts were organized predominantly by White 'women of means' (Tyler et al. 2009, p. 30). Examples of this in the US South include Hoelscher's (2003, p. 657) study of the performance of elite White women in establishing the Natchez Pilgrimage as a 'bedrock of cultural hegemony based on white supremacy', and Gulley (1993) who highlights the role of White Southern women in establishing the United Daughters of the Confederacy, known for glorifying the 'Old South' through the symbolic metamorphosis of Confederate veterans into a largely positive image.

But other women – beyond the wealthy, White woman typically associated with Southern heritage or memory work – have also taken up the banner of memorial entrepreneur (Dwyer and Alderman 2008). For example, Davis (2012, p. 309) examines how Black women appropriate and perform in upper-class antebellum clothing at Civil War re-enactments and thus 'inject alternative historical knowledges into a variety of public spheres . . . us[ing] historical re-enactment as a means of critiquing the dominant contemporary images of black women through interrogation of their root – the history, memory, and legacy of slavery'. Alderman (2002) highlights the work of Black female activist Jacqueline Smith, who has protested the National Civil Rights Museum in Memphis since its opening to contest the 'official' version of Dr Martin Luther King, Jr's memory presented in the museum.

Turning specifically to research on the role of heritage from below in plantation tourism, much of the existing literature tends to focus on the narrative of guided plantation tours or on visitors' experiences and feedback (for example, see Eichstedt and Small 2002; Modlin 2008; Carter et al. 2014). However, Potter (2016) argues that guides exercise varying degrees of control over their own tours, and tours themselves are highly unpredictable, performative and dependent upon the audience. Thus, more attention should be paid to the role of the guide in plantation tourism. In her study of guides working at River Road (Louisiana) plantation sites, Potter identifies 24 of the 28 interviewed guides as White while four identified as Black. Summarizing the guides' demographics, Potter found guides sought work in plantation tourism for a variety of reasons, with economic motivations (simply needing a job, especially while in high school and college or after graduation if they had difficulty obtaining a job in their chosen degree field) as the primary factor. Beyond sheer economics, however, the predominantly White interviewees listed several other reasons for working as guides, such as retirement boredom, plantation tourism as a place to put foreign language (specifically, French)[8] skills to use, and theatrical or entertainment experience sought out by plantation ownership.

Many of these motivations stand out as capitalizing on various social, educational and racial privileges, in contrast to the motivations of the Black women interviewed for this chapter. For example, Toni,[9] a Black woman working at a Charleston-area plantation, commented that she pursued guiding because she was only three generations removed from slavery and took up an interest in history because of her daughters (Interview, 20 February 2016):

Toni: My background is my interest in history, and that started after I was married and had two little girls and thought about ways of teaching them history about slavery, which is a part of my heritage. . . . I wanted them to understand and know about that heritage. Well, part of that I had to reach out and learn on my own, and that's what I did. I started learning, going to libraries, research facilities, and then I started volunteering at an African-American history [museum].

Me and my daughters were part of a group of women that have children, well, that told women's side of the story and talked about where Black women would've been and during this time of the Civil War and what would have been happening with them, which we found the part of the story that's left out. People don't think about the women and children. Where were they in the midst of all this chaos going on hunt at the time while men are going off to war and women are left or they're running away, things like that?

Rachael, another Black woman who works at the same plantation site, also discussed the importance of historical and ancestral connections as motivating factors for why she worked in historic interpretation (Interview, 28 February 2016):

Rachael: I've had some people come out and ask: 'Why aren't you in period dress?' I'm thinking like 'So you want me to be dressed as a slave?' I'm not ashamed that my ancestors were enslaved, but for me it's very important to present myself as a modern, present-day Gullah woman because very often people perceive Gullah culture as a relic, a historical slave culture, something that's dead. And it's present.
. . .
I'm often told that they can tell how passionate I am. I think people are interested in Gullah culture. And also, I think people feel that it is more authentic coming from me as opposed to someone else. I get that, and I respect it.

Rachael's identification as Gullah and incorporation of Gullah culture in her tours adds another layer of complexity to the exploration of Black sense of place and heritage from below, beyond the Black/White binary that often conflates all the nuances of Black experiences and histories into one generic, amorphous culture. Gullah/Geechee[10] culture has tradition-ally had a deep sense of place on coastal islands in the Southeastern United States, centred predominantly off the coast of South Carolina and Georgia.[11] The Gullah/Geechee sense of place is under threat from displacement caused by tourism and land development (Faulkenberry et al. 2000).

Edie, a Black guide at a large plantation tourism site in Louisiana, grew up in the same small town where the plantation is located and put herself through college working part-time at the site. Unable to find a job after graduation, the plantation hired Edie full-time and began to develop a slavery-specific tour to add to their traditional house tour. She developed her slavery tour based on archival research at Tulane University, which included public records and letters from the original plantation owners. In describing how she felt about being encouraged by management to create a slavery-themed tour, Edie said (Interview, 6 March 2015):

Edie: I think the most exciting part is just sharing with people something that they don't usually get to see. Especially in the house. I mean we do mention slavery – but it's just impossible to condense everything into one tour and so that's why we have so many other exhibits. . . . it's just really exciting to just add another facet to [this site] and just make it that much more valuable where people can learn about the whole experience.

And instead of it just being an afterthought or just in the back of your mind that 'Hey, slaves are the ones that built this planta- tion', you actually get to see it and hear about it first hand and it's kind of brought to the forefront that this was built with, you know, with slavery, and it was not a good part of history: its very ugly, but its history.

Edie's words speak to the importance of Black women teaching the counter narratives of slavery at Southern plantation sites that have whitewashed slavery for decades and instead focused on the White planter class family's history, home and grounds. By bringing slavery out of the margins – both historically and bodily – women like Edie, Rachael and Toni are obvious examples of memorial entrepreneurs who denaturalize overwhelmingly White-dominated spaces and recover the 'places and spaces of blackness . . . [that were] formerly identified as irrelevant and/or nonexistent' (McKittrick 2006, p. 32). Toni described how she crafted her tour specifi- cally to de-emphasize the planter family and quickly focus the main part of her tour on the history of the enslaved and their transition to freedom.

Toni: For me, I talk a little bit about the [planter] family – who it's named after. But then the majority of my conversation is about the enslaved. My main piece is from slavery to freedom, so I'm covering antebellum plus to 1865 and then to beyond and how that relates just to [this] plantation . . . My perspective is another path still in that freedom period, but how this site per- sonally relates, from the house to the outbuildings. (Interview, 20 February 2016)

In keeping with Potter's (2016) observation that tours are ephemeral and often change depending on the audience, we noticed several different counter narrative strategies employed on tours that emphasize slavery. The historical and geographical counter narrative content differed from other tours by de-emphasizing the slave-owners, their family and their property and instead emphasizing the living and work quarters of the enslaved with many details about their everyday work, their family structure and the hardships and brutalities they routinely encountered. While approaches vary at different sites and with different guides, they generally fall into the categories of textual, performance and artifact-based strategies (Cook 2016). The textual category of counter narrative strategy includes the fac- tual information presented on tours and within the plantation landscapes on informational signs and brochures. Performance strategies include the actions of the guides and other employees, both in terms of performance as movement through the former spaces of the enslaved and sometimes *lit- erally* performing the roles in first person (though none of the three women interviewed here were first-person performers like Azie Dungey at Mount Vernon). Artifact-based strategies are intimately entwined with performative strategies, though differ in that they go beyond the bodily movements of the guides to include the engagement with historical material objects such as chains, cabins and whips to help visitors make empathetic connections with the enslaved (Alderman and Campbell 2008).

Moore (2015, p. 105) highlights how the overall shortage of Black museum staff serves to amplify concerns over the interpretation of slavery:

> They [historic house museums] rely on the perception that black people are seen as more credible and as telling a more affective story of slavery. Some black interpreters are often looked upon as the logical choice to give voice to enslaved people. A visitor may expect them to be a more natural, logical, and empathetic channel for the thoughts and emotions associated with being enslaved. This dilemma can almost paralyze some sites in terms of what site directors feel they can and cannot interpret, and it stops some white interpreters from talking about slavery at all, leaving the burden of the narrative solely on the shoulders of their black counterparts.

Like Moore (2015), we argue that the responsibility to interpret the history of slavery should not fall solely on the shoulders of Black guides. The ability of the women highlighted in this chapter to operate as memorial entrepreneurs promoting heritage from below does not come without great struggle. Even in some of the better circumstances, such as the plantation sites that permit guides to discuss slavery in a critical manner – or even at sites that *centre* slavery in most aspects of their historic interpretation – many guides still struggle with how to deal with the intricacies of teaching and talking about slavery:

Researcher 2:	Is there something that you would want to talk more about, um, that you're not able to, either because of not enough time or space or is there a theme or topic that you would like to cover that you just don't ever get to do it . . .?
Edie:	Not so much. The only thing that I would say, uh, just in the interest of time I guess is, uh, just talking a little bit more about the individual slaves. You know and their stories because I mean, uh, there's you know – at one time at their height there were about 120 slaves and we, we highlight maybe three or four of them on the actually slavery tour. You know you can't talk about all of them. (Interview, 6 March 2015)

The quote below clearly shows how incredibly difficult working with a predominantly White – and often rude or racist – public can be:

Edie: This is just a personal thing because, you know, I am an African American and working in the house occasionally I, you know, do get a lot of negativity that a lot of other people will not get ... It's not uncommon for me to be at the house saying hi, welcoming someone and then, 'Oh hi, are you here for the tour?' that kind of thing, and they'll look at me kind of like, oh what are you doing here, shouldn't you be out in fields? I mean ... it's amazing how rude people can be. (Interview, 6 March 2015)

The emotional toll of the work of crafting heritage from below became a consistent theme in the interviews with all three women (Tyson 2013).

Rachael: I think the majority of tourists come to this site because they want to hear new history. They want to hear something that they haven't heard and that they know that they're not going to hear at other places. So, there are a few of them who are readily able to draw connections between the past that we're interpreting and the present that we're living in. Not everybody, but there are people who come out here who have said 'Yeah, I went by the church [Mother Emmanuel AME] as well.' Or at least they're aware of Walter Scott, even though that case didn't get the amount of love and support that Emmanuel Nine did. ... But there are some people you realize are still very, very disconnected. ... I need people to understand that, so that has changed just over the things that have happened, things that I've seen, my own experiences. Like, 'You've really got to know. I need you to understand. This is important'. Just the things that I say, whether I raise my voice or drop it – you know, I cry. I'm about to cry now. I cry all the time. ... It's serious stuff. (Interview, 28 February 2016)

As this quote from Rachael illustrates, the work of tour guiding can have long-lasting emotional effects that go beyond the daily work of leading tours. Rachael and Toni worked in 2015–16 at the same Charleston-area plantation that focuses primarily on the lives of the enslaved, and both discussed the emotional toll that working as a Black history interpreter at a plantation had on them. In interviews with members of the NSF research team and in private conversations with one of the authors, Rachael and Toni both referred to their familial connection to their work and how that played a role in how they craft the historical narratives and emotional emphases that went into their tour.

Rachael: My major goal was to make the enslaved people *people*, make them human so people understood that these were human beings that we're talking about. So, I really wanted to humanize them, give them experiences, make them relevant to the people who were coming. Like 'How would you feel in this case?'

Because it's so very easy to – one, use the word slave, which is so objectifying; but to then think of that and not apply human emotions or human experiences to that. So that was really important to me. That was my major goal. Because it is my heritage, I was able to provide some personal family stories. I got to talk a lot about my grandmother, which is really special. She died last year at 101. That was hard. She died when they had to come out here, and I was always talking about her. So, it's been a real transition to say 'My grandma is . . .' to 'My grandma was . . .'. (Interview, 28 February 2016)

At another point in the interview, Rachael described how the financially strapped plantation site limits the guides' work hours to part-time and the impacts this has on her ability to continue in this line of work:

Rachael:	The reason I emphasize we only work four days is because we can only work part-time. They don't want us to be full-time. So obviously that doesn't require benefits. You can't live off of part-time. So, going home really on the weekends, I go back to Georgetown – which is where my parents live. During the week, I stay various places because I can't afford to stay there. So I've just really been reflecting recently on how much . . . There's not even any balance. You need some form of stability when you are coming to work in this, and I haven't really had it the majority of time I've been working in this job. So that's made it . . .
Interviewer:	So how are you going to continue?
Rachael:	Well, I don't really know. I'm reviewing things, and I don't know. That might not be a question for me. That might be a question for [the site's management]. I don't know. I've been very empowered and fulfilled by this work. I know how important it is. I don't know that you're ever going to find someone – maybe in this part of the South – to pay for the gravity of what we're doing. (Interview, 28 February 2016)

We later found out in an email follow-up conversation with Rachael that she quit working at the site because she felt the management was ill-equipped to support the sensitive and important work of guides, in terms of both financial and emotional support. She also reported that she perceived an increased racist climate in Charleston, which weighed heavily on her so she moved away to start a graduate program in public history.

Despite the struggles guides face, we captured visitor data that suggest these guides' efforts in creating more inclusive spaces on their tours had been successful. Interviews with management at the Charleston plantation site where two of the guides worked revealed that visitors often request these particular guides by name, and in a survey of 53 people at the same

Charleston site, seven visitor respondents positively identified these two guides by name in at least one survey question. One response read: '[tour guide's name] was outstanding and her connection from slavery to freedom with personal stories made this experience one to remember'. At the same site, of 49 respondents who answered the question, 'Did your visit cause you to think differently about your views on historic and current race relations, justice, or inequality in America?', 32 (65 percent) said yes. While we acknowledge there are statistical limitations to our survey, including the sample size of n = 53, self-selection bias among participants, as well as the presence of other guides, we nonetheless maintain that these responses are instructive even if we cannot speak to their representability of larger populations.

Similar to our findings in the first case study, there are a mix of benefits and challenges that Black women plantation guides experience while operating from the position of 'below' in heritage from below. Interviews with these women demonstrate that there is excitement at the ability to work in a position that enables them to engage in the daily, bodily work of teaching Black histories and geographies to visitors, yet the ongoing struggles – particularly the lack of financial and emotional support from management – was a real factor that led two guides to leave the site for other historical interpretive career choices.

CONCLUSION

Returning to the question from McKittrick in the introduction: what kinds of new and possible spaces uncovered through the use of the past can be observed through the work of the women presented here? We believe that these women demonstrate through their very bodies the importance of heritage from below, working from the margins as women who occupy the 'last place they thought of' as discriminated against for both their gender and race. However, we also argue that these women operate from the *frontlines* of resisting simplified and racist historical narratives while fighting for social justice in the present. While some may take issue with this geographic conflation of margin and frontline, we believe this is a fruitful topological tension. McKittrick (2006) takes the margins to be more than metaphor, conceptualizing them as sites of political agendas that are often under-acknowledged in geography. She also argues that the geographic conceptualization of margins is problematic because it flattens reality into a *bifurcated* dimension – the centre *or* margin, core *or* periphery – with no room for contestation or heterogeneity.

As the examples in this chapter demonstrate, if we consider the margins to be a space within which heritage from below can indeed present a challenge to AHD, then reality *must* necessarily be messier than the neat binary of centre/margin. In our analysis of social media, for instance, heritage from below can challenge AHD for some people while reinforcing it for others. bell hooks (1984, p. 161) adds that the margin is a site one does not want to lose – it is *central* for the production of liberating, counter-hegemonic discourse: 'To build a mass-based feminist movement, we need to have a liberatory ideology that can be shared with everyone. That revolutionary ideology can be created only if the experiences of people on the margin who suffer sexist oppression and other forms of group oppression are understood, addressed, and incorporated'.

The spatial concept of the frontlines, which we add to the concept of margins, draws upon the metaphor of battle to describe the conflict over Black Geographies moving outward from margin toward the mainstream. This is obviously an unfinished geographic project, since many, if not most, Black women are still not afforded access to those frontline positions from the margins because of racist power structures still inherent in the United States today. These women are restricted by structures that allow them to work toward a Black sense of place at these sites in the first place. While things may be slowly changing toward greater equality, the current structures still speak to disparities in power at heritage sites across the United States.

Hartman (2008, p. 4) says that 'narrating counter-histories of slavery has always been inseparable from writing a history of present, by which I mean the incomplete project of freedom'. After hearing the voices of the women memorial entrepreneurs foregrounded in this chapter, we want to conclude by arguing that it is of critical importance to highlight in our research the role of people who are working tirelessly (and sometimes thanklessly with little emotional and financial support) to be the public face of Black lives, Black History and Black Geographies.

NOTES

1. While we are unable to reproduce the lyrics of this spiritual here for copyright reasons, we encourage readers to take a few minutes to listen to a recording of a recent arrangement of 'Hard Trials' by US composer Craig Hella Johnson, available online at https://www.youtube.com/watch?v=rsq_CLLSpW4 (accessed 8 March 2018).
2. We specifically avoid saying African American women, though they comprise the majority of women represented in this piece, because one – owner of the @AfAmHistFail account – is White.
3. NSF Grant #1359780; Principal Investigator, David L. Butler; Co-Principal Investigators, Derek H. Alderman, Perry L. Carter, Stephen P. Hanna and Amy E. Potter.
4. Both authors conducted interviews with guides and management staff at the plantation tourism sites, and while we did not conduct all of the interviews included in this chapter,

all interviews come from the collective team research. Interviews were transcribed by undergraduate team members and an independent transcription company.

5. The information in this section is derived from a personal interview with the account owner and publicly accessibly information, including the account bio, found on Twitter for @AfAmHistFail at https://twitter.com/afamhistfail (accessed 22 July 2017).
6. All episodes are available online at http://askaslave.com.
7. Available at https://www.youtube.com/watch?v=X1IYH_MbJqA (accessed 22 July 2017).
8. Louisiana attracts tourists from France because the state's tourism industry primarily promotes its French heritage.
9. Given that tour guides at plantation sites are usually all White, the guides included in this case study have been given pseudonyms randomly selected using an Internet name generator.
10. Gullah are predominantly found in the Carolinas while Geechee are located in Georgia.
11. Their heritage corridor stretches from North Carolina to northern Florida.

REFERENCES

Alderman, D.H. (2002), 'Street names as memorial arenas: the reputational politics of commemorating Martin Luther King Jr. in a Georgia County', *Historical Geography*, **20**, 99–120.

Alderman, D.H. and R.M. Campbell (2008), 'Symbolic excavation and the artifact politics of remembering slavery in the American South: observations from Walterboro, South Carolina', *Southeastern Geographer*, **48** (3), 338–55.

Alderman, D.H., D.L. Butler and S.P. Hanna (2016), 'Memory, slavery, and plantation museums: the River Road Project', *Journal of Heritage Tourism*, **11** (3), 209–18.

Bright, C.F. and P. Carter (2016), 'Who are they? Visitors to Louisiana's River Road plantations', *Journal of Heritage Tourism*, **11** (3), 262–74.

Burleigh, Harry T. (arranger) (1919), *Hard Trials*, New York: G. Ricordi & Co. Music Publishers.

Butler, D.L. (2001), 'Whitewashing plantations: the commodification of a slave-free Antebellum South', *International Journal of Hospitality & Tourism Administration*, **2** (3/4), 163–75.

Buzinde, C.N. and I. Osagie (2011), 'Slavery heritage representations, cultural citizenship, and judicial politics in America', *Historical Geography*, **39**, 41–64.

Carney, N. (2016), 'All lives matter, but so does race: black lives matter and the evolving role of social media', *Humanity & Society*, **40** (2), 180–99.

Carter, P., D.L. Butler and D.H. Alderman (2014), 'The house that story built: the place of slavery in plantation museum narratives', *The Professional Geographer*, **66** (4), 547–57.

Cook, M.R. (2016), 'Counter-narratives of slavery in the Deep South: the politics of empathy along and beyond River Road', *Journal of Heritage Tourism*, **11** (3), 290–308.

Cook, Matthew and Derek H. Alderman (2017), 'Classroom as memory workspace: the educational and empathetic potentials of *Twelve Years a Slave* and *Ask a Slave*', in Jeremy D. Stoddard, Alan S. Marcus and David Hicks (eds), *Teaching Difficult History Through Film*, New York: Routledge, pp. 160–77.

Cope, Megan (2002), 'Feminist epistemology in geography', in Pamela Moss (ed.),

Feminist Geography in Practice: Research and Methods, Oxford: Wiley-Blackwell, pp. 43–55.

Davis, A. (1981), 'Reflections on the black woman's role in the community of slaves', *The Black Scholar*, **12** (6), 2–15.

Davis, P.G. (2012), 'The *other* Southern Belles: Civil War reenactment, African American women, and the performance of idealized femininity', *Text and Performance Quarterly*, **32** (4), 308–331.

Domosh, M. (1998), 'Geography and gender: home, again?', *Progress in Human Geography*, **22** (2), 276–82.

Dungey, A. (2013), 'Ask a slave: the web series', accessed 22 February 2017 at http://www.askaslave.com.

Dwyer, Owen and Derek Alderman (2008), *Civil Rights Memorials and the Geography of Memory*, Chicago, IL: Center for American Places at Columbia College.

Eichstedt, Jennifer and Stephen Small (2002), *Representations of Slavery: Race and Ideology in Southern Plantation*, Washington, DC: Smithsonian Institution Press.

Faulkenberry, L.V., J.M. Coggeshall, K. Backman and S. Backman (2000), 'A culture of servitude: the impact of tourism and development on South Carolina's Coast', *Human Organization*, **59** (1), 86–95.

Gulley, H.E. (1993), 'Women and the lost cause: preserving a Confederate identity in the American Deep South', *Journal of Historical Geography*, **19** (2), 125–41.

Hall, Stuart (2005), 'Whose heritage? Un-settling "the heritage", re-imagining the post-nation', in Jo Littler and Roshi Naidoo (eds), *The Politics of Heritage: The Legacies of 'Race'*, London: Routledge, pp. 23–35.

Hartman, S. (2008), 'Venus in two acts', *Small Axe*, **12** (2), 1–14.

Hoelscher, S. (2003), 'Making place, making race: performances of whiteness in the Jim Crow South', *Annals of the Association of American Geographers*, **93** (3), 657–86.

hooks, bell (1984), *Feminist Theory: From Margin to Center*, Boston, MA: South End Press.

Horton, James and Lois Horton (eds) (2006), *Slavery and Public History: The Tough Stuff of American Memory*, Chapel Hill, NC: University of North Carolina Press.

McElya, Micki (2007), *Clinging to Mammy: The Faithful Slave in Twentieth-Century America*, Cambridge, MA: Harvard University Press.

McKittrick, Katherine (2006), *Demonic Grounds: Black Women and the Cartographies of Struggle*, Minneapolis, MN: University of Minnesota Press.

McKittrick, K. (2011), 'On plantations, prisons, and a black sense of place', *Social & Cultural Geography*, **12** (8), 947–63.

Modlin, E.A. (2008), 'Tales told on the tour: mythic representations of slavery by docents at North Carolina Plantation Museums', *Southeastern Geographer*, **48** (3), 265–87.

Moore, Nicole A. (2015), 'Perceptions of race and identity and their impact on slavery's interpretation', in Kristin L. Gallas and James D. Perry (eds), *Interpreting Slavery at Museums and Historic Sites*, Lanham, MD: Rowman & Littlefield, pp. 101–18.

Potter, A.E. (2016), '"She goes into character as the lady of the house": tour guides, performance, and the Southern plantation', *Journal of Heritage Tourism*, **11** (3), 250–61.

Price, P.L. (2010), 'At the crossroads: critical race theory and critical geographies of race', *Progress in Human Geography*, **34** (2), 147–74.

Robertson, Iain J. (ed) (2012), *Heritage from Below*, Burlington, VT: Ashgate Publishing.

Smith, Laurajane (2006), *Uses of Heritage*, London: Routledge.

Tyler, Norm, Theodore Ligibel and Ilene Tyler (2009), *Historic Preservation: An Introduction to its History, Principles, and Practice*, New York: W.W. Norton & Company.

Tyson, Amy (2013), *The Wages of History: Emotional Labor on Public History's Front Lines*, Amherst, MA: University of Massachusetts Press.

Wynter, S. and D. Scott (2000), 'The re-enchantment of humanism: an interview with Sylvia Wynter', *Small Axe*, **4** (1), 119–207.

7. Stolpersteine and memory in the streetscape

Danielle Drozdzewski

INTRODUCTION

The Stolpersteine (stumbling stones) are small bronze plaques embedded in the pavements of many German but also other European cities. There are 53,000 Stolpersteine in 1,400 places in Europe. Each stumbling stone recalls the fate of one person under Fascism. They locate the memory of that individual to place(s) – to the individual's last known residence in that city, and to places of transportation and death (if both are known). This brief inscription denotes one person, one name, one fate (Demnig 2015). The Stolpersteine spatialise remembrance, affixing those place names to the streetscape to the point where that person's fateful journey began. In localising remembrance to place and focusing on the individual, the Stolpersteine are a distinctive form of war remembrance. They are small in material scale and are part of the everyday landscape. Their unique local and grassroots origin juxtaposes the normative state-driven impetus of many large-scale memory projects commemorating war. Commemoration of war is commonly used by the state for nation-building. That each stumbling stone is laid into a nation's territory (at the place where individuals were deported) signifies that the nation, and often more than one nation, is present in the memory installation. Yet, the overriding impetus for this memory project has been to foreground the individual.

Gunter Demnig, the German artist of non-Jewish descent, cites the Talmud when outlining his motivation for initiating the Stolperstein project, stating: 'a person is only forgotten when his or her name is forgotten' (Demnig 2015). The Stolpersteine are small brass plates, 96 x 96 mm wide and 100 mm high (Figure 7.1). The inscription on each stumbling stone notes:

> **'Here Lived'**, followed by the individual's name (their maiden name if applicable);
> **'Born'**, followed by their date of birth;
> **'Deported'**, followed by the date and location; and,
> **'Murdered'**, followed by the date and location.

Source: Author's own.

*Figure 7.1   Stolperstein for Gertrud Baruch at Gipsstraße 4. The text
              reads: Here Lived Gertrud Baruch, Born 1876, Deported
              24.10.1941 to Lodz/Litzmannstadt (Poland), Murdered
              4.5.1942*

The inscribed text is replicated across all stones, but translated into the
language of the country where the stone is laid. The text alters only slightly
in a small number of stones if the individuals' circumstances deviated from
this unfortunate norm; for example, 'Missing' (*Verschollen*) is used in cases
where the individual's location remains unknown. The stones cost 120
Euros to install. The installation process can now take more than a year
and requires official verification of the individual's address (in addition to
personal family information) as well as permission from local authorities.
Permission varies between cities in Germany and in different countries.
In Berlin, for example, there is a dedicated organisation that handles the
application and processing of the stones. The first stones were installed

there illegally in 1996; there are now approximately 6,686 Stolpersteine in Berlin.

In this chapter, I focus on how these distinctive features of the Stolpersteine – their small commemorative scale, everyday location, and individual-led focus – are encountered by the people passing by, on and/ or over them in the course of their daily routines. Their positioning within the streetscape means that different demographics living in different temporalities to the events being commemorated can encounter the Stolpersteine. A key point of departure from visitation to other forms of war commemoration is that encounters with the Stolpersteine are often unintended; people literally do 'stumble upon them'. I focus on this type of inadvertent encounter to better understand how the Stolpersteine's form and locale influence how the public interact with them (or not). I have positioned these potential interactions as proxies for how memory of World War II (WWII) is interpreted but also how it is conceived of outside official commemorations or designated memory-sites.

The chapter draws from fieldwork conducted in Berlin, a city of many memory projects and a concomitant corpus of work on memory-making and contested memory (see, for example, Ladd 1997; Till 1999, 2001; Brockmeier 2002; Stangl 2003; Åhr 2008). In Berlin, as elsewhere in Germany, the *Vergangenheitsbewältigung* (coming to terms with the past) has influenced the number, type and form of war-related memorialisation. In her comprehensive *New Berlin*, Karen Till (2005, p. 5) casts it as 'a city where, more than any other city, German nationalism and modernity have been staged and restaged, represented and contested'. She has also referred to it as a 'wounded city' – referencing its past traumas and how these simultaneously overlay and scar the city's landscape. Berlin is a 'highly memorial-laden landscape' (Drozdzewski 2016, p. 21). Cook and van Riemsijk (2014, p. 142) have noted that the proliferation of 'faceless and nameless memorials that often focused solely on the victims as groups or numbers rather than individual victims and perpetrators' have contributed to a contested memorial landscape, especially among younger generations of Berliners. The Stolpersteine sit amid and within the many layers of Berlin's memory but their material stature is dwarfed by larger-scale projects, such as the Topography of Terror, Neue Wache, The Monument to the Murdered Jews of Europe, the Jewish Museum. Yet cumulatively as monuments commemorating war, these are all sites of memory – regardless of size – and are beacons of the symbolic transmission of national identity positioned in public space. Their materiality and memory narrative link historic events of national significance to the present day; through collective remembrance the linkages between a nation's past and its present persist.

MEMORY AND THE NATION

The synergetic relationship between memory and the nation endures because memory has both a 'sticky' quality (Ahmed 2010) *and* a politics. A politics of memory 'operates in, on and with (re)productions of places *and* identities' (Drozdzewski et al. 2016a, original emphasis). Memory's stickiness resonates in national memory through the remembrance of trauma, especially trauma associated with war and conflict (Drozdzewski et al. 2016b). 'Memories of territorial subjugation' (Drozdzewski et al. 2016b, p. 3) have longevity, both with the individual but also in the material structures of a nation's cities and towns – in its monuments and memorials, and the material and immaterial ruins of the wounded city (cf. Till 2012b). The placement of sites of (national) memory in the everyday landscape is purposeful and demonstrative of a politics of memory. It communicates nation-based ideologies to publics, in public places. Johnson (1995, p. 54) has contended that war memorials are key spatial markers for discerning how 'national cultures conceive of their pasts and mourn the large-scale destruction of life' (see also Till 1999). Said (2000, p. 177) also has stated that national memories 'are shaped in accordance with a certain notion of what we [the public] or, for that matter, they [those in power] really are'. Material representations of war memory function to solidify a collective cultural memory – purposefully chosen – amongst a national citizenry. In this portrayal of the nation, Renan (1882 [1990]) has argued that the elements of sacrifice and suffering were essential to the continuance of collectively remembered and articulated national narratives. Further, and focussing on the geography of memorialisation, Atkinson and Cosgrove (1998, p. 32) have shown how, through nineteenth-century Italy, large public monuments were strategically located in 'key metropolitan locations' to ensure that the portrayal of the nation's past was overt and unavoidable.

The stickiness of a politics of memory, then, relates not only to the choice of which elements of a nation's past to commemorate, but also to the location of their commemoration. A politics of memory codifies normative rituals of commemoration; it creates 'stable' sites and narratives of remembrance – most successfully achieved through the founding of symbolic places, dates and events (Johnson 2002). Said's (2000, p. 179) reminder that memory is 'rather useful' is especially apt in research that examines the positioning of memories of war into public spaces (see Logan and Reeves 2009; Sather-Wagstaff 2017; Viejo-Rose and Stig Sørensen 2015). While the Stolpersteine are not a state-driven initiative, they are still positioned in public space; they are 'stuck' literally to the territory of the nation and metaphorically to its collective narrative(s) of

war. While the purpose of each Stolperstein is to reinforce memory of the
individual, as a form of public memorialisation, they are also susceptible
to the same critique of memorial forgetfulness propounded by Young
(1993, p. 5), who has suggested that 'once we assign monumental form to
memory, we have to some degree divested ourselves of the obligation to
remember'. Such critique expounds that the onus of the memory-work
transfers from the individual to the memorial once taking material form,
and can actually incite forgetfulness rather than remembrance. In the case
of the Stolpersteine, because they are so small, I wondered whether this
forgetfulness would be augmented by the fact that they are easy to miss
and that often one does not purposefully go looking for them.

MEMORY METHODS

To think differently about the capacity of the Stolpersteine to commemorate war from below and amid the busy city, I used an ethnographic
approach operationalised by a qualitative mixed methodology. Thinking
about engagements with memory, Sather-Wagstaff (2017, p. 21) has argued
that 'memorial landscapes are still designed with intentional, specific
symbolic elements' – they are planned for purposeful engagement. In
the case of the Stolpersteine, as with other heritage from below installations, encounter is often unforeseen. Thus, designing a methodology
that captures 'encounter' and the 'affect' of those encounters requires
consideration of how such happenstances are mediated or even constrained by individual subjectivities (Sather-Wagstaff 2017), as well as an
alert cognisance of the context of the everyday streetscape. In conducting
research on the experience of ruins, Light and Watson (2017, p. 165) have
argued for an 'extended repertoire of research methods', as well as 'an
openness to innovation'. To investigate the Stolpersteine in their everyday
environs, I combined video ethnography, vox pops, participant observation
and auto-ethnography to examine the affective engagement and encounter
with the past through the Stolpersteine laid out in the Berlin suburb of
Mitte. I chose three different streets: Gipsstraße 3 and 4; Ackerstraße 1;
and Große Hamburger Straße 30 and 31. The streets were chosen based
on their busyness, their residential character, that they were close to parks
and local cafes (as important vantage points) and that multiple stumbling
stones were located at these sites (four at Gipsstraße, four at Ackerstraße,
and 11 at Große Hamburger Straße).

At each of these streets, I used a field diary, photography and GoPro
HERO 3+ to record encounters and engagement. Pink (2007, p. 243) has
argued that the 'videomaking process [is] a form of place-making'. In this

research, I used video to sensorially make place and to make 'sense of place' (Pink 2007, p. 243). At each stumbling stone, I recorded five-minute video grabs, positioning the GoPro on the ground near to the stumbling stone so only people's feet were visible in the screenshot. I chose this arrangement to emulate the position of the stumbling stone in the ground. In the observational component of the method, I watched people's encounters with the Stolpersteine; I paid attention to their mobility to them, over them, onto them, and/or past them. I watched people walk up and down the streets I had chosen; I also traversed the streets of Berlin. Hill (2013, p. 391) has contended that 'walking creates powerful recollections because it provokes a distinct and familiar tactility with the world'. Further, being attentive to walking presented an opportunity to examine the 'experiential flow of successive moments of detachment and attachment' in the streetscape (Edensor 2010, p. 70). Because people were mobile around, on and over the Stolpersteine, they interacted, either knowingly or unconsciously, with 'how that same environment was encountered in the past' (Degen and Rose 2012, p. 3279).

I documented my observations and reflexivity in field notes. My autoethnographic notes meant I remained cognisant of 'reflexive engagement with the way of . . . knowing [encounters with the Stolpersteine] in practice' (Pink 2008). I counted the number of people passing or stopping and the number of cyclists; I also recorded the types of encounters by passers-by, for example, whether they stopped, trod on them, read the stone, bent down, photographed it or discussed it with an acquaintance. As Grasseni (2004, p. 16) has summated, the participant observation and my field notes were 'a process of sensory apprenticeship in order to appreciate' and help 'see' the research field. Each observation period lasted 30 minutes per day over a seven-day period, at different times of the day. On the third day of observation and for the remainder of the week, I also included a vox pop with passers-by. Via a translator, I asked five questions to 38 respondents pertaining to reasons for stopping (or not), links to national identity, the everyday setting, and whether they considered the Stolpersteine to be associated with German nationhood.

At the commencement of my field research, I was fortunate to be escorted by one of Demnig's small team and followed him around Berlin for two days of installing Stolpersteine. Originally, Demnig made and inscribed all the stumbling stones, as well as laid them. However, he now employs another artist to make and inscribe them. Until January 2015, Demnig had also been solely responsible for laying all Stolpersteine. Since that time, his foundation has been responsible for running and organising the Stolpersteine project. Currently, the webpage states that: 'Demnig tries to place as many STOLPERSTEINE as possible himself – he ALWAYS places the first STOLPERSTEINE in a new place' (Demnig 2015, original emphasis). Demnig never envisaged that every person who suffered the atrocities of National Socialism could be commemorated. To this end, the Stolpersteine project was never envisaged to be all-encompassing. Demnig has stated that the project is and always has been envisaged as symbolic – by keeping it this way 'the Stolpersteine team has made a conscious decision to not expand production – in direct opposition to the mass murder that the Nazis engaged in between 1933 and 1945' (Demnig 2015). However, such is its popularity that more and more people every year apply to have stumbling stones made and laid. So much so that Demnig's timetable is somewhat overwhelming.

During the two days of Stolpersteine installation, Demnig moved from site to site with purpose and haste. At each site, he quickly lifted the original pavement stones, watered the pavement so the cement would seal the new Stolperstein(e). He then replaced the original pavement stones with the purpose-made Stolperstein. Once the stone is laid, those that may have gathered for its emplacement usually conduct a short ceremony or reflection. On my trip, the type of reflection depended on who had sought to install the stone; commonly this would be a relative, the current residents of the building where it was laid, school groups or local Jewish organisations. I encountered one group of relatives from North America, a school group, members of the local synagogue and residents of the building. It was common for a photographic image of the person, or people, to be placed alongside the newly installed stumbling stone(s) and for white roses to accompany the photo (Figure 7.2). If time permitted, Gunter stayed for a photo with the group or individual who had ordered the stones. As Matthew Cook (Cook and van Riemsdijk 2014) also found on his 'journey' with Demnig, time was tight and Demnig moved with determination through the sites, he rarely lingered for any official ceremony or for protracted conversation. Following these initial two days, watching the Stolpersteine become part of the streetscape, I began my other field research. In the remainder of this chapter I thus focus on engagement, encounter and tactility with the Stolpersteine and the memories they narrate. I discuss how the stumbling stones afford the opportunity for the passers-by to interact with memory in the everyday streetscape. I also detail how the stumbling stones engender tactile and affective engagements with memory.

WALKING PAST, OVER, ON STOLPERSTEINE

Tim Ingold (2004, p. 331) has argued that 'locomotion, not cognition, must be the starting point for the study of perceptual activity'. Following

Source: Author's own.

Figure 7.2   Stolpersteine for Alfred and Olga Kalmus, with flowers on Schivelbeiner Straße 49

his reasoning, by walking past, over or on the stones, the passer-by is afforded the opportunity to think on, and of, them. Indeed, to encounter a Stolperstein one must walk. But walking does not necessarily guarantee contact. Their compactness and positioning below our feet meant that, more often than not, passers-by do not notice them. They do not neces-sarily stop. Rather, they walk on by, or over, or on the stumbling stones. During my observations at Gipsstraße, 255 people passed the Stolpersteine, 2 people looked down at them and 2 people stopped. At Ackerstraße, 296 people passed them, 5 people looked down at them, 2 people stepped on them, no one stopped. At Große Hamburger Straße, the busiest site frequented by tour groups specifically stopping at the Stolpersteine, 511 people passed them, 17 people looked down, 27 people stepped on them and 21 people stopped at them. These latter figures do not include counts from designated tour groups as it was difficult to observe the stones directly when they were surrounded by larger groups; I approximate, however, that an additional 70 people stopped as part of groups. Watching this process of people walking by, on, or over the Stolpersteine, on repeat, reminded me of Tyner et al.'s (2012) adage 'hidden in plain sight'.

Law (2005, p. 440) argues that the 'the street looks and feels differently depending on the perspectives of those inhabiting urban spaces'. While I had chosen the locations based on their busyness, their residential character, and that they were close to parks and local cafes, residents of those neighbourhoods already knew where the stumbling stones were and were not necessarily going to stop every time they passed one. Further explanations proffered in the vox pops demonstrate varying levels of attachment and detachment to stopping at the Stolpersteine mediated by the necessity to walk (Edensor 2010). For example, one participant noted: 'maybe, if the weather is nice, but often one is in a rush' (Respondent 49, 6 May 2014), and another said: 'only when I had time to stop' (Respondent 43, 3 May 2014). A city tour guide who was interviewed noted: 'I can tell you from our experience, yes they do [see the stones], not all of them, also a lot of people they know them already, so they just want to walk because they are living here' (Respondent 20, 1 May 2014). Similarly, at a recent conference presentation on this chapter, one participant suggested that she knew the exact locations of the stumbling stones near her house, could picture them, and thought of them as she walked over them every time, but she did not stop. In these examples, the 'movement of walking' constituted 'a way of knowing' (Ingold and Vergunst 2008, p. 5). Here 'knowledge' has a dual meaning; it relates to an awareness of the locations of the Stolpersteine as they are passed over but also to erudition of the narratives of that place – who had lived there, when and where they were taken, when they died. Passing over the stumbling stones 'momentarily fuses or brings into phase the otherwise divergent and unsynchronised life trajectories of individual . . . [passers-by and former residents] . . . into a unified take of belonging to this place' (Ingold and Vergunst 2008, p. 9). Through this knowledge the place in the present becomes linked to the past.

A key aim of the vox pop questions was to explore the positioning of the Stolpersteine in relation to other German WWII memory-work. Cook and van Riemsdijk (2014, p. 138) have argued that in Berlin's memorial landscape the Stolpersteine provide a sharp contrast with the 'state-sponsored memorials that present the outcomes of the Holocaust as large, incomprehensible numbers'. They do this by individualising the commemoration of the same event but by singling out individuals murdered by Nazi Fascists. Indeed, this is Demnig's intention to remember the many people whose names and lives have become part of the unfathomable whole of totalitarian mass extermination. To understand how this individual focus was conceived by respondents, I asked: 'Do you think this memorial is different because of where it is in an everyday street (as opposed to a larger memorial like the Holocaust memorial)?' I provided a prompt of the Monument to the Murdered Jews of Europe, near Potsdamer Platz, as an example of a larger memorial if required. I chose this comparison point because of its contrasts to the Stolpersteine in scale, size, target audience, contestation and scope of representation; while the Stolpersteine are small scale, individual-focused and grassroots-led, the Monument to the Murdered Jews of Europe is strategically placed within an existing conflict zone (near to Hitler's Bunker, the former wall, Tiegarten, Potsdamer Platz and the American Embassy), the murder of all Jews are encompassed in its remit, and facilitated by the state. The majority of respondents stated that they preferred the stumbling stones to the larger monument (Box 7.1).

This process of individualising examples of Fascist-led murder enabled these (and other) respondents to think about the nation through the individual. References to the nation were both figurative and spatial. Symbolic nation-led memory narratives were all-encompassing and often positioned as necessary to assuage perpetrator guilt. The nation was also thought of as the place where these events took place. I argue that the latter place-based representation of the nation provides both palpable and more incontestable connection points to memory.

Being in place and linking memory to place stimulates recognition(s) of the past, in the present. Jones (2011, p. 878) has contended that 'notions of being-in-place are powerful, even fundamental to everyday life . . . memory is key as it is one means by which people are in place/landscape'. Walking through Berlin (for this and subsequent field research) I frequently encountered the Stolpersteine. Often, I had unknowingly trodden on or over them, not noticing them until my movement(s) over them. Of course, while walking, my eyes, like those of the field respondents, were often not directed towards the ground, but on the direction in which I was travelling. Missing the Stolpersteine was inevitable; their purposefully small stature is not attention-drawing and even spurred one respondent to comment: 'they could be higher, so you see them better' (Respondent 31, 2 May 2014). Yet, when noticed, some respondents did stop. Respondents noted how stepping on the stumbling stones compelled them to think about the past in that place. For example, one respondent noted: the 'symbolic meaning [of the stones] is more significant when you step on it' (Respondent 34, 2 May 2014); another cautioned: 'I try not to step on them' (Respondent 50, 6 May 2014); while another highlighted that it is: 'most interesting that you step on it' (Respondent 30, 2 May 2014). These comments indicate that interest in the stumbling stones is sparked when the respondents come in contact with them or purposely avoid them. The power of this tactile encounter with memory occasions two further pathways of discussion. First, the placement of the Stolpersteine into the streetscape is frequently not premeditated, meaning that the past is recalled spontaneously and unexpectedly. Second, the corporeal engagement with the memory-site stimulates consideration of what is being commemorated. In the following sub-sections, I detail the influence of the everyday setting and discuss the affective capacity of the stumbling stones.

BOX 7.1   EXAMPLE RESPONSES TO: 'DO YOU THINK THIS MEMORIAL IS DIFFERENT BECAUSE OF WHERE IT IS IN AN EVERYDAY STREET AS OPPOSED TO A LARGER MEMORIAL LIKE THE HOLOCAUST MEMORIAL?

'This [the stolpersteine] is more personal to me. You are given a name. Whereas if you deal with something at Potsdamer Platz, it's a group of people, and this is individual' (Respondent 40, 3 May 2014).

'I think the idea of a Stolpersteine is much better than a large memorial. Because most people do not know what the memorial is about or for. Children play and the idea gets lost. Most people think it's an artwork' (Respondent 23, 1 May 2014).

'[The] stolpersteine are more decent and more personal than the memorial at Potsdamer Platz. I like this more' (Respondent 36, 3 May 2014).

'This [the stolpersteine] is more everyday. [It] brings attention to the fact that they were taken' (Respondent 51, 6 May 2014).

'These [memorials] are two categories. One is more commercial, but good because it represents Germany and Berlin, and show[s] what happened here. Whereas the stolpersteine are more for residents and people living here' (Respondent 41, 3 May 2014).

'In my opinion, these are two different types of memories. Stolpersteine are individual and tell the story of how someone died, whereas larger memorials are a more general reminder [of what happened]' (Respondent 39, 3 May 2014).

'[The stolpersteine are] more personal therefore its more appealing to me. Instead of just a bunch of stones lying around and [that] nobody understands the meaning [of]' (Respondent 23, 1 May 2014).

'In comparison with big Memorials, Stolpersteine are more sensible and they refer directly to the house. And also, people walk like this (looking to the ground) and look in front of their feet. I think, it fits very well to the city life, where people walk a little bit dreamily and introverted and suddenly stumble on the stolpersteine' (Respondent 19, 1 May 2014).

'It is interesting that this Memorial is not located in one particular place, but is spread all over the city and refers directly to the house. But it is nice and important that there are two different ways of presentation' (Respondent 21, 1 May 2014).

'This idea has been created by an artist. it's not the initiative of the State of Berlin but rather an individual project. I like it!' (Respondent 23, 1 May 2014).

Memory and the Everyday

Unless we are purposefully locating a particular Stolpersteine or partaking in an installation of one, more often than not encounters with them are extemporaneous. The serendipity of these meetings with the past was explained by one respondent: 'it affects me personally, to stop somewhere is always different than to look at something [on purpose]' (Respondent 31, 2 May 2014). Another respondent explained it as: 'more of a random recognition, by chance I recognise them' (Respondent 28, 2 May 2014). The unpredictability of this type of encounter with the past – and often with the concomitant thoughts of the violent past and probable death of that individual – intrudes into the everyday landscape and the daily routines of those who pass by them. These abrupt incursions mean that, when noticed, the stumbling stones can 'force' us to think about Fascist-led genocide, even when we may be on the way to work, to a cafe, or to shop, for example. These moments are summarised aptly by Till (2008, p. 104) in her work on another small-scale memory project in Berlin:

> When situated in the now mundane spaces of what was once a residential area known for its professional and upper-class Jewish community, these seemingly innocent signs permeate the comfortable world of everyday routine and ask viewers to move between past and present spaces of social exclusion, legal separation, expulsion, and murder in their city.

That everyday locations have grievous histories is (sometimes) unnerving and unwelcome. Anecdotally, I was told of people who refused to buy houses with Stolpersteine in their doorways because they provide such enduring reminders of the past. Indeed, the Stolpersteine do 'give a wider bird's-eye view of the particular history of places' (Muzaini 2016, p. 39). They also challenge us to 'think more fluidly about the ways that social memories are constituted throughout society at different scales and in mundane and everyday places' (Atkinson 2007, p. 521). For example, some respondents specifically noted the influence of the everyday setting: 'Jews were our neighbours, our parent's neighbours. It's important to revitalise memories as they disappear from everyday life' (Respondent 46, 6 May 2014). Others stated: 'It's everyday life. It's everywhere. The mass of stones makes people aware' (Respondent 50, 6 May 2014); and, 'I think the important thing about these Stolpersteine is that they are focusing on the life of people, showing the places where they lived and not the place where they died' (Respondent 22, 1 May 2014). The stones invoke life and loss; they also represent a persistent present absence of those former residents. For example, one respondent commented: 'I just read the name and thought how this person would have developed and what they would have done if they were still alive' (Respondent 34, 2 May 2014). The confrontation with this absence and how it is wrapped up in the heinous events of the nation's and city's past is ominous. Shields (2012, p. 15, original emphasis) has contended that:

> disappearance does not offer the body such solace. The mind reels to repopulate place and the body is led to turn *without gesture* around a gap, a space of absence that is both a material and abstract representation.

In Berlin, the Stolpersteine reference that 'gap', which prompts rumination on the absence of people who were once neighbours in those same places – as Demnig has intended them to. These encounters stimulate us to think about that city's past; in Berlin, like in other places, we frequent places with tragic and heinous histories. Indeed, residents live in the houses of people who were deported and murdered. The everydayness of our contemporary settings can shield us from these histories and prompt a forgetfulness of how an event relates to us through the place where it occurred. These unnerving happenstances expose the wounds of the city (Till 2012a, p. 22) and show that 'trauma does not occur from an event or occurrence that caused pain or suffering per se, but from an individual's inability to give the past some sort of story'.

Touching Stones?

Again Ingold (2004, p. 330) has suggested that 'it is surely through our feet, in contact with the ground (albeit mediated through footwear), that we are more fundamentally and continually "in touch" with our surroundings'. The affective capacity of the stumbling stones can derive from their palpability. At each stone that I noticed and/or trod on, I was compelled to dwell. My feet were stepping on the surrounding ground creating the direct physical connection to that place – there was a sense of that place in the past. I wondered what this spot might have looked like on the day when that person was removed from their home. What sounds in the street preceded the knock on the door? Were the residents prepared? What did the neighbours do, did they try to help? Were people crying? Did they protest? Was physical violence involved? . . . What happened in the spaces in between the timeline on the stones? The questions about that moment in time and what followed from that place ferociously bombarded me. They prompted an awareness of the spatial separation in my corporeal and perceptual encounter with these Stolpersteine locales. The uneasiness of my thoughts meant that the temporal distance between the dates recorded on the Stolpersteine and the present moment shortened. My dwelling feet were no longer compelled to settle. They had a sense of urgency, a sense of wanting to flee, to move on, move away.

While some respondents had noted that their contact with stumbling stones impelled consideration of the information provided on them, others avoided touching them altogether. When I could avoid it, I would not touch them. Most often my feet were touching the ground surrounding them, which comprised a different surface material from the shiny brass plates. They always seemed too scared to purposefully touch. Furthermore, my feet, like other passers-by, cannot feel the actual stumbling stone. We can only sense a change from rough pavement stone to smooth Stolperstein through our shoes. Our tactility with the Stolpersteine, then, derives from our perceptual engagement with the surrounding locale and our physical contact with the adjoining ground. Thus, in addressing Ahmed's (2010, p. 29) question of 'what sticks', I argue that the places where the Stolpersteine are embedded stick. I take place to include both the locale and the sense of place proximate to the Stolpersteine (Agnew 1987). These places stick in our minds, they create urgency in our movement, they are 'the stuff' that can sustain and preserve our connections between ideas, values and objects' and the past (Ahmed 2010, p. 29). Returning to Shield's quote above, the stumbling stones are both material and abstract representations of memory. We can touch the Stolpersteine; indeed, they are often trodden on, but we need knowledge of that sense of place and their narrative to connect the person and the place in the past to our being in the present day. Perhaps the Stolpersteine are touching stones that do not necessarily have to be touched to enable engagement with the past. Scattered around the city, cumulatively they reference the enormity of this city's traumatic history, something that in itself is unparalleled.

STUMBLING UPON MEMORY

The Stolpersteine are distinct entry points of remembrance. While they are often missed in the harried everyday mobilities accompanying modern cities, when noticed they remind passers-by of the small and hidden places of memory within our cities, and their grievous histories. These reminders – encountered under our feet, through the closeness of touch, and visually – differ in character from other forms of war memorialisation. The extemporaneous nature of our engagement with the Stolpersteine often means we have little or no time to process our thoughts or prepare ourselves to encounter narratives of deportation and death, or indeed totalitarianism. Their positioning and size are strategic elements of their design; when noticed, their placement in the pavement necessitates the

viewer to stop, look down, bowing their head in a familiar stance of reverence. Cheng (2014, p. 212) has contended that such memory projects in the
everyday streetscape are a particular way of gathering stories 'from below'
from the 'street level perspective' because they 'open up a series of spaces
for critical reflections on what constitutes urban life and cities'. The stories
that unfold in the locales of Stolpersteine are of the individuals' fate in the
war-wounded city.

The Stolpersteine seemingly offer an opportunity to escape the politics
of memory that enshrouds war commemoration in Berlin (and Germany
more generally), because they are small-scale and they individualise the
victims of state-led terror. They do not attempt to draw visitors to specific
commemorative places or to be part of nation-led calendar rituals. They
are not commissioned by any governmental body, but by individuals who
choose to be part of a grassroots memory project. Further, because they
commemorate all victims of Nazi Fascism regardless of nationality, faith,
social creed or gender, it is more difficult to charge the project for privileging one victim group over another. Yet, they are still public sites of memory
and as such choices have been made about how to present the information
on the stones. For example, Demnig has staunchly defended his choice of
the word 'murdered' over 'died' in the inscriptions; he has also refused to
alter inscriptions to suit the purchasers' requests. Further, and despite the
project's popularity, issues of the equality of representation – who can
afford to buy a stone and perhaps travel to see a stone laid – raise further
questions of forgetfulness of the individuals not remembered in this project
(as previously mentioned, Demnig and the team have indicated that they
will not expand the project, and for good reason). Moreover, while it is
individuals who choose to commemorate other individuals, choices of representation are still open to potential bias and selectivity of the individual's
commissioning stones – arguably, such partiality may be less transparent
in this case than with state-led commemoration. By including these admit-
tances, I do not seek to detract from the enormity of the project Demnig
has devoted himself to, or its substantial accomplishment in sidestepping
many of the debates that have surrounded other memory installations (see,
for example, Åhr 2008). Rather, I provide a small aide-memoire that all
public memory-work has a politics because someone always chooses what
to portray and how that portrayal takes form in public space.

The Stolpersteine's memory narratives are deeply entrenched in wider
histories of mass destruction of WWII. These linkages have the potential
to (re)direct the intended focus of the individual back towards the nation.
Notwithstanding this caution, the Stolpersteine are incomparable in their
capacity to locate memory to place and to compel otherwise unintended
rumination on victims of Nazi Fascism. I contend that as a memory

project, the Stolpersteine do not embody Young's (1993) contention of memorial forgetfulness precisely because they do not beckon collective engagement. Rather, they seek to engage the individual in a very different capacity, serendipitously and through movement. Integral to their ability to resist forgetfulness is that we encounter them while walking in the everyday city. The bodily interactions with the Stolpersteine locales prompt remembrance while highlighting an individual's intimate engagement with memory. While watching Gunter work digging and laying the Stolpersteine, I was struck by the stillness of the small crowd at each installation. We all dwelled in that small part of the Berlin sidewalk and watched memory-making in action. These moments of stillness were probably the only time in the life of the Stolpersteine that people stood still around them, for any great length of time. Once they were laid, the words spoken, people moved on, but the stones remained.

REFERENCES

Agnew, John (1987), *Place and Politics*, Cambridge, MA: Allen & Unwin.

Ahmed, Sara (2010), 'Happy objects', in Melissa Gregg and Gregory J. Seigworth (eds), *The Affect Reader*, Durham, NC: Duke University Press, pp. 29–51.

Åhr, J. (2008), 'Memory and mourning in Berlin: on Peter Eisenman's Holocaust-Mahnmal', *Modern Judaism*, **28**, 283–305.

Atkinson, D. (2007), 'Kitsch geographies and the everyday spaces of social memory', *Environment and Planning A: Economy and Space*, **39** (3), 521–40.

Atkinson, D. and D. Cosgrove (1998), 'Urban rhetoric and embodied identities: city, nation, and empire at the Vittorio Emanuele II monument in Rome, 1870–1945', *Annals of the Association of American Geographers*, **88**, 28–49.

Brockmeier, J. (2002), 'Introduction: searching for cultural memory', *Culture and Psychology*, **8**, 5–14.

Cheng, Y.E. (2014), 'Telling stories of the city: walking ethnography, affective materialities, and mobile encounters', *Space and Culture*, **17** (3), 211–33.

Cook, M. and M. van Riemsdijk (2014), 'Agents of memorialization: Gunter Demnig's Stolpersteine and the individual (re-)creation of a Holocaust landscape in Berlin', *Journal of Historical Geography*, **43**, 138–47.

Degen, M.M. and G. Rose (2012), 'The sensory experiencing of urban design: the role of walking and perceptual memory', *Urban Studies*, **49**, 3271–87.

Demnig, G. (2015) 'Stolpersteine', accessed 23 May 2015 at http://www.Stolpersteine.eu/en/home/.

Drozdzewski, Danielle (2016), 'Encountering memory in the everyday city', in Danielle Drozdzewski, Sarah De Nardi and Emma Waterton (eds), *Memory, Place and Identity: Commemoration and Remembrance of War and Conflict*, London: Routledge, pp. 27–57.

Drozdzewski, D,. S. De Nardi and E. Waterton (2016a), 'Geographies of memory, place and identity: intersections in remembering war and conflict', *Geography Compass*, **10** (11), 447–56.

Drozdzewski, Danielle, Sarah De Nardi and Emma Waterton (eds) (2016b), *Memory, Place and Identity: Commemoration and Remembrance of War and Conflict*, London: Routledge.

Edensor, T. (2010), 'Walking in rhythms: place, regulation, style and the flow of experience', *Visual Studies*, **25**, 69–79.

Grasseni, Cristina (2004), 'Video and ethnographic knowledge: skilled vision and the practice of breeding', in Sarah Pink, Laszlo Kurti and Ana I. Afonso (eds), *Working Images*, London: Routledge, pp. 12–27.

Hill, L. (2013), 'Archaeologies and geographies of the post-industrial past: landscape, memory and the spectral', *cultural geographies*, **20**, 379–96.

Ingold, T. (2004), 'Culture on the ground: the world perceived through the feet', *Journal of Material Culture*, **9**, 315–40.

Ingold, Tim and Jo Lee Vergunst (2008), *Ways of Walking: Ethnography and Practice on Foot*, Cornwall, UK: Ashgate.

Johnson, N. (1995), 'Cast in stone: monuments, geography, and nationalism', *Environment and Planning D: Society and Space*, **13**, 51–65.

Johnson, N. (2002), 'Mapping monuments: the shaping of public space and cultural identities', *Visual Communication*, **1**, 293–8.

Jones, O. (2011), 'Geography, memory and non-representational geographies', *Geography Compass*, **5**, 875–85.

Ladd, Brian (1997), *The Ghosts of Berlin: Confronting German History in the Urban Landscape*, Chicago, IL: University of Chicago Press.

Law, Lisa (2005), 'Sensing the city: urban experiences', in Paul Cloke, Philip Crang and Mark Goodwin (eds), *Introducing Human Geographies*, London: Arnold, pp. 439–50.

Light, Duncan and Steve Watson (2017), 'The castle imagined: emotion and affect in the experience of ruins', in Divya P. Tolia-Kelly, Emma Waterton and Steve Watson (eds), *Heritage, Affect and Emotion: Politics, Practices and Infrastuctures*, Abingdon: Routledge, pp. 154–78.

Logan, William and Keir Reeves (2009), *Places of Pain and Shame: Dealing with 'Difficult Heritage'*, London: Routledge.

Muzaini, Hamzah (2016), 'Personal reflections on formal Second World War memories/memorials in everyday spaces in Singapore', in Danielle Drozdzewski, Sarah De Nardi and Emma Waterton (eds), *Memory, Place and Identity: Commemoration and Remembrance of War and Conflict*, Abingdon: Routledge, pp. 38–55.

Pink, S. (2007), 'Walking with video', *Visual Studies*, **22**, 240–52.

Pink, S. (2008), 'Mobilising visual ethnography: making routes, making place and making images', *Forum Qualitative Sozialforschung/Forum: Qualitative Social Research*, **9** (3), Article 36, accessed accessed 18 Janaury 2017 at http://nbn-resolving.de/urn:nbn:de:0114-fqs0803362.

Renan, Ernest (1882), 'What is a nation?', in Homi K. Bhabha (ed.) (1990), *Nation and Narration*, London: Routledge, pp. 8–22.

Said, E. (2000), 'Invention, memory and place', *Critical Inquiry*, **26** (2), 175–92.

Sather-Wagstaff, Joy (2017), 'Making polysense of the word: affect, memory, heritage', in D.P. Tolia-Kelly, E. Waterton and Steve Watson (eds), *Heritage, Affect and Emotion: Politics, Practices and Infrastuctures*, Abingdon: Routledge, pp. 12–30.

Shields, R. (2012), 'Urban trauma: comment on Karen Till's "Wounded Cities"', *Political Geography*, **31**, 15–16.

Stangl, P. (2003), 'The Soviet war memorial in Treptow, Berlin', *Geographical Review*, **93**, 213–36.

Till, K.E. (1999), 'Staging the past: landscape designs, cultural identity and *Erinnerungspolitik* at Berlin's *Neue Wache*', *Ecumene*, **6**, 251–83.

Till, K.E. (2001), 'Returning home and to the field', *Geographical Review*, **91**, 46–56.

Till, Karen E. (2005), *The New Berlin: Memory, Politics, Place*, Minnesota, MN: University of Minnesota Press.

Till, K.E. (2008), 'Artistic and activist memory-work: approaching place-based practice', *Memory Studies*, **1**, 99–113.

Till, K.E. (2012a), 'Reply: trauma, citizenship and ethnographic responsibility', *Political Geography*, **31**, 22–3.

Till, K.E. (2012b), 'Wounded cities: memory-work and a place-based ethics of care', *Political Geography*, **31**, 3–14.

Tyner, J.A., G.B. Alvarez and A.R. Colucci (2012), 'Memory and the everyday landscape of violence in post-genocide Cambodia', *Social & Cultural Geography*, **13**, 853–71.

Viejo-Rose, Dacia and Mary L.S. Sørensen (2015), 'Cultural heritage and armed conflict: new questions for an old relationship', in Emma Waterton and Steve Watson (eds), *The Palgrave Handbook of Contemporary Heritage Research*, Basingstoke: Palgrave Macmillan, pp. 281–96.

Young, James E. (1993), *Texture of Memory Holocaust Memorials and Meaning*, New Haven, CT: Yale University Press.

8. Adoption, genealogical bewilderment and biological heritage bricolage

Meghann Ormond

INTRODUCTION

> I should have liked there to be a voice behind me which had . . . carried me to the threshold of my story . . . I think a good many people have a similar desire to be freed from the obligation to begin, a similar desire to be on the other side of discourse from the outset, without having to consider from the outside what might be strange, frightening and perhaps maleficent about it. (Foucault 1970 [1980], p. 51)

My mother was born to a young American Catholic woman of Scottish and English descent in 1952 in the Our Lady of Victory home for unwed mothers run by the Catholic Church in Lackawanna, New York, along the United States (US)-Canada border. She spent the first months of her life there with the birth name 'Virginia', after which time she was adopted by a Catholic German-American couple from rural Ohio and was renamed 'Mary'. Over the seven decades that have followed, she has sought to discover her repressed biological 'truth' (Foucault [1970] 1980). In the following pages, I recount my mother's experience by drawing on her wealth of personal writings and communications, everyday conversations with her over the years and my own lived experience as her biological daughter, witness and research sidekick to reflect on her gradual discoveries and harnessing of elements she has understood as key to bringing her closer to piecing together her biological 'truth' and the enfolding of these elements into her personal heritage beliefs and practices.[1]

I have found Hirsch's (2008) work on 'post-memory' helpful for exploring how ordinary people understand and feel their inheritance of the past and the ways in which these understandings and feelings are used. Her work on descendants' relationships 'to powerful, often traumatic, experiences that preceded their births but that were nevertheless transmitted to them so deeply as to seem to constitute memories in their own right' (Hirsch 2008, p. 103) has frequently been applied to the intra- and transgenerational transmission of trauma and memory by those who survived violent and repressive regimes (e.g., the Shoah and other modern genocides, South American dictatorships, the Spanish and Lebanese civil wars and so on). However, Stein's (2009, p. 294) work on trauma, memory and genealogy suggests that Hirsch's concept of post-memory can also be helpful in grasping adoptees' feelings and experiences since both adoptees and descendants of traumatised survivors have been subjected to 'a severing of familial roots' that generates belief in possessing incomplete or 'false' stories about their origins. Individuals in both groups may be prone to what has come to be known as 'genealogical bewilderment' (Sants 1964), a profound feeling of disorientation I describe in detail in the following section, as a result of the absence – whether through destruction, suppression, distortion or inaccessibility – of public records key to institutionalised memory; ruptures and failures in the transmission of familial memory through intimate social relations; and heavy reliance on publicly available narratives and tropes to complement, fill in gaps regarding or render intelligible what scant knowledge of one's genealogical heritage has been transmitted (Halbwachs 1980; Hirsch 2008).

In exploring my mother's shifting subjectivity relative to societal and technological transformations that actively shape notions of what constitutes biological 'truth', how to identify and codify it as heritage, and how to manage it within the contemporary moral economy of trauma, reconciliation and redemption (Fassin and Rechtman 2009; Smart 2009), I excavate the ways in which layers of discursive and material configurations of politically, legally, religiously, scientifically, commercially and familiarly authorised and authorising narratives have accreted over time, allowing certain strains and understandings of her biological 'truth' to percolate to the surface while trapping potential others below. In so doing, I seek to call attention to the variety of sedimented layers of power relations – ones that are not neatly identifiable as top-down or bottom-up – that serve as the fundament of personal and collective memory and steer action, demonstrating the need for nuanced analyses of heritage that challenge the simplistic dualism heroically pitting a popular 'heritage from below' (Robertson 2012) against an elitist 'Authorised Heritage Discourse' (AHD) (Smith 2006), a problematic binary I seek to de-couple and blur with a bevy of examples in the following sections and to which I will return explicitly at the end of this chapter.

CLOSED ADOPTION

My mother's birth and adoption in 1952 occurred during a period popu-
larly known as the 'Baby Scoop' Era in Australia, Canada, Ireland, New
Zealand, the United Kingdom (UK) and the US, a period bookended on
one side by the end of the Second World War and, on the other, the widespread availability of oral contraception ('the pill') by the late 1960s. and
legalisation of abortion in most of these countries in the late 1960s
and early 1970s (Kahan 2006). This was a time of significant social, legal
and cultural transition in these countries linked to increasing governmental
reach in the recording of vital statistics and demographic data, persisting
laws on illegitimacy, the rise of the 'psy' sciences and professions, profes-
sionalisation of social work and the consolidation of child welfare movements (Smart 2009, p. 552). These together served to normalise and codify
specific 'ideal' family configurations, leading to the phasing out both of
practices encouraging mothers to raise their illegitimate children and of
informal adoption practices – where children were often taken in by others
within a mother's extended family, the burden of proof for their legitimacy
attenuated by the previously poor official record-keeping practices (Smart
2009, p. 557). Instead, unwed, pregnant, young, white women – societally
stigmatised as deviant – during the 'Baby Scoop' Era were actively discour-
aged from keeping their babies and pressured, even forced,[2] to formally
give them up for adoption in the widespread belief that it was in the best
interests of both the infants and mothers to have a chance at life without
the legal, social and economic stigma of illegitimacy (Mandell 2007).
Homes for unwed mothers increased in number during this time, shielding
the mothers' identities and providing maternity care services to many free
of charge (Hartel 2006).

In the US, the 'Baby Scoop' Era movement to formalise adoption
generated increased supply to meet rapidly expanding demand – heavily
racialised and classed – in the 'adoption market' by involuntarily childless,
white, middle-class Americans for healthy, white babies whose physical
traits would allow adoptive parents and children to physically 'match' and
visibly 'pass' as a 'real' biological family (Briggs 2012). In support of the
secrecy and anonymity deemed requisite for adoptive parents and children
to 'pass' as a biological family and for biological mothers to avoid social
shaming, statutes were widely enacted in states throughout the US and
in other countries in the 1950s and 1960s to seal adoption case records
(Kahan 2006). This enabled adoptive parents to conceal from outsiders
– sometimes even the children themselves – that their children had been
adopted, thus 'protect[ing] the child born out of wedlock from the stigma
of illegitimacy' (Carp 1992, p. 28). The act of sealing records rendered an

adoption 'closed', meaning that hospitals, adoption agencies and courts were not permitted to provide family information from adoption case records to anyone, including adopted persons and birthparents searching for their biological kin. Secrecy around biological parentage grew more impenetrable through not only the sealing off of existing records but also by the drawing-up of entirely new ones (e.g., the reissuing of adopted children's birth certificates with the names of their adoptive parents replacing those of their biological ones and children's adoptive names replacing those given to them at birth to give the appearance of biological legitimacy).

The practice of closed adoption in itself has increasingly come to be recognised in English-speaking Western countries as psychologically traumatising for both biological mothers who gave up their babies and adoptees victimised by the Era's prevailing societal mores (Verrier 1993; Higgins 2011). Indeed, given the state-fostered severing of adoptees from their biological roots, adoption rights advocates have called for the 'Baby Scoop' to be compared to the 'Sixties Scoop' (Canada) and 'Stolen Generation' (Australia), where tens of thousands of aboriginal infants and children were forcefully removed from their families of birth and placed with white adoptive families, policies for which the Australian government and the lone Canadian provincial government of Manitoba have only issued formal apologies in the last decade (Barta 2008). These forced adoption practices in Canada and Australia – recognised as acts of cultural genocide (Crichlow 2002) – not only reduced the size of aboriginal communities but also cut children of aboriginal origin off from their cultural heritage of birth and, via adoption into non-aboriginal families, placed them in contexts in which they might come to see their cultural heritage of birth as inferior to that into which they were adopted. A recent Canadian court decision found that

> there is no dispute that great harm was done ... the 'scooped' children lost contact with their families. They lost their aboriginal language, culture and identity ... the loss of their aboriginal identity left the children fundamentally disoriented, with a reduced ability to lead healthy and fulfilling lives. The loss of aboriginal identity resulted in psychiatric disorders, substance abuse, unemployment, violence and numerous suicides. (Judge Belobaba, cited in Gignac 2017)

It should be noted that the racialised state violence inflicted during the Sixties Scoop and Stolen Generation differed in severity, form and function from that of the Baby Scoop, which, by contrast, largely served to solve the social 'problem' of rising white middle-class illegitimacy in the wake of the Second World War. However, it is highly significant that the Canadian judge's argumentation above rests upon the concept of 'genealogical bewilderment', a diagnosis developed in the 1950s and 1960s in the US to describe the psychological condition of anyone who – regardless of their racial or ethnic background – 'either has no knowledge of his [*sic*] natural parents or only uncertain knowledge of them . . . [which results in] confusion and uncertainty . . . [and] fundamentally undermines his security and thus affects his mental health' (Sants 1964, p. 133).

Many, both within and outside adoption communities,[3] in English-speaking Western countries have taken up the condition of 'genealogical bewilderment' to draw attention to the psychological trauma caused during the Baby Scoop Era, where children were not raised by their 'real' (i.e., biological) parents, and by its closed adoption practices, more specifically, where sealed records inhibit adoptees from learning about their heritage of birth. The conscious deployment of 'genealogical bewilderment' by the 1970s by so many signalled growing belief that the emotional desire to know one's heritage of birth or genealogical heritage was not at all a psychological condition exclusive to 'maladjusted' individuals but was instead central to *all* people in developing their sense of self and identity (Sorosky et al. 1974). As Leighton (2012, p. 65) observes, 'the diagnosis of genealogical bewilderment seems to displace former worries about the harmful effects of illegitimacy onto worries about the effects of adoption itself'. Reflecting this growing trend, the Adoptees' Liberty Movement Association (ALMA) was launched in the US in 1971 to support adoptees in their search for their biological parents and campaigned to do away with closed adoptions, a practice considered to be an affront to basic human dignity given that 'western cultures tend to equate biological origins with identity' (Homans 2006, p. 5).

Societal perceptions continued to change gradually, such that, by 1989, the United Nations (UN) Convention on the Rights of the Child stipulated that a child should, as far as possible, have 'the right to know and be cared for by his or her [biological] parents' (UNHR 1989, p. 3). Today, due to the use of contraceptives, legality of abortion and reduced stigma surrounding unwed young mothers, far fewer children are given up for adoption within the US (though this has subsequently led to controversial growth of the international adoption market and so-called 'transracial' adoption (DellaCava et al. 2004)). Furthermore, while adoption records remain inaccessible to the general public, nearly all US states have now modified their statutes on adoption to enable biological parents, adoptive parents and adoptees to access non-identifying information (e.g., date and place of birth, physical traits, ethnicity, religion, educational level, occupation and medical history of biological parents; reason for placing the child for adoption; and the existence of other children born to the biological parents) and, where the person whose information is sought has consented, his or her identifying information (e.g., names and addresses). Out of concern for the potentially negative psychological impacts of search and contact with biological kin, however, some US states require adopted persons to receive counselling prior to the disclosure of identifying information (Child Welfare Information Gateway 2015).

While it would appear that the era of coerced and closed adoptions is now coming to a close in the US, thus enabling greater transparency, new challenges are emerging. With advances in assisted reproductive technologies since the 1980s, for instance, anonymous gamete donation has been framed as depriving the donor-conceived of their 'true genetic identity' (Leighton 2012, p. 65), knowledge of which might offer insight into their medical history and genealogical and ethnic heritages, leading to legal challenges regarding the responsibility of donors to disclose information about themselves to their biological offspring. This has led to great debate among bioethicists about the significance of legal transparency and biological 'truth' to a person's sense of ontological security (Smart 2009). In addition, with the growth of 'transracial' and international adoption in recent decades, an industry has emerged to enable adoptive parents to help their adopted children develop and retain 'a sense of native group identity' through 'culture-keeping' socialisation practices that involve the 'selective appropriation and consumption of renovated cultural symbols, artefacts and events that serve as the source of [cultural and racial] identity construction for adopted children' (Quiroz 2012, p. 528), like 'ethnic' dolls, folk music, cookbooks, 'culture camps' and 'roots trips'. Such legal challenges regarding biological 'truth' and heritage cultivation practices speak to the persistent and profound Western societal preoccupation with the notion that knowledge of one's 'real' (biological) heritage is essential to the healthy development of an individual's sense of self and that deprivation of it is not only psychologically (i.e., individually) but also morally (i.e., socially, collectively) traumatic (Fassin and Rechtman 2009).

BIOLOGICAL BELONGING

My mother does not recall when she was told that she had been adopted. Rather, she 'just always sort of knew'; her adoptive parents did not try to conceal that she and her (non-biological) younger brother were adopted. By the time she was in high school, however, her adoptive mother offered her the first clue to her biological origins: a slip of paper on which her biological mother's name and address prior to the time of her birth were written. In a meeting during the adoption process, the nuns running the orphanage left a file folder with information about her biological mother open on the desk and briefly stepped out of the meeting room, perhaps intentionally, allowing them to gather whatever information they wished to have. The information on this slip of paper was acquired in a way that simultaneously acknowledges yet undermines the state's authority in enforcing legal secrecy regarding information about biological kinship and heritage. It brings to the fore the significance of arbitrary record management practices by both institutional and familial authorities that can usurp and render the seemingly impenetrable penetrable. Still, it was considered so powerful, so private, that it was held in the adoptive family's safe and could only be accessed by specific people at the 'right' time.

While the identifying information she came to possess in high school about her biological mother undoubtedly facilitated her later search, looking for one's biological parents in a pre-internet era required significant energy, navigational know-how, delicacy and persistence but also heavy reliance on others' good will and belief in adoptees' right to know about their origins. In mid-1978, after statutes began to be relaxed in US states, thus enabling adoptees to access non-identifying information about their biological parents, my mother handwrote a letter to the director of the Catholic orphanage in which she spent the first three months of her life, making no reference to the 'secret' knowledge of her biological mother's name and the complicity surrounding that knowledge:

> . . . Having been an elementary school teacher for the past five years, I have had contact with many adopted children who are full of questions about adoption – why they were given up or what their 'real' parents were like. I only hope honest answers from their parents will help them.
> . . .
> The reason for this correspondence is to request any and all information you have concerning the circumstances of my adoption, names/addresses of my birth parents, birth siblings and relatives. Medical histories of my natural parents are necessary as my husband of four years and I will soon be expecting a child. (Having the possibility of someone *looking* like me is overwhelming!) I also want facts dealing in my birth parents' backgrounds, physical descriptions, special interests (employment), etc.
> . . .
> Rest assured that I am not aiming for a reunion (although that possibility has always been in the back of my mind) – unless it is desired by my natural mother or father also. Have they ever inquired about me? Just insatiably curious . . .
> . . .
> I am a very stable person. I enjoy my life, my husband, my family. It seems quite natural to me to desire this information.
> . . .
> I firmly believe that adoptees have the undeniable right to know everything about the circumstances surrounding their adoption and any other requested information. I am happy to see many states making great strides in improving the status of adoption 'veil of mystery' laws. It is unfair to force people to suppress these

yearnings. For a well-adjusted person, 'finding out' can only be a relief from a feeling of biological non-belonging. (Mary, 1978, original emphasis)

The excerpt above, with its carefully framed appeals to the presumed empathetic nature of its reader (a nun), reflects my mother's and other adoptees' profound feelings of powerlessness as they seek to scale the walls erected by diverse institutional authorities around official records. Characteristic of the era in which it was written, my mother makes delicate efforts here to quell any potential concern from the orphanage director that the desire to possess information about her biological parents and to lift the 'veil of mystery' surrounding her origins might be related to some sort of psychosocial 'maladjustment'. She instead roots the yearning to assuage her sense of 'genealogical bewilderment' as an adoptee – what my mother here calls feelings of 'biological non-belonging' – in no-nonsense language that indicates the discursive weight of biological arguments. Despite loving her adoptive and elective kin, not physically resembling anyone around her is used as evidence of the adoptive family unit failing to convincingly 'pass' as a 'real' biological family. This failure to 'pass' is further concretised by not being able to draw on the medical histories of her adoptive parents to infer about her own health and that of her yet-to-be-born child. Finally, part of the joy of giving birth to her own biological child – me – resides in creating someone who not only resembles her but, perhaps, also possesses characteristics of her biological parents, offering up a partial reflection of a denied past.

Like many adoptees, interest in finding her biological parents introduced a painful rift between my mother and her adoptive mother, despite receiving encouragement from the latter – an ardent lover of history and of amateur genealogy – to look for her biological mother. Smart (2009, p. 555) suggests that this may be due to biological kinship links 'occupy[ing] a kind of iconic status in the cultural and personal imaginary'. Regardless of the actual quality of such links, they deeply condition everyday lived relationships with adoptive and elective kin. Still, my mother's sense of 'genealogical bewilderment' persisted and, armed with the identifying and non-identifying information about her biological parents, she began her search in earnest. I recall seeing the long telephone cord tautly stretched across the length of the kitchen to the dining table, where in the evenings my mother would sit and make long-distance cold calls to people throughout the country with her biological mother's surname, sharing her desire to find her biological parents. Telephone books from different parts of the US – sacrosanct founts of potential clues, perhaps holding the phone number of her biological mother or someone who might be able to guide her towards her – were pored over within different Ohio libraries. Advocacy organisations that emerged in the 1970s to alter adoption policy in the US, like ALMA and the Concerned United Birthparents (CUB) (DellaCava et al. 2004), were joined and drawn upon for up-to-date information on legislative changes, tips for contacting the right agencies for information and their support networks for members searching for their biological kin. A New York member of CUB, who had herself given up a baby for closed adoption in her youth, helped my mother by undertaking the necessary local footwork (e.g., filing information requests at courthouses and so on) as she carried out her search. In adoption community lingo, she would today be known as a 'search angel'. Through a combination of these methods and networks, my mother located her biological mother in 1988.

Shortly after she found her, we ended up in a car heading to central New York to meet her, her husband and three adult daughters, my mother's biological half-sisters. My mother reflected on the journey some years later in writing:

> All of my life I have looked into the faces of strangers. I have searched those faces for traces of my own likeness. I have scanned crowds at street fairs and observed passers-by on city sidewalks and in airports – for eyes like mine. Eyes that might hold the secrets of my beginnings. At times, perhaps, for eyes that are gazing back at me, wondering if I am 'The One'. . . . What began as a burning desire to unearth my roots is soon to become a reunion of strangers. . . . Will she look like me? . . . Will she play piano, guitar, have a music collection? Has she read Madeleine L'Engle's books, felt frightened in thunderstorms, wondered about past lives? . . . Sometimes I would sink into silent reveries when I was pregnant with Meghann. And often thereafter, when I would study this child's features. This child who'd been part of my human body. . . . I don't remember getting out of the car, but here I am walking toward the people pouring out of the house. I frantically look from face to face. I see Her . . . I recognize those eyes. I have seen those eyes in the mirror every day of my life. (Mary, 19 June 1991)

Every few years, my mother revisits this particular text with me, looking at it when we are together or forwarding it by email. The photographs that sometime accompany this revisiting recall my mother gleefully comparing nose shapes and the location of moles on her body with those of four people with whom, other than me, she shared an uncanny physical resemblance.

BEING IN THE TREE

My mother discovered half of her biological parentage, was able to partially fill in the gaps in her medical history and could very easily physically 'pass' as part of her biological family. Yet, at the same time, while 'real' biological kin, they were not immediately recognisable to each other as 'true' family. They had not grown up together; neither she nor they had played a part in the events and stories that constitute the collective imaginary of family life (Hirsch 2008, p. 113). As such, the next step my mother took to overcome her 'genealogical bewilderment' was to immerse herself in her biological mother's genealogical heritage and, for the first time, to claim it also as her own. She began by collecting copies of old family photos and asking for stories about the people, places and events depicted in order 'to diminish distance, bridge separation, and facilitate identification and affiliation ... [to] look not only for information or confirmation, but also for an intimate material and affective connection' (Hirsch 2008, p. 116) with those in her immediate and extended biological family. Her biological mother acquiesced, providing the information she could. My mother then turned to genealogy, with its great appeal lying in the essentialist notion that one's 'true' identity can be revealed through the discovery of one's ancestral lineage, that who and where we come from determines who we are. Her interest in her biological mother's genealogical heritage and her ensuing prominent role in curating her biological mother's family tree were not only to learn about those already in the family tree but also to firmly emplace herself legitimately within that tree, explicitly and implicitly counteracting and 'overriding the desires of some family members to forget' (Nash 2008, p. 72).

Through the photos, stories and family trees, Anglo-Saxon and Scottish surnames and names of cities and villages not only in New York but also across the Atlantic in England and Scotland flooded in. Social narratives constructed around descent lead to certain ancestors being cherished, with stories about them passed down from one generation to the next in order to assert social status and maintain kinship and ethnic bonds, while others might be completely forgotten or deliberately suppressed – a selective remembering and forgetting of ancestors determined by ever-shifting societal conventions and norms (Basu 2004; Nash 2008). My mother's entry into these social narratives and connection with her biological mother's familial heritage 'pantheon' served to orientate her sense of self. Her heritage was no longer singular; it was multiple. Though she grew up making apple butter, eating sauerkraut and making routine family pilgrimages to the neighbouring state's 'Little Bavaria' for its quaint nineteenth-century German ambiance, she was no longer 'just' part of her adoptive parents' rural Ohio, German-American Catholic farming family and community. She was now suddenly 'also' a direct biological descendent of a major American bookseller, the first female physician in the state of New York and other illustrious figures who, together, drastically reconfigured her 'genealogical imaginary' (Kramer 2011) by entering her pantheon.

The popularity of genealogy as a pastime in recent decades in contemporary Western societies has been described by Basu (2004) as a reaction to depersonalised modernity, fragmentation and dissolution of traditional family structures and mobile, consumption-based lifestyles. This is especially the case among adoptees. In their study of how adopted children narrate their life stories, Brookfield et al. (2008) deploy Hirsch's concept of 'post-memory practice' to capture the interplay between facticity (what actually happened) and construction (the imaginative piecing together of events and artefacts) in order to make sense of one's experience and/ or position within a broader context through compelling fiction. More intensely than those confidently and consistently steeped in the details of their biological ancestors, therefore, they argue that adoptees engage in creative bricolage practices, cobbling together sometimes scarce and incongruent fragments from a bevy of sources in order to create origin stories – explanatory narratives about their genealogical descent. Indeed, as Hirsch (2008) observes, a lack of inherited genealogical artefacts can lead to collectively circulated cultural artefacts and tropes taking on greater significance. Thus, my mother quickly came to see herself not only as the biological fruit of a particular family tree but also, more generally, as a 'true' descendent of Scottish Highlanders and undertook efforts to claim her legitimate place as a 'card-carrying' member of the vast Scottish diaspora. Scottish Highland games were now attended in the Rocky Mountains and Appalachians, the film *Braveheart* (1995) stirred yearnings for a homeland, clan-specific tartans and other accoutrements were purchased and proudly worn, Scottish history and landscapes were studied and, at world music's height of popularity, Celtic music was constantly played at home and in the car (Basu 2004). She eventually legally reverted to her Scottish pre-adoption surname, thus – ironically, symbolically – requiring her post-adoption birth certificate to be officially adjusted and reissued by authorities to reflect the change back to her surname of birth. Such consumerist and legal acts of celebration and resistance enabled her to assert greater personal control and ownership over what she understood as both her biological and adoptive heritages.

As my mother gained access to her biological (mother's) genealogical heritage, great advances were being made in both information and communication technologies and genomic sequencing technologies. While I focus on the latter in the next section, here I wish to touch upon the significant role of the internet and public and private collections of big data in facilitating adoptees' access to and sharing of genealogical information (Nash 2002; Basu 2004). Consumer-orientated websites like Ancestry.com, FamilyTreeDNA.com and FamilySearch.com, all of which emerged in the mid-1990s with the expansion of internet access, have enabled countless amateur and professional genealogists to tap into an ever-growing wealth of digitised public records and print media coverage (e.g., census, immigration and military enlistment records, wedding announcements and obituaries in newspapers and so on). These sources are sometimes digitised by public bodies themselves and accessible free of charge, but others – due to the prohibitive financial and time investments associated with digitisation – are digitised by Ancestry.com and other for-profit services in exchange for exclusive rights to them for a set amount of time (see, e.g., Mullis 2016). Through such private-public partnerships – perceived as a boon for cash-strapped public authorities – private enterprises are increasingly becoming significant repositories, and marshals over the appropriate use, of 'public' information.

Yet, it is the powerful interlinkage of 'public' records with families' private record-keeping and heritage practices that renders services like Ancestry.com so powerful. Their genealogical value is exponentially increased by not only serving as exclusive storehouses of 'public' records but also of consumer-collaborators' own privately uploaded familial artefacts (e.g., intragenerationally documented family trees, photographs, letters, summaries of orally transmitted anecdotes and so on). It is via these services' special tools to sort the big digital datasets from public and private records that informational overlaps between individual consumers' family trees and official records (e.g., names, dates and so on) can be identified. Ancestry.com, for instance, offers a 'Hints' feature that enables consumers with overlaps in their trees to link up with one another and share and assimilate data not only from official public records but also from each other's private trees and familial artefacts in order to shore up the documental veracity upon which the sturdiness of their own trees relies. These 'Hints' – which graphically appear as tiny, quivering green leaves of a tree – have been likened by Clancey (2015) to digital tombstones, an example of collective memorialising in the age of big data and online databases.

Ancestry.com and services like it may both enhance and supplant more conventional forms of collective memorialising with more personalised, self-interested – if also more collaboratively generated – 'roots' practices (Filene 2012). Being networked with other amateur genealogists via the Ancestry.com site – who are themselves somehow related to her, albeit in widely varying degrees – has allowed my mother to exhaustively explore the lives of her biological mother's documented ancestors[4] in the privacy and comfort of her home by accessing the boon of co-generated/pooled visual artefacts and records archived on the site and by using additional online tools, like Google Maps, to see what the places mentioned in official records and private letters look like today. In the special folder dedicated to

'Ancestry' in my e-mailbox sit innumerable messages from my mother with attachments comprising old newspaper clippings detailing and celebrating her biological mother's documented ancestors' lifetime accomplishments as well as grainy, scanned black-and-white photos found in others' family trees depicting distant relatives accompanied by messages from my mother that ask, consistently and with only subtle variation, 'Do you think they look like me/you/my biological mother?' The heavily curated tree on Ancestry.com, to draw on Clancey's (2015) metaphor above, has become the sacred burial ground or temple at which she can come to know, relate with and honour a set of ancestors she has come to recognise as her biological tribe – for only USD 35 per month.

THE OTHER 50 PER CENT OF HER GENETIC MATERIAL

US immigration and shipping records available on Ancestry.com revealed the Estonian national to me one evening in front of the computer screen in 2011. A ship electrician with the merchant marine, US immigration records indicated that he worked on cargo ships bringing, among other goods, fruit to the US from Cuba and Brazil, docking from time to time in New York City, where my mother's biological mother was studying nursing in the early 1950s. While unable to provide many details about the identity and origins of my mother's biological father, my mother's biological mother corroborated my findings: while omitting his good dancing skills, the official records appeared to accurately depict what little she knew about him.

Despite exhaustive efforts, little else has been able to shed light on his life trajectory or whereabouts since his time with the merchant marine. It would seem that we had reached an impasse. However, as Nash (2008, p. 221) observed in the early days of direct-to-consumer (DTC) personal genomic testing, 'Genealogy is no longer limited by the availability of documentary sources. Those who have reached a dead-end due to the lack of recorded information can turn to genetics.' First, my mother's saliva made its way to the DTC personal genomic testing company 23andMe's California processing laboratory in a vial tucked safely inside a padded envelope marked with an alarming orange biohazard sticker, then mine, then that of her biological mother. The results confirmed that her identified biological mother was indeed her biological mother and – in a twenty-first-century-style paternity test – that her biological father, whose whereabouts and background were largely unknown, was indeed of Scandinavian/Baltic descent.

My mother's sleuthing led to the triangulation of chromosomal data gleaned from kin found on 23andMe and GedMatch with the conventional family tree data she could tap into by examining others' family trees on Geni and Ancestry.com through hypothesising linkages via Ancestry.com's 'Hints' feature. Developing and accessing genetically confirmed biological kin's family trees enabled my mother to build speculative family trees backward, forward and horizontally in time in order to gather identifying information about kin closer in relation to her biological father. At the same time, she sought out 'search angel' assistance and information from other amateur and professional genomic genealogists on numerous public internet bulletin boards and chat groups and in private emails. She also approached people online that she suspected were related to her biological father, delicately requesting that she would pay for them to do the 23andMe test in order to find her biological father's family. A university-aged Estonian woman studying in Denmark agreed to do the test, the results of which confirmed third-degree biological kinship. Tracing her family tree revealed new connections, enabling contact with more Estonian biological cousins and revealing more about her biological father's family. Yet, while she has managed to locate many in his family, the fate of my mother's biological father remains unknown. The lack of institutional records during the period immediately following the Second World War and the continued reluctance of older Estonians to talk about what happened during the war and the Soviet period have effectively erased him from collective memory at the national, local and extended familial levels.

In the absence of knowledge about her biological father, as she had done earlier with all things Scottish, she began to embrace Estonian crafts, music, documentaries and so on to immerse herself in yet another canon representing part of her cultural heritage of birth, a heritage that heretofore had been previously unknown and largely irrelevant to her. Upon learning that her biological paternal grandfather was sent to the Gulag Angara prison labour camp in Siberia for a decade immediately following the Second World War, she explored how Estonians fared during the Soviet era. At the time of Estonia's independence and the fall of the Soviet Union in 1991, her third cousin played in a well-known band – their song served as the anthem for the country's transition. In a diary entry, my mother celebrates her biological ancestral link to this important historical event:

> My adoptive family gave me my first compass. Discovering [my biological Estonian kin] has restored my compass settings. There is music and there are musicians in my bloodline – my ancestral family! (Mary, January 2015)

With these new stories, new figures entered her personal heritage pantheon, once again shifting her genealogical imaginary. What was once someone else's heritage and another country's history suddenly felt very much her own; tapping into others' personal and collective memories helped her to further construct her sense of self and develop her origin story.

Nordgren and Juengst (2009) suggest that DTC personal genomic testing via companies like AncestryDNA, Family Tree DNA and 23andMe attract consumers through their appeal to seemingly incongruous yet simultaneously overlapping pre-modern, modern and post-modern definitions of identity: the pre-modern desire for a twenty-first-century essentialist genetic narrative (akin to Social Darwinism in the nineteenth and twentieth centuries) that purports to explain one's identity; the modern desire for a scientific route to unlocking the secrets of one's genealogical heritage; and the post-modern desire to have individual control, choice and ownership over the components contributing to one's self-identification. In spite of growing appeals by regulators like the US Food and Drug Administration (FDA) and genetic ethicists to heed the social risks of genetic testing to personal privacy, (mis)interpreted results on family dynamics and individual health and lifestyle decision-making, and essentialist genetic discrimination, as at July 2017, 23andMe alone had some two million genotyped customers (23andMe 2017a). DTC personal genomic testing has offered adoptees (those who can afford it, at least) in particular the ability to access genealogical and medical information far beyond what has been made available to them through (partially accessible) adoption records (Baptista et al. 2016). It is estimated that at least 6 per cent of 23andMe customers are adoptees (Petrone 2015), significantly more than the estimated 2–4 per cent in the general US population (The Adoption History Project 2012).

Those in search of their 'real' biological identities find scientific evidence of their genealogical lineages and ethnic origins and the medicalised decoding of their bodies' genetic proclivities to be a significant lifeline. Thus, when the US FDA placed what became a nearly three-year-long moratorium in 2013 on the release of health data by 23andMe to its customers, my mother worriedly forwarded on an email to another adoptee she met on 23andMe for whom she served as a 'search angel' and to me:

> People who signed up for their service did so primarily because they heavily advertised their ability to predict the odds of getting various diseases. Finding possible relatives was only an additional benefit. However, the FDA put them out of business as far as testing for the possibility of getting certain diseases. Therefore, the only product they have left to offer is finding possible relatives. Only recently we learned that their default is NOT to be notified of close relatives. This is a serious problem for the many subscribers to 23andMe who have been adopted at birth and are trying to find their birth parents through DNA testing. The situation is that the policies of 23andMe are blocking these people

from receiving the information that they desperately want to get. . . . Just about everybody interested in genealogy wants to find and be found by their nearest relatives. The question is how to convince 23andMe to do the right thing by, among other things, letting adoptees find their real parents. My suggestion is to approach 23andMe like this: the only new customers they are going to get is [*sic*] genealogy people. If these genealogy people find out that their closest relatives will be prohibited from knowing about them, they are not going to pay their money to join. (Sam Sloan 2014, emailed by Mary, September 2014)

Though outrage spread within the 23andMe adoption community, one that notably began to articulate itself through the lenses of both biological citizenship (Rose and Novas 2004) and political consumerism (Micheletti 2003), the company's default option for new genotyped customers remains 'opt-out' to date likely because, while its customers may wish to find out about their broader ancestral genetic origins (e.g., having African or Jewish heritage) and health risks (e.g., having a genetic predisposition to breast cancer), they may be less interested in coming into contact with living genetic kin (23andMe 2017b). This time, a company – not a government body – has effectively institutionally 'sealed off' significant portions of genomic data in order to protect individual customers' rights to privacy regarding their potential biological relationships to other customers. The tantalising promise of potential biotechnical revelation has been placed just out of reach for adoptees seeking greater control over their biological heritage. Paradoxically, as with Ancestry.com in the earlier section, for adoptees to be able to take greater ownership of their biological heritage, they must rely heavily on others' non-proprietary willingness to collaborate by sharing data depicting their own biological matter/heritage and being open to the consequences of such collaboration – not only for themselves but also for close biological kin with whom they share a non-negligible percentage of genetic material. The adoption community's 'right to know' stance – a hard-fought one that has benefited so immensely from more democratised, if also increasingly commoditised, access to all kinds of public and private data being made available via the internet and social media outlets in recent years – contrasts sharply, therefore, with contemporary societal fears about the implications of DTC genomic testing, for example, on individual freedom relative to government paternalism, health data ownership and privacy in the face of possible genetic discrimination (Chow-White et al. 2017).

CONCLUSION

While acknowledging that notions of 'true' and 'false' selves and origin stories are formulated through discourse and situated in time and space, the deep-seated, widespread and persistent belief in the existence of one's 'true' self and origins and the possibility of their revelation remains far from trivial. I recall here this chapter's opening excerpt from Foucault's (1970 [1980]) lecture regarding 'the will to truth' that acknowledges the ontological security afforded by privileged positioning within discourse. Those who have always 'known', never had reason to question or never had the 'truth' of their biological heritage challenged have been 'freed from the obligation to begin' (Foucault 1970 [1980], p. 51) contemplating (much, at least) the ways in which the knowledge of biological 'truth' has come to structure everyday lives and how the absence of that knowledge has come to be recognised as an impediment to 'healthy' development and self-actualisation within contemporary society.

My mother's liminality within such discourse offers valuable insights into the construction of, stakes in and effects of that knowledge. Like many others who have been impacted by the Baby Scoop Era's closed adoption statutes, she has struggled not only to simply assert her right to be able to know her biological 'truth' but also to assume greater control and ownership over it by individually and collaboratively commandeering an increasingly diverse range of publicly and privately accessible heritage resources to fashion an origin story with elements deemed suitably 'truthful' against the backdrop of dominant societal narratives about the role of family heritage in forging and sustaining the ontological security required for 'healthy' personhood. This desire for a coherent origin story has required the active analogue, digital and biotechnical acquisition and cobbling-together of disparate fragments of politically, legally, religiously, scientifically, commercially and familiarly authorised and authorising 'heritages' from among an increasingly diverse cast of heritage-makers and resources rendered intelligible and relevant by ongoing societal and biotechnological refinements of what constitutes personal and collective 'truth' and the relation between them.

In this sense, my mother's journeying through the dense thicket of 'genealogical bewilderment' has not been one in which 'heritage from below' (Robertson 2012) practices are intentionally united and locked in battle with some monolithic AHD (Smith 2006). Rather, there has been a far less spectacular and frequently tacit and messy, if uneasy, complicity between everyday personal heritage practices and dominant discourse regarding the ontologically rewarding promise of biological 'truth'. That tantalising discourse drove her to desire and capture 'truth' fragments with the conceptual and material tools and resources at hand. Fragments of her repressed biological 'truth' were slowly revealed first by defiant nuns, a heritage-of-birth-appreciating adoptive mother and open adoption advocates, and later on by witting and unwitting biological and documented kin – closely and distantly related, living and deceased, circulating public records and private artefacts and stories or featuring prominently in them, and supplying genetic material evidencing their and her biological connections to past, present and future populations – and the for-profit companies' digital platforms and partnerships that made such a surfeit of information both available and intelligible. At the same time, this assemblage of different actors only authorised the 'appropriate' release of certain 'truths' when they saw fit, curating 'truths' that were not only hers but also those of others with the aid of technological tools that themselves reinforced dominant societal narratives about the significance of biological 'truth' and its relevance to a 'healthy' sense of self. My mother's journeying demonstrates how normative notions of biological 'truth' can be desired and conjured through a diverse range of practices with the aid of an increasingly diverse cast of witting and unwitting heritage-makers and resources. The multiplicity, ambiguity and arbitrary nature of such practices and resources merits greater attention by heritage scholars who have, to date, focused more heavily on intentionality.

NOTES

1. I closely consulted with my mother throughout the research and writing process and she approved the final text. While several adoptees have undertaken scholarly reflections on their autoethnographic research (see, for e.g., Kim 2000; Wall 2008), I have yet to find similar work by descendants of 'closed adoption' adoptees. For this reason, Hirsch's (2008) work on post-memory practices among descendants of trauma survivors seeking to honour and pass on the memory of their forebears' experiences while at the same time grappling with their own complicated relationships with those simultaneously distant and intimate experiences has been instructive and comforting.
2. Films like *The Magdalene Sisters* (2002) and *Philomena* (2013) depict the experiences of young 'fallen' Irish women forcibly detained, punished with hard labour and required by the Catholic Church (and, it was to be discovered later, with the complicity of the Irish state) to relinquish their babies for adoption. Beyond such depictions of these extreme circumstances, however, the 'Baby Scoop' Era – enacted less severely in the US and other English-speaking Western countries – has received little attention.
3. This term encompasses those who comprise the so-called 'adoption triad': adoptees, biological mothers and adoptive parents.
4. They, of course, may not themselves be biologically related kin.

REFERENCES

23andMe (2017a), 'About us', accessed 14 July 2017 at mediacenter.23andme.com/about-us/.

23andMe (2017b), 'Privacy and display settings in DNA relatives', accessed 14 July 2017 at customercare.23andme.com/hc/en-us/articles/212170838-Privacy-and-display-settings-in-DNA-Relatives.

The Adoption History Project (2012), 'Adoption statistics', accessed 14 July 2017 at pages.uoregon.edu/adoption/topics/adoptionstatistics.htm.

Baptista, N.M., K.D. Christensen, D.A. Carere, S.A. Broadley, J.S. Roberts and R.C. Green (2016), 'Adopting genetics: motivations and outcomes of personal genomic testing in adult adoptees', *Genetics in Medicine*, **18** (9), 924–32.

Barta, T. (2008), 'Sorry, and not sorry, in Australia: how the apology to the stolen generations buried a history of genocide', *Journal of Genocide Research*, **10** (2), 201–14.

Basu, P. (2004), 'My own island home – the Orkney homecoming', *Journal of Material Culture*, **9** (1), 27–42.

Briggs, Laura (2012), *Somebody's Children: The Politics of Transnational and Transracial Adoption*, Durham, NC: Duke University Press.

Brookfield, H., S.D. Brown and P. Reavey (2008), 'Vicarious and post-memory practices in adopting families: the re-production of the past through photography and narrative', *Journal of Community and Applied Social Psychology*, **18** (5), 474–91.

Carp, E.W. (1992), 'The sealed adoption records controversy in historical perspective: the case of the Children's Home Society of Washington, 1895–1988', *Journal of Society and Social Welfare*, **19** (2), Article 5, accessed 14 July 2017 at scholarworks.wmich.edu/jssw/vol19/iss2/5.

Child Welfare Information Gateway (2015), 'Access to adoption records', June, accessed 14 July 2017 at http://www.childwelfare.gov/pubPDFs/infoaccessap.pdf.

Chow-White, P., S. Struve, A. Lusoli, F. Lesage, N. Saraf and A. Oldring (2017), '"Warren Buffet is my cousin": shaping public understanding of big data biotechnology, direct-to-consumer genomics, and 23andMe on Twitter', *Information, Communication and Society*, **21** (3), 1–17.

Clancey, G. (2015), 'The diaspora of the dead: civic memorialization in the age of online databases', *Mortality*, **20** (4), 390–407.

Crichlow, W. (2002), 'Western colonization as disease: native adoption and cultural genocide', *Canadian Social Work*, **5** (1), 88–107.

DellaCava, F.A., N. Kolko Phillips and M. Engel (2004), 'Adoption in the US: the emergence of a social movement', *Journal of Society and Social Welfare*, **31** (4), Article 8, accessed 14 July 2017 at http://scholarworks.wmich.edu/jssw/vol31/iss4/8.

Fassin, Didier and Richard Rechtman (2009), *The Empire of Trauma. Inquiry into the Condition of Victimhood*, Princeton, NJ: Princeton University Press.

Filene, B. (2012), 'Passionate histories: "outsider" history-makers and what they teach us', *The Public Historian*, **34** (1), 11–33.

Foucault, Michel (1970), 'The order of discourse', reprinted in Robert Young (ed.) (1980), *Untying the Text: A Post-Structuralist Reader*, London: Routledge, pp. 51–78.

Gignac, J. (2017), 'Canadian judge rules in favour of forcibly adopted First Nations survivors', *Guardian*, 14 February, accessed 14 July 2017 at http://www.theguardian.com/world/2017/feb/14/canada-sixties-scoop-ruling-first-nations-children.

Halbwachs, Maurice (1980), *The Collective Memory*, trans. F.J. Ditter, Jr and V.Y. Ditter, London: Harper & Row.

Hartel, H.A. (2006), 'Producing Father Nelson H. Baker: the practices of making a saint for Buffalo, NY', Doctoral dissertation, University of Iowa.

Higgins, D. (2011), 'Unfit mothers . . . unjust practices? Key issues from Australian research on the impact of past adoption practices', *Family Matters*, **87**, 56–67.

Hirsch, M. (2008), 'The generation of postmemory', *Poetics Today*, **29** (1), 103–28.

Homans, M. (2006), 'Adoption narratives, trauma, and origins', *Narrative*, **14** (1), 4–26.

Kahan, M. (2006), 'Put up on platforms: a history of twentieth century adoption policy in the United States', *Journal of Sociology and Social Welfare*, **33** (3), Article 4, accessed 14 July 2017 at http://scholarworks.wmich.edu/jssw/vol33/iss3/4.

Kim, E. (2000), 'Korean adoptee auto-ethnography: refashioning self, family and finding community', *Visual Anthropology Review*, **16** (1), 43–70.

Kramer, A.-M. (2011), 'Mediatizing memory: history, affect and identity in Who Do You Think You Are?', *European Journal of Cultural Studies*, **14** (4), 428–45.

Leighton, K. (2012), 'Addressing the harms of not knowing one's heredity: lessons from genealogical bewilderment', *Adoption and Culture*, **3**, 63–107.

Mandell, B.R. (2007), 'Adoption', *New Politics*, **11** (2), 63.

Micheletti, Michele (2003), *Political Virtue and Shopping*, New York: Palgrave Macmillan.

Mullis, S. (2016), 'Huge collection of Indiana public records now digitized', *Evansville Courier and Press*, 4 June, accessed at 14 July 2017 at http://archive.courierpress.com/news/local/huge-collection-of-indiana-public-records-now-digitized--343fa6b0-e285-777a-e053-0100007f9181-381856701.html.

Nash, C. (2002), 'Genealogical identities', *Environment and Planning D: Society and Space*, **20** (1), 27–52.

Nash, Catherine (2008), *Of Irish Descent: Origin Stories, Genealogy and the Politics of Belonging*, Syracuse, NY: Syracuse University Press.

Nordgren, A. and E.T. Juengst (2009), 'Can genomics tell me who I am? Essentialistic rhetoric in direct-to-consumer DNA testing', *New Genetics and Society*, **28** (2), 157–72.

Petrone, J. (2015), 'As consumer genomics databases swell, more adoptees are finding their biological families', *GenomeWeb*, 25 September, accessed 14 July 2017 at http://www.genomeweb.com/applied-markets/consumer-genomics-databases-swell-more-adoptees-are-finding-their-biological.

Quiroz, P.A. (2012), 'Cultural tourism in transnational adoption: "staged authenticity" and its implications for adopted children', *Journal of Family Issues*, **33** (4), 527–55.

Robertson, Iain J.M. (ed.) (2012), *Heritage from Below*, London: Ashgate.

Rose, Nikolas and Carlos Novas (2004), 'Biological citizenship', in Aihwa Ong and Stephen J. Collier (eds), *Global Assemblages: Technology, Politics, and Ethics as Anthropological Problems*, London: Blackwell Publishing, pp. 439–63.

Sants, H.J. (1964), 'Genealogical bewilderment in children with substitute parents', *British Journal or Medical Psychology*, **37**, 133–41.

Smart, C. (2009), 'Family secrets: law and understandings of openness in everyday relationships', *Journal of Social Policy*, **38** (4), 551–67.

Smith, Laurajane (2006), *Uses of Heritage*, New York: Routledge.

Sorosky, A.D., A. Baran and R. Pannor (1974), 'The reunion of adoptees and birth relatives', *Journal of Youth and Adolescence*, **3** (3), 195–206.

Stein, A. (2009), 'Trauma and origins: post-Holocaust genealogists and the work of memory', *Qualitative Sociology*, **32** (3), 293–309.

UNHR (United Nations Human Rights) (1989), 'Convention on the Rights of the Child', accessed 14 July 2017 at http://www.ohchr.org/Documents/ ProfessionalInterest/crc.pdf.

Verrier, Nancy N. (1993), *The Primal Wound: Understanding the Adopted Child*, Baltimore, MD: Gateway Press.

Wall, S. (2008), 'Easier said than done: writing an autoethnography', *International Journal of Qualitative Methods*, **7** (1), 38–53.

Afterword

Iain J.M. Robertson

This is the 'stuff' of heritage from below. If this heritage is made material, or if it is material, then this occurs almost spontaneously and (seemingly) organically. It is heritage without fuss and with minimal commercial interest. (Robertson 2012, p.17)

The chapters here also make evident how AHD and HFB are, more often than not, overlapping and intertwined, such that it is problematic to pit one against the other; rather, we should seek to refine their relationships and promote their collaborations towards mutually beneficial purposes. (Muzaini and Minca, this volume)

It seems odd at best, disingenuous at least, to be quoting oneself. It feels appropriate in this current context, however, for if any three sentences can encapsulate the ontology of Heritage from Below, it is these. Where that ontology has now been taken must be the subject of some debate and will be contemplated, albeit briefly, in this Afterword. The second opening quotation, taken from the Introduction to this collection does just that, a central part of a convincing attempt to set the agenda for driving both concept and relationship forward. And yet, almost by necessity, this rethinking remains intriguingly situated within, and draws on, strands of thought the genealogy of which is traceable back to the foundational texts of heritage studies.

Although it is not the principal intention of this Afterword to detail the lineage, genesis and, indeed, heritage of Heritage From Below as concept and category, the close connection between HFB and the foundations of (critical) heritage studies means that a few words by way of contextualisation and reflection are required. Whilst Hamzah Muzaini and Claudio Minca have provided an excellent summary by way of introduction, if we are to look forward to future developments then a brief backward glance establishes a solid base from which to proceed. Pausing to look back on the development of HFB as originally formulated brings the realisation that it is important, nay imperative, to appreciate that its birth was a protracted one. Significantly much of the thinking out of which HFB emerged took place in an intellectual environment that predates the turn, and rise to prominence, of two paradigm-shifting ways of thinking: non-representational theory and critical heritage studies. Under the latter's banner, a fascinating range of approaches to the multiple manifestations and valorisations of the past in the present became loosely corralled with the formal launch of the Association of Critical Heritage Studies at its first conference in Gothenburg in 2012, marking the point at which changed perspectives accelerated.

The Association's Manifesto, also launched in Gothenburg, set the agenda from the outset. Here was the call for the 'ruthless criticism of everything existing' (Manifesto 2012) in which heritage was viewed as a political act and the interests of the marginalised and excluded explicitly foregrounded. No small part in the rise to prominence of this approach was played by Laurajane Smith's hugely influential and important monograph, *Uses of Heritage* (2006). Indeed, the thinking that went into HFB was both shaped by, and foreshadowed, key aspects of Smith's thesis with the concept first essayed in 2008 (Robertson 2008). In part at least, this conjunction is the product of the fact that elements of both Smith's still powerfully persuasive Authorised Heritage Discourse (AHD) and HFB first surfaced in conversations had, and papers presented (in the early 2000s), at the Public History workshops run by Hilda Kean at Ruskin College, Oxford.

Prior to this, whilst the world of heritage studies was far from static, it was influenced by a heavy dose of landscape theory and, in particular, the view which saw landscapes as representations (Cosgrove 1984; Cosgrove and Daniels 1998). In this understanding of 'landscape-as-text' can be found the tap root of HFB based on the assertion that landscapes, and heritage landscapes in particular, emerge from both material and immaterial processes. Landscapes, it was argued, are comprised of multiple layers of meaning which, when approached iconographically, can be exposed to reveal the processes that go into the making of these landscapes. They are, in short, social and cultural constructs and product, representation and means to maintain relationships of power as well as to manifest and materialise class relations. Critical too was the assertion that such configurations were at the same time products of class conflict and, on occasion, counter-hegemonic impulses.

Undeniably, heritage landscapes offer perhaps the most potent terrain for this way of seeing, even though the utility of subsequent developments and the turn away from the purely representational equally cannot be denied. More satisfying, perhaps, is the perspective that is captured in Hayden Lorimer's (2005) near-ubiquitous aphorism, the 'more-than-representational'. Whatever the form they take, whether tangible or intangible, landscapes of heritage are undeniably social and cultural constructs. As such, they are symbols, representations and materialisations of relationships of power and control. So, drawing all of this together, and filtering it through, and recognising both tangible and intangible expressions of the past in the present, the notion of HFB emerged out of the belief that, if the power of heritage is a means to ensuring that the world view of those in power is accepted as entirely 'natural' by the essentially powerless, then, because there are always spaces of and for the assertion of counter-hegemonic views, there are equally spaces for the assertion of counter-hegemonic heritages. HFB is therefore both category and concept, identifying landscapes of counter-hegemonic pasts wherever, whenever and however they may be found. Equally undeniably, this remains a fundamental principle (accepting a very broad definition of landscapes) for the individual chapters in this current collection; where, intriguingly and importantly, this collection builds on, critiques and develops this perspective is largely, and correctly, beyond this culturally-dominated realm and that of the personal and dialogic. Seeking, remarkably, to identify and promote collaborations between AHD and HFB.

In this collection, time and again heritage expressed for and 'from below' is seen as the everyday, as ongoing performance. And that is no bad thing. It was certainly the intent of the original collection to contrast spatially fixed, concretised memory markers with the fluid, dynamic and ongoing ways of remembering and reconstituting the past that appeared in those forms of heritage which eschewed much that was material, or, at the very least, much that was formal. In this turn to the everyday, the spacing of the heritage performance – the process of quotidian heritagisation (Harvey 2001) – was seen as significant. As such, this drew on one of the most important trends in the study of the rise of the heritage industry, that is, the emphasis on space. Consistently, commentators, perhaps revealing the preponderance of geographers amongst their ranks, have demonstrated that space matters. This collection is no exception. From James A. Tyner's opening chapter, the tone and ambition is set. Tyner both subtly reworks the important relationship between the AHD and HFB and powerfully reminds us that space matters. It matters, he shows, because it is an important part of the nexus of power and social relations. This tone and argument is of course one of the important stepping off points for HFB as originally conceived. Indeed, in his drawing together of the processes and forms of grassroots memorialisation with the more transgressive and spectral, Tyner takes the interrogation of spaces associated with heritage from below on an interesting journey. Such ghostly hauntings, we may suggest, are deeply suggestive of the motifs and dualism of presence/absence conjured up by John Wylie (2009, p. 277) in his engagement with the memorial benches at Mullion Cove (on the Lizard

Peninsula in the South-West of England). In gazing on the benches put there to *remember*, Wylie suggests, we are also engaged in a complex nexus of *watching* that involves '*looking with* . . . a host of ghosts and memories' [his emphasis].

This sense of the power and complexity of looking with, of the absence/presence dualism, and of the affective realm of 'love', is not confined to this one chapter; it permeates the collection and helps to strongly reinforce the notion that to engage with HFB involves an important fore-grounding of the individual. Here too we uncover, in its most vivid and obvious form, the transgressive, fluid and conflictual nature of all herit-ages. That much is revealed in Danielle Drozdzewski's simple but potent claim that, in Berlin, the first *Stolpersteine* were illegal emplacements. Whilst it lay at the heart of the original collection, a discussion of the role of illegality expressed, perhaps, as counter-hegemony, is not the central concern of Drozdzewski's chapter. Nevertheless, there remains room for such a consideration in studies of HFB more generally. It is moreover apposite to raise this point in the context of Drozdzewski's chapter as it was in Germany where the anti-monument movement was born, found its most powerful expressions, and was an inspiration for this strand of the thinking that went into HFB. In attempting to generate alternative memory work, and in celebrating and commemorating illegality, so the argument went, these anti-monuments created distinct and ephemeral landscapes of belonging that drew on landmarks to the memory of an alternative culture. As heritage from below was originally understood, such landmarks were seen to contain the possibility for the celebration, perpetuation and materialisation of oppositional meanings and practices. In so doing, landmarks of HFB unlock the possibility for the emergence of social movements framing an assertion of a structure of feeling that runs counter to the hegemonic. It remains the cause of some regret that subsequent research, including the present volume, failed to uncover many instances of this landmark 'work' outside the examples offered in the original collection.

Moving away and on from this rather polemical and didactic view, the stated aims of this current collection are to both question all forms of herit-age produced 'from below', and escape from the understanding of heritage performances as hierarchical, the clearest examples of which are the chap-ters by Meghann Ormond and Danielle Drozdzewski. Undoubtedly, the ontological emphases underpinning these aims are in part the consequence of the significant turn away from the search for those aspects of a sense of inheritance from the past that appear to have the capacity to function as a resource for social movements once it was realised that this was something of an intellectual blind alley. If this concept is to have any purchase going forward, then this was probably necessary, although there are two factors which may well suggest otherwise.

First, is the fact that there is a close intellectual lineage between HFB and the direction Laurajane Smith took after *Uses of Heritage*. In collaboration with a number of other authors, Smith turned to the exploration of the parameters and possibilities of 'working class heritage' which, in adopting a celebratory tone, sought to focus on 'the positive uses . . . heritage is being put to in the present' (Smith et al. 2011, p. 1). Once again, the concern here was very much with the role of the past in identity making and maintaining, assertion and reassertion. The aim was also to show that working class understandings of the past eschew the more overt and naïve forms of nostalgia and romanticisation closely associated with Authorised representations of working class heritage. Nostalgia, the authors asserted, had the capacity to evoke 'critical and mindful memorial work' (Smith et al. 2011, p. 3). Moreover, these are themes that were, in part at least, prefigured in essays in the original HFB collection, most notably by Roy Jones whose work focussed on a close reading of a number of formal and informal workers' memorials in Perth, Western Australia.

The belief in heritage, quotidian and vernacular, as enfolding the possibility for catalysing and coalescing social movements is given further potency and legitimacy through the parallel assertion that this unfolding involves active and performative engagements with the past that run counter to dominant discourses and which perform new forms of expression into space. Inspiration for this realisation came, of course from the pioneering work of Gaynor Bagnall (2003) in heritage studies but also, and more significantly, the general turn to ideas of embodied performance across the social sciences more generally (see, for instance, Butler 1998; Gregson and Rose 2000; Crouch 2003, 2010a, 2010b; Thrift 2004, 2008). This practical ontology undoubtedly lends considerable weight to our attempts to understand the 'work' heritage (and HFB) does, not least from the fact that heritage is, in every sense of the word, constantly performed and in performance, but also because one of the key precepts in play here is the recognition of a world far messier than hitherto imagined. Messiness means holes and tears, gaps through which HFB can flood to perform identities of all sorts into being.

It can be further suggested in this context that it is a sense of destabilising ghost or guerrilla memorialisation which offers the most potent means to opening up and propping open these necessary holes and tears. Indeed, here too is an interesting point of contact between the original and the present collections. In a chapter in *Heritage From Below*, Alan Rice considered a wide range of memorials (broadly defined) to point up the ways in which their traditional role can be re-worked to draw attention to that which has been elided (as with a number of chapters in this current collection). Central to this discussion was the Wye Plantation House, home both of the slave-owning Lloyd family, and Frederick Douglass, slave of the plantation overseer and celebrated autobiographer. Neither Wye nor Douglass feature in Matthew R. Cook and Amy E. Potter's chapter in this collection; nevertheless, they too seek to explicate ways in which forms of heritage, in this case 'women – particularly, though not exclusively Black women – may shape public memory and historical interpretation of Black History in the United States'. Through this, as with Rice's reading of the Wye Plantation House, and the ongoing performance of alternative meanings, dominant narratives are challenged. This challenge, Cook and Potter assert, is undertaken largely through the women's own bodies and via an important margin/frontline dualism which mirrors and points to the less hierarchical and rather more interactive and relational nature of the HFB/AHD dualism this book aspires to elucidate.

The thread of embodied practice is picked up again in Drozdzewski's chapter and taken by foot in a stimulating direction. Perambulatory practice is a key motif in this direction as method, way of thinking and means to interact (even passively) with *Stolpersteine*. The broader link here is to the view which revels in the power of walking as performative and autobiographical creative practice, with the rhythmic and muscular nature of walking in, on and over the present, drawing together 'personal cultural and collective memory' (Huyssen 2003, p. 28). And whilst it is appropriate to speculate that, in these performances, walking may well bind 'thickly laid temporal dimensions' (Mock 2009, p.8) into an embodied performance which often draws on a sense of nostalgia, Roberta Mock asserts that this is not the nostalgia of a romanticised and mythologised national past but one which is both individual and works against the grain of the homogenising narrative.

There are strong elements of this in James A. Tyner's chapter, occasioned, it must be suggested, by an approach that carries unconscious echoes of the essaying of encounters with various 'scapes whilst walking a long-distance coastal path. In these essays, Wylie (2005, 2009) sought to respond to Thrift's call to 'weave a poetic' (Wylie 2005, p. 237) of the commonplace – to move beyond the straightforwardly narrative and towards the embracing of the creative register. Wylie's writing, therefore, echoes both the non-linear nature of the walks he undertook and offers much to the student of heritage 'hidden in plain sight' (to borrow a key trope of the current work). Here, Tyner asserts that the everyday heritage of violent deathscapes in Cambodia is fully practiced and performed only by those with first-hand experience of the horrific conditions occasioned by the Khmer Rouge. And if this assertion carries some echoes of the

AHD bad/HFB good binary cautioned against by Muzaini and Minca in their Introduction, this is more than counterbalanced by the realisation that, more often than not, HFB serves less to counter AHD and the power structures it supports and manifests, and more to expand 'our remembrance and interpretation of the past' (Tyner this volume). Nevertheless, the opportunity here was to engage with elements and manifestations of the 'more-than-human' in the way that say Waterton and Watson (2015) have done for the Battle of Towton (UK). The opportunity to look for moments of affect was eschewed here but has something of a foothold in heritage studies more generally (Crouch 2015) and offers much by way of insight into the 'work' heritage, and HFB in particular, may be said to do.

Layering memory, embodied performance/practice and landscape in the way that both Tyner and Drozdzewski achieves here, and which Cook and Potter engage with in some detail, is deeply reminiscent of Mike Pearson's (2007) artistic practice and his reflections thereon. In *In Comes I*, Pearson takes a powerful interdisciplinary approach, drawing upon performance studies, landscape theory, and cultural geography to name but three. He weaves these diverse perspectives together and embodies and embeds them into a landscape/text that is itself a performance and a record/reflection of performances. It is no disservice to, or reduction of, the complexities of this most stimulating text to identify it as an attempt to write a 'deep map' as this is how Pearson characterises it. In its autobiographical centring, *In Comes I* further serves to both emplace the individual simultaneously in the past and present and to speculate on future trajectories.

Deep mapping is both research method and output. In both forms, it is a deeply attractive way of working for those who seek to take HFB forward. In the hands of its most prominent advocate (Biggs 2011, 2012; Bailey et al. 2014), at the very least, here is an approach to research which engages with place in temporal depth and interweaves art and ethnographic practices 'to evoke "place" as lived landscape of multiple connectivities' (Bailey et al. 2014, p. 159). In taking up this richly creative palette, deep mapping weaves together multiple narratives, conversations, the authorial voice, and images and stories in a way of doing that can frame future work in HFB. In its arts-science hybridity, it mirrors deployments of the past in the present.

Deep mapping as output, as in the 'Either Side of Delphy Bridge' project (Bailey et al. 2014), can take the form of multimedia digital landscapes, in this case, comprised of 'fragments' harvested from the fieldwork. This is an alluring possibility. As Muzaini and Minca correctly identify in their Introduction, the earlier essaying of the concept rather ignored the democratising and popularising possibilities offered by computer mediated communication. This is far from the case for the current volume, with a number of essays drawing attention to the ways in which social media provides the means to challenge both the AHD and representations of HFB in an ongoing dialogue that appears considerably more fluid than hitherto imagined. This is certainly the lesson to be learned from Richard Carter-White's exploration of the use of Instagram to memorialise touristic visits to former concentration camps (this volume). There is, of course, something of the self-evident about the claim that even HFB is contested and contestable. But, in exactly the same way as Duchamp's *Readymades* and Tunbridge and Ashworth's *Dissonant Heritage*, to be the first to identify this and make it problematic is important. For here, as with images of the large-scale impact of the 2007 floods in Gloucestershire (UK), are informal archives (McEwen 2012; McEwen and Jones 2012) that provide a resource for resilience and future Heritage From Below.

The heritage wateryscapes conjured up through flood memories; the use of social media to offer counter-narratives of chattel slavery; Instagrammable memorialisations of Thanatourism; all offer the possibility of counter-mapping the Authorised and, indeed, the Below. This heightened sensitivity to the multiple layers in play in any 'scape is enhanced, it can be suggested, by drawing on the perspectives offered by Tim Ingold's 'dwelling perspective' (1993). This casts a light both on shadow worlds and the active and dynamic relations made and maintained by 'scapes of all sorts. To do so is to recognise that heritage landscapes (in any form) embody, through a particular set of emotional relations, a desire to dwell and a deep sense of rootedness in particular places and spaces. Ingold's taskscapes, therefore, are made up of both practical human engagements with the world and bodily agency and the interactions between them. Ingold's emphasis here is on the interactions between people and environments in which the boundaries between self and landscape, culture and nature, 'dissolve altogether' and emerge as 'agents of change and that which is changed' (Ingold 2000, p. 56, 133; also Wylie 2007). Culture, and therefore heritage, we may suggest, is continuously made through this interaction. The crux of Ingold's view is that it is always activity; always contextualised lived practices that create spaces. Such practices, Ingold argues (1993, p. 155–158), are based on Merleau-Ponty's aphorism that 'I am "at my task rather than confronting it"', and are principally, but not exclusively, work tasks. In this construction, the everyday lives of individuals, immersed in the fabric of the landscape, ensure interaction between the material space and the senses, 'forges identities and senses of place and landscape of practice' (Ingold 1993, p. 164; Jones 2011), and comes together in the taskscape. Critically, therefore, performed repetition can be seen as a key way in which people articulate and construct their sense of their pasts and historical identities. In this, moreover, the emphasis is often placed on the dust and decay of domestic spaces and routine material culture as signifiers of everyday memory work and hence heritages of the mundane; accidental and informal archives that inform and shape hardscrabble heritages (DeSilvey 2007a, 2007b; McEwen and Jones 2012; Robertson 2015). In these discursive realms, then, as with many of the chapters in this volume, equal weight is given to the presence of the fragmentary, the ephemeral and the 'urban ghosts and hauntings' (Atkinson 2008, p. 385; Edensor 2008) that constitute a significant element of 'the histories of our contemporary places'.

This turn towards the exploration of heritages that are local, particular and mundane is, in fact, along with the parallel turn to the affective realm, one of the most important in the growing maturity of heritage studies as signified by the prominence of the Association of Critical Heritage Studies. And if the focus on both the affective realm and explicitly *critical* heritage studies is given less prominence here than in other explorations of memory work, this attempt to suggest a further layering of HFB is not intended to detract from the fact that the great achievement of this collection is that it subtly reworks the relationship between the AHD and HFB into something that has greater utility than the original, in which quotidian heritages were recognised as signifiers of class, conflict and contrast, and inherently and inescapably antithetical to 'set piece' sites. This collection, by contrast moves forward from the convincing assertion that 'every form of heritage valorisation . . . is inherently selective and responds, in various degrees, to the position of the respective promoters and advocates. There is no neutral ground out there where to stage an apolitical and objective actualisation of history' (Muzaini and Minca this volume).

In practice and in performance, it is impossible to deny the fact that all heritage is permanently entangled. Often engaged in a permanent spatial dance between authorised and 'from below' forms, and most often made and maintained as embodied performance. In embracing this perspective, we are opened up to the recognition of the public consumption of the past and interlinked social memory as fluid, polysemic and multi-layered (see, for instance, Crouch 2005, 2010; Edensor 2008). In this collection, perhaps most obviously with Jamie Gillen's motorbikes and Tyner's more sombre essay on the memorialisation of the Cambodian genocide, various chapters show how mundane practices and performances weave and enfold the multi-layered and multi-consumed past into the present. In this reading, the relationship between the Authorised and 'from below' forms of heritage appears both hidden from plain site and constantly in the making; an ongoing and constitutive relationship. What Gillen in particular suggests, then, is that heritage is seen as almost exclusively presentist – concerned only with the present and future enrolments and mobilisations of the past (Gillen, this volume).

This was an emphasis rarely given voice in the original collection but convincingly obvious in retrospect. It importantly prioritises how selected histories are actualised in terms of today's practices which, in turn, lead the various authors to a concern to unravel and lay bare engagements and entanglements with the past at the most individual and personal level. What this is not, however, is a reductionist agenda – reducing these engagements and entanglements to their most basic manifestation. Instead, in Meghann Ormond's chapter, for instance, banality is an asset, a device and means to reveal that heritage expressed both from below and in its Authorised form can exist in mutually co-constitutive and complementary ways in the bodily performances of an individual.

As concept, category and call to arms, Heritage From Below has proven to be of variable utility. The readings offered in this collection offer, at one and the same time, the possibilities of 'holding on' and 'going further'. This is a considerable achievement.

REFERENCES

Association of Critical Heritage Studies, http://www.criticalheritagestudies.org/, accessed 21/03/18.

Atkinson, David (2008), 'The heritage of mundane places', in Brian Graham and Peter Howard (eds), *The Ashgate Research Companion to Heritage and Identity*, Aldershot: Ashgate, pp. 381–95.

Bagnall, G. (2003), 'Performance and performativity at heritage sites', *Museum and society*, **1** (2): 87–103.

Bailey, Jane, Iain Biggs and Daniel Buzzo (2014), 'Deep mapping and rural connectivities', in Catherine Hagen Hennessy, Robin Means and Vanessa Burholt (eds), *Countryside Connections: Older People, Community and Place in Rural Britain*, Bristol and Chicago: Policy Press, pp. 159–92.

Biggs, I. (2011), 'The spaces of "Deep Mapping": A partial account', *Journal of Arts & Communities*, **2** (1): 5–25.

Biggs, Iain (2012), 'The Southdean Project and beyond – "Essaying" site as memory work', in Owain Jones and Joanne Garde-Hansen (eds), *Geography and Memory: Explorations in Identity, Place and Becoming*, London: Palgrave Macmillan, pp. 109–23.

Butler, J. (1988), 'Performative acts and gender constitution: An essay in phenomenology and feminist theory', *Theatre Journal*, **40**, (4): 519–31.

Cosgrove, Denis E. (1984), *Social formation and symbolic landscape*, London: Croom Helm.

Cosgrove, Denis and Stephen Daniels (eds) (1998), *The Iconography of Landscape: Essays on the Symbolic Representation, Design and Use of Past Environments*, Cambridge: Cambridge University Press.

Crouch, D. (2003), 'Spacing, performing and becoming: tangles in the mundane', *Environment and Planning A*, **35** (11): 1945–60.

Crouch, D. (2010a), 'Flirting with space: thinking landscape relationally', *cultural geographies*, **22** (1): 5–18.

Crouch, David (2010b), 'The perpetual performance and the emergence of heritage', in Emma Waterton and Steve Watson (eds), *Culture, Heritage and Representation*, London: Ashgate, pp. 57–74.

Crouch, David (2015), 'Affect, heritage, feeling', in Emma Waterton and Steve Watson (eds), *The Palgrave Handbook of Contemporary Heritage Research*, London: Springer.

DeSilvey, C. (2007a), 'Salvage memory: constellating material histories on a hardscrabble homestead', *cultural geographies*, **14** (3): 401–24.

DeSilvey, C. (2007b), 'Art and archive: memory-work on a Montana homestead', *Journal of Historical Geography*, **33** (4): 878–900.

Edensor, T. (2008), 'Mundane hauntings: commuting through the phantasmagoric working-class spaces of Manchester, England', *cultural geographies*, **15** (3): 313–33.

Gregson N. and Rose G. (2000), 'Taking Butler elsewhere: performativities, spatialities and subjectivities', *Environment and Planning D: Society and Space*, **18** (4): 433–52.

Harvey, D.C. (2001), 'Heritage pasts and heritage presents: temporality, meaning and the scope of heritage studies', *International Journal of Heritage Studies*, **7** (4): 319–38.

Huyssen, Andreas (2003), 'Trauma and memory: a new imaginary of temporality', in Jill Bennett and Rosanne Kennedy (eds), *World Memory: Personal Trajectories in Global Time*, London: Palgrave Macmillan, pp. 16–29.

Ingold, T. (1993), 'The temporality of the landscape', *World Archaeology*, **25** (2): 152–74.

Ingold, Tim (2000), *The Perception of the Environment*, London: Routledge.

Jones, Owain (2011), 'Materiality and identity – forests, trees, and senses of belonging', in Eva Ritter and Dainis Daukstra (eds), *New Perspectives on People and Forests*, Dordrecht and New York: Springer, pp. 159–77.

Lorimer, H. (2005), 'Cultural geography: The busyness of being "more-than-representational"', *Progress in Human Geography*, **29**: 83–94.

Manifesto (2012), Association of Critical Heritage Studies, http://www.critical heritagestudies.org/history/, accessed 01/03/2018.

McEwen, L., Reeves, D., Brice, J., Meadley, F.K., Lewis, K. and Macdonald, N. (2012), 'Archiving memories of changing flood risk: interdisciplinary explorations around knowledge for resilience', *Journal of Arts & Communities*, **4** (1–2): 46–74.

McEwen, L. and Jones, O. (2012), 'Building local/lay flood knowledges into community flood resilience planning after the July 2007 floods, Gloucestershire, UK', *Hydrology Research*, **43** (5): 675–88.

Mock, Roberta, (2009), 'Introduction' in Roberta Mock (ed.), *Walking, Writing and Performance: Autobiographical Texts*, Bristol: Intellect Books.

Pearson, Mike (2007), *In Comes I: Performance, Memory and Landscape* (Exeter Performance Studies), Exeter: University of Exeter Press.

Robertson, Iain J.M. (2008), 'Heritage from below: class, social protest and resistance', in Brian Graham and Peter Howard (eds), *The Ashgate Research Companion to Heritage and Identity*, Aldershot and Burlington: Ashgate, pp. 143–58.

Robertson, Iain J.M. (ed.) (2012), *Heritage from Below*, Farnham and Burlington: Ashgate.

Robertson, I.J.M. (2015), 'Hardscrabble heritage: The ruined blackhouse and croft-ing landscape as heritage from below', *Landscape Research*, **40** (8): 993–1009.

Smith, Laurajane (2006), *Uses of Heritage*, London: Routledge.

Smith, Laurajane, Paul A. Shackel and Gary Campbell (eds) (2011), *Heritage, Labour, and the Working Classes*, London: Routledge.

Thrift, N. (2004), 'Performance and performativity: A geography of unknown lands', in James Duncan, Nuala C. Johnson and Richard H. Schein (eds), *A Companion to Cultural Geography*, London: John Wiley & Sons, pp. 121–36.

Thrift, Nigel (2008), *Non-Representational Theory: Space, Politics, Affect*, London: Routledge.

Waterton, E. and Watson, S. (2015), 'A war long forgotten: feeling the past in an English country village', *Angelaki*, **20** (3): 89–103.

Winter, T. (2009), 'The modernities of heritage and tourism: interpretations of an Asian future', *Journal of Heritage Tourism*, **4** (2): 105–15.

Wylie, J. (2005), 'A Single Day's Walking: narrating self and landscape on the Southwest Coast Path', *Transactions of the Institute of British Geographers*, **30** (2): 234–47.

Wylie, John (2007), *Landscape*, London: Routledge.

Wylie, J. (2009), 'Landscape, absence and the geographies of love', *Transactions of the Institute of British Geographers*, **34** (3): 275–89.

Index

abortion, legalisation of 150
Abrasevic Youth Center 68
adopted children
  genomic testing of 160–63
  life stories of 158
Adoptees' Liberty Movement
  Association (ALMA) 152, 156
adoption
  Ancestry.com 158–61
  biological belonging 153–6
  biological parentage 151
  Braveheart (1995) 158
  children's birth certificates 151
  closed 150–53
  family information 151
  family tree and 156–60
  middle-class illegitimacy 151
  transracial 152
  true genetic identity 153
African Americans
  slavery *see* slavery
  Spiritual 'Hard Trials' 107
  Transatlantic Slave Trade 111
  using social media to voice dissent
    113–18
American Atrocities Museum 28
Ancestry.com 158–61, 163
AncestryDNA 162
Angkor Wat, Cambodia 9
  as World Heritage Site 33
Asian forms, of heritage-making
  8
Ask a Slave 109, 113–14, 117
aspirational heritage
  fundamental aspect of 60
  idea of 54, 61
  markers of 49
  motorbikes in Vietnam, status of
    55, 60
  object-focused 60
  process-oriented 60

Association of Critical Heritage
  Studies 170, 177
attention economy, characteristic of
  98
Auschwitz-Birkenau Memorial and
  Museum (ABMM) 87
  advantage of 88
  as archetypal digital media object
    92
  Auschwitz selfies, rise of 92
  dark tourism 88, 89
  digital recontextualization of 99
  dominance of 88
  iconic photographs of 90
  images related to Nazism and the
    Third Reich 97
  Instagram photographs of 92–102
  motivations for visiting 88
  official account on Instagram 93
  as site of Holocaust heritage 88
  social media remediation of 96
  'Yolocaust' controversy 92
authenticity
  concept of 24
  of heritage sites 24
  of S-21 site in Cambodia 31
Authorized Heritage Discourse (AHD)
  1–2, 66, 69, 126, 149, 170, 176
  biases of 8
  concept of 3–7
  consequences of 110
  of slavery 108, 116
  top-down 13

'Baby Scoop' Era 150, 152, 164
Battle of Towton (UK) 175
being-in-place, notion of 139
Berlin 139, 142, 144–5
bicycles, in Vietnam
  as conventional heritage-making 49
  'foreigner' status of 51

ISBN 978-

Printed and bound by CPI Group (UK) Ltd, Croydon, CR0 4YY

16/04/2025

14658489-0001